THAT'S DEBATABLE

60 YEARS IN PRINT

TONY THOMAS

Connor Court Publishing Pty Ltd

Published in 2016 by Connor Court Publishing Pty Ltd

Connor Court Publishing Pty Ltd.
PO Box 7257
Redland Bay QLD 4165
sales@connorcourt.com
www.connorcourt.com
Phone 0497 900 685

ISBN: 978-1-925501-03-2

Cover design, Maria Giordano

Printed in Australia

Table of Contents

PART 3: CLIMATE UNFROCKED

PART 4: THE MILITARY BRASS VS FEMINISTS – NO CONTEST

PART 5: THE HORROR OF ABORIGINAL VIOLENCE

PART 6: A MISCELLANRY OF ITEMS

PREFACE
About Tony Thomas

I was raised in a Perth Communist household where political faith was transmitted much as faith in a creed would be transmitted in a religious household.

I remember lying on the lounge-room floor with a Soviet calendar, painstakingly copying its noble portrait of Stalin. No-one suggested I do that, but I was keen for approval of my parents. Or rather, mother and a sternly-distant stepfather. My father in 1946 left Perth by air for Brisbane. Whenever I heard the buzz of a four-propeller airliner, I would rush out the kitchen door, wave at the plane and rush inside shouting, "Mum! Daddy's coming back, I saw him in that plane!" Whatever dampener Mum responded with, I ignored.

The Soviet calendar had weeks illustrated by black-and-white photos of Soviet tanks, artillery, fighter planes and grim-faced infantry. I was so thrilled that I took the calendar to school for show-and-tell. I relished every caption about Hitlerite defeats – always 300,000-plus per battle.

I joined the Communist Party's Junior Eureka Youth League at about 13 and got around at weekends in the white shirt and red scarf of my peers in the Soviet bloc. It was a colorful childhood I had – and useful grist for essays about Youth Carnivals, Five-Power Peace Pacts and security snoopers.

At Intermediate level (age 16) the plan was for me to go to sea with the Communist-led Maritime Union, but my paternal grandmother Violet offered board so I could stay at school to matriculate. This kind deed by a hard-pressed grannie changed my life for the better.

I joined the Communist Party at age 18 as a matter of course and spent until age 22 on such mundane activities as demarcating streets for letter-box drops and planning demonstrations at which few ever showed up. A year ago, when I got my ASIO file, I discovered that our Willagee branch of at most a dozen included at least one ASIO plant. I still wonder which of my "friends" he (or she) was.

Discovery of dormant TB in 1962 nailed me to a hospital bed for six months and I gladly let my CPA membership lapse. Thereafter I veered to conservatism, coupled with permanent anger at the horrors of 20th Century Communism.

I had followed my father and mother into journalism in Perth, and my eldest daughter has followed me, making three generations in Perth journalism.

The West Australian took me on as a first-year cadet in 1958 and I wrote for it until 1969. I was Economics Writer for *The Age* in the Canberra Press Gallery through the 1970s, including the excitements of the Whitlam Labor government. But political excitements were nothing compared with the nightly stress of getting our stories transmitted from the Press Gallery to *The Age's* Melbourne office. We had an imperturbable telex operator moonlighting from the GPO who re-keyed all our typewritten copy down the telex from 6.30pm, while we did dances of impatience as deadlines came and went.

Late in the piece fax machines arrived, but with a gruesome tendency to transmit only hot black smudges. Similarly burnt-out by 1979, I went to Melbourne for 20 years with Fairfax's *Business Review Weekly* (BRW) from its precarious launch in 1981 to my retirement in 2001.

At BRW I was handed the job of writing about public accountants, a proverbially dull cohort who happened to be the all-important subscriber base of the magazine. For more than a decade my minimum weekly quota was four pages of accountancy drama. The last on-line remnant of BRW expired a fortnight ago.

In 2000 I self-published my own monograph for practitioners: *Invasion of the Practice Snatchers*. This analysed the global fad for rolling up small businesses into a listed conglomerate – a model which, in practice, didn't work and left many an investor out of pocket. The Institute of Chartered Accountants (ICAA) gave the book an award for "A Substantial Contribution to the Literature of the Industry". Pity it wasn't a best-seller.

In recent years I've written close to 200 essays for *Quadrant Monthly* and *Quadrant Online*, enjoying the freedom that comes with unpaid work. Climate, current affairs, history, the Cold War, Indigenes and whimsical autobiography – I write what and how I like. My favorite topic is the foibles of my social self and foibles of by-gone eras. I recall, for example, interviewing a West Australian Minister for Police in 1968 about policy towards then-illegal homosexual activity, and getting the reply, *"Personally, I'd have their balls out!'*

My original career plan was to become a lecturer in English literature. After slaving a decade as a part-time uni student, I finally earned my entry ticket – an MA in 1970 on Australian novelist Christina Stead. At the time most of her books were out of print. When I got my hands on them, my late-night photocopying sprees regularly disabled The West's primitive photocopier. But economics writing for The Age seemed a better job, even if it involved another four years of studies after work.

A side-interest is Aboriginal affairs. This arose firstly from undergraduate lectures by top-notch anthropologists (Catherine and Ronald Berndt and Peter Lawrence) in the late 1950s when WA's north-west and PNG Indigenes still had continuity to ancient traditions. Some years later, linguist Dr Carl Georg von Brandenstein co-opted me to help him put together *TARURU – Aboriginal Song-Poetry from the Pilbara* (Rigby, 1974) documenting the fast-disappearing songs of four Pilbara language groups.

In an odd collaboration in 2010 with historian Keith Windschuttle, I produced a 90-page pocket edition of Keith's 650-page *Fabrication of Aboriginal History – The Stolen Generation 1881-2008*. I'd been concerned that Keith's original and startling volume was too detailed for non-specialists. In a strange conjunction, I wrote the preface to the pocket-book in the evening after a day at the Theresienstadt ex-concentration camp in the Czech republic, where thousands of Jewish children passed through en route to Polish death camps. That was a stolen generation indeed.

Outside work, I've been an obstreperous member of Rotary for two decades, a frequent advocate-speaker for Myanmar's oppressed dissidents and latterly, for climate-change skepticism.

My wife of thirty years, Margaret, has suffered the fate of all writers' spouses, to be short-changed of attention and left to do the chores while her would-be Tolstoy cranks out his "literature". My cancer diagnosis last January has made me doubly dependent on her support. Thanks, beloved Margaret!

13 March 2016

1

MAD MEMOIRS

The Madman of Tullamarine

There is much to be said about the joys of children, but words are apt to fail any parent marooned without a car key in an airport's tow-away zone. Well, not all words …

◇◇◇

I was required to deliver one of my daughters, Briony, to Melbourne's Tullamarine Airport the other day. She drove her car with me in the passenger seat.

On arrival at Tullamarine, the 3-minute parking bays for departures were pretty full. I pointed to a small gap and said, "Stick your bonnet in there, it doesn't matter if the car's backside is sticking out because I'll be on my way home with the car in no time."

I got out and gallantly went round to the boot to unload her uber-heavy cases. With an affectionate farewell, daughter disappeared into the terminal, bound for Singapore.

I paused to give the sigh of fatherhood, then went round to the driver's seat and leaned forward to key-start the car. But the key was not there. Daughter had taken it with her into the terminal.

I felt like a lab rat in an experiment designed to induce mental collapse. I could stay in car and hope daughter would re-emerge from the terminal. That would mean overstaying the 3 minutes and moreover, every minute I sat there increased the chance that daughter would find her way into the one-way immigration hall.

I could instead abandon the car and dash into the terminal in the hope of discovering daughter and wrenching the keys violently from her. This would mean the security guards would notice an abandoned car parked at 45 degrees to the footpath and with its backside sticking out a metre or two (all the other cars had meanwhile driven away leaving daughter's car alone and prominent). At best, car would be towed away; at worst, blown up.

I chose to abandon car and locate daughter, and dashed into International Terminal. Milling crowds everywhere, and I had no idea which airline Briony was using. So I took up a position 5 metres inside, and shouted at the top of my lungs: "B-R-I-O-N-Y !!" This caused a sensation as people wondered who the elderly male was and why he was screaming. Briony failed to appear.

I checked the departures: a QANTAS 380 was boarding for Singapore. I dashed to the right to the special QANTAS section where hundreds of travellers were coiling around the people-barriers like a snakes and ladders game. Briony is short and if there, she would be undetectable. So I again bellowed, 'B-R-I-O-N-Y!!' Again the crowd gave a startle-response but no Briony emerged. Staff are still talking about "the madman of Tullamarine" they saw that day.

By this time I was fearful about my daughter's abandoned car. I dashed outside and sat in it, not realising that I could at least release the handbrake and push the car to align it with the kerb. But Briony by now could possibly be ticketed and heading for Immigration. I needed to go back again to seek her out among the multitude.

I dashed back into the terminal, dashed here, dashed there, and then looked back and caught sight of a group of officers outside the terminal, some armed, warily inspecting my daughter's grey runabout. I dashed outside again to liaise with the security squad. "This is your car?" they asked, grim-faced.

Myself, doing a little dance of anxiety: "Yes, that's right, no, daughter's! She's in there somewhere [gesticulating towards terminal]. Suitcases… she drove… Singapore… no key…a good girl, usually…sure to come out soon with key…on my mother's grave, I'm not al Qaeda! Can one of you please hotwire this car? Please don't tow an old pensioner away!" [Actually I have a Senior's Card but am not a pensioner].

None of my pleas impressed the bomb squad. They circled round the car like it was a wild beast, or a big pile of steaming ordure. Some wrote copiously in black-covered notebooks, others dialed up colleagues or maybe the SOGGIES [Special Operations Group] on their radio. They were joined by a parking inspector demanding to know of me why my car was so badly parked. While I was again explaining, a familiar figure holding car keys burst out of the terminal, my daughter Briony!

She explained all to the blue-clad commandos. She had been excited about her big trip to Singapore. She got her tickets. She remembered she had a letter to post and went to the airport Post Office. She pulled the letter out of her handbag and noticed the car keys. She put two and two together and thought I might need them. That's all, officers, it's quite a simple mistake.

The security squad conferred and wandered off, disappointed. The parking lady continued tapping busily into her fines device, ignoring my daughter's increasingly shrill protests. Parking lady: "I'm just doing my job. Have a nice day". And to me, "On your way, please."

"Heck Dad! It's your fault. You should pay the fines. Why didn't you ask me for the keys!"

With another fatherly sigh, the madman of Tullamarine headed for home in Briony's grey Nissan Tiida.

Quadrant Online, 31 October 2012

Reflections on a Youth Carnival by a Primary-School Stalinist

Did Mr A.T. Jelly, probably of Nedlands, Perth, WA, play some small role in 1952 in ameliorating Cold War tensions and bringing about a more peaceful world?

He was walking along the Stirling Highway footpath near the then State Saw Mills, and I, as an 11-year-old, blocked his way. I presented him with a petition for a Five Power Peace Pact between the US, UK, France, the Soviet Union and China. I explained why it was a good idea, and he became about my tenth signatory that morning.

I was a keen collector of signatures, so keen that I won the prize from the Eureka Youth League and/or its parent the Communist Party of Australia. The big prize! I became the sole delegate from Perth's Junior Eureka Youth League (JEYL) to Sydney's Youth Carnival for Peace & Friendship.

At this distance it is safe to make a confession. I did forge 10-15% of my signature tally, enough to knock my sister, 12, out of the short-list for the prize. My parents, inspecting my petition sheets, immediately queried the authenticity of "Mr Jelly". But Mr Jelly's signature was authentic. I was righteously indignant. Even today I notice two Jelly families in Perth's White Pages, possibly Mr A.T. Jelly's descendants.

At 11, I was already a petition veteran. At ten I had taken the World Peace Council's petition to ban the atom bomb to Nedlands State School and got a lot of kids to sign before school – they were flattered to be asked. By playtime, to my disgruntlement, the kids virtually queued to scratch their names off my petition sheet. At a lunchtime interview, the doubtless horrified deputy headmaster at this conservative school, Mr Thorpe, instructed me to cease and desist from signature collecting among his flock.

Joseph Stalin was my ultimate boss as the mainspring of the Five Power Peace Pact petition. Some press man interviewed him in February 1951. Comrade Stalin highlighted the need for the pact, which had been languishing as a topic since Foreign Minister Vyshinsky broached it in the UN a year earlier. (Vyshinsky had presided over the pre-war Zinoviev-Kamenev trial, remarking judicially, "Shoot these rabid dogs… Let's put an end once and for all to these miserable hybrids of foxes and pigs, these stinking corpses!").

Insensitively, the General Assembly had voted against Vyshinsky's peace pact, opting instead for an American protocol for 'peace through deeds'.

After the Stalin interview, instructions about the petition speedily went out via Alexsander Fadeyev, of the Soviet Writers Union, and Ilya Ehrenburg, the writer, who were Stalin's conduits to the Peace Council. What do you know, by December there were 600 million signatures, including Mr Jelly's.

The predecessor petition against the atom bomb (then a US hegemony) had not done nearly as well, gathering only 500 million signatures, including the vestigial tally from my Nedlands State School peer group. Most of the signatures were from Soviet bloc citizens, where declining to sign involved a career setback.

We JEYL members in Perth, aged to about 15, wore the white shirts and red scarfs that were a la mode for Communist youth globally. Our troop mother was a nice but humourless young woman called Dot Calvert.

One morning about eight of us boarded a Stirling Highway bus for the beach, and half-way there Dot instructed us brightly, "Let's sing the peace song!" We immediately piped up, "For peace, world peace! United for peace! For peace, world peace! U-u-NIGHT-ed for PEACE!" We then launched into the many verses between choruses, such as "Everywhere the youth are singing freedom's song…We are the youth! And the world acclaims our song of truth!"

How co-passengers on the bus viewed this performance, I do not know. I think Dot imagined that our peaceful enthusiasm would inspire them to join the Communist Party.

Our main JEYL assignment was fielding a soccer team in the Saturday juniors. We played for two seasons, winning no games but memorably drawing one, at one-all. I was goalie. Our ability to field an 11-boy team, given JEYL's miniscule numbers, was zero. Normally we fielded between 7 and 9 players, and the opposing team would assign us a couple of their spare players to make a better game of it. Those seconded players seldom put their heart into the game.

There was a Jewish team called the Maccabeans, probably boosted by recent arrivals from Yugoslavia, Hungary and the Ukraine. The Maccabeans, if you will excuse my anti-semitism, were bastards. They wouldn't donate their spare players to our team, and they spent their hour banging goals past me into my net. Our or my worst score was 35-nil.

I'm a bit annoyed that our Eureka Youth League sponsors were so busy creating a better world that they never gave a thought to putting down our mortally-ailing little soccer team.

Or perhaps they were just too busy cramming for EYL study courses. I turned up the curriculum for Victorian EYL studies, July 1951 – maybe they used the same one in Perth. Lesson 6 was 'Historical Materialism'. The poor EYL sods not only had to ingest Stalin's work, "On origin and role of ideas" but do further reading including Zhdanov's views on "Marxism and Linguistics" and even Boris Hessen's tract on "Social and Economic Roots of Newton's Principia."

Zhdanov died in 1948, and in 1953 Stalin used the death as the fulcrum of his planned "Doctors' Plot Trial" to deport 2 million Jews to extinction beyond the Urals. Boris Hessen had been tried and shot (on the same day) in Moscow in 1936 so his work shouldn't actually have been on the Victorian EYL curriculum in 1951, although Hessen was rehabilitated posthumously in 1956.

Sorry, I'm rambling. Anyway, I was soon Sydney-bound for the Peace Carnival on the Trans-Continental Train. I can't remember much about the Youth Carnival, except that I had a starring role in a big campfire evening where I sang Walter Scott's song about "Bonny Dundee", except I precociously substituted rhymes about NATO and its UK Labor supporter Clement Attlee. This went down a treat among the evening's sausage eaters and keg-dwellers.

I still recall the atmosphere of excitement and self-importance. Much to my surprise, I found a newsreel about the carnival online (http://tinyurl.com/l7ahuad).

and I've transcribed the commentary below. The background music was the march from Tchaikowsky's Sixth Symphony, perhaps a musical pun on Russian influence on the Carnival. The newsreel opens with a Russian-language sign:

> Russian for 'Peace & Friendship' – one of many signs at Fairfield's Hollywood Park where the Youth Carnival for Peace & Friendship opens. The Carnival itself has been give little publicity but Cinesound presents these pictures, [shot of crowds, families, kids] because the Australian public should know what is going on in their midst. Suppression too often breeds strength.
>
> [People march past under flags bearing the Carnival symbol, a dove plus a boomerang which seem slightly sinister/fascist in black-and-white footage].
>
> Ten thousand people attended the opening day. Noticeable among flags missing from the carnival was that of the United Nations, of which Russia is also a member.
>
> The Federal Government and the Australian Labor Party have both described the carnival as Communist inspired. [State delegations go past, and nice-looking female teenagers and young women are singing but not audible]. The procession of youth, the flags, the banners and marching songs are strangely reminiscent of the Nuremburg rallies of

the late unlamented Hitler Youth. [Broad-chested young men march in T-shirt uniforms]. Not so many flags, not so many people, but the first German rallies were small too. To a man (sic) sitting in the centre, it is often difficult to tell the far Left from the far Right.

We seem to have gone all European suddenly don't we? For this is hardly an Australian scene...

Yes Madam, [matronly woman applauds enthusiastically] it is impressive but it is the start of what?

'Peace', and marching in the procession are Chinese. [The Chinese, all locals, are in androgynous Confucian or Tai Chi sort of costumes, eschewing any militancy]. We seem to recall that Red China today is at war with the world in Korea...that Australian youth is dying there to restore peace.

Communist Waterside Workers leader Healy marches – a rather mature youth. [With a large tummy, too].

Perhaps the greatest job these people [Greeks and New Zealanders sweep past] could do would be to convince Russia that the whole world wants peace with a passionate longing. [A big truck float goes past, massively decorated with flowers forming the dove/boomerang symbol]. Frankly we can't see how the cause of World Peace can be aided by a semi-theatrical parade in a picnic ground 15 miles from Sydney. We wonder too how many of those marching today and those who watch, really know what is going on – these children for instance. [Yay! A truckload of cheering, waving kids. Is that cute kid leaning out, me? Well, maybe!]

Let's not fool ourselves. There is war in the world today and it was started not by the democracies. Maybe the Youth Carnival could start right there, if the authorities would let them. [Women in hats, a toddler wildly waves a flag in each hand]. Because if this were a democratic procession it could not happen in Moscow's Red Square!"

And you thought ABC News was subjective?

An ASIO plant was in a cinema when the newsreel was originally shown. As described by historian Dr Phillip Deery, the field officer reported:

The commentary itself was so biased and unfair that it drew groans from the audience...The audience consisted, not of Carnival supporters, but of suburban housekeepers in town for shopping and members of the public and their girlfriends sheltering from the rain ['members of the public' must have all male, unless the agent also spotted some lesbians] …the obvious injustice of the commentary provoked a sympathetic reaction.

Dr Deery, of Victoria University of Technology, in his excellent study of the Carnival, lavishly appropriated below by myself, complains that most historians of the post-war peace movement have ignored or downplayed it. The most detailed work has been by the 'unremittingly hostile' historians, including (Quadrant stalwart) Hal Colebatch of Perth, who treat it as a Communist stunt and ignore its broader community participation, Deery says.

He notes that the Carnival was the first outside Eastern Europe and was the child of the August 1951 3rd World Youth Festival in East Berlin (two years before the East Berlin uprising by less-conformist types). The 1951 show was attended by 26,000, compared with 10,000 at Sydney. Among those at Berlin were 135 Australians including Frank Hardy.

One delegate was 24 year old Frank Townsend, a lab assistant and former Student Council president at Melbourne Technical College. Although a political cleanskin in ASIO's view, he became full-time organiser of the Sydney carnival in early 1952, keen to repay hospitalities involved in his Berlin trip. He envisioned that the carnival would, in the words of a pamphlet:

> light a torch which will shine in a world where the people's are kept too much apart from each other. This torch can light up the road to the happy, sane and peaceful Australian (sic) that we all hope and strive for.

Getting 10,000 attendees was a good effort considering the hostile State apparatus. Attendees ran the gamut of refusals by 25 councils of halls, stadiums, parks, ovals and even beaches. The planned venue, the Harold Park trotting stadium, was withdrawn a bare fortnight before start-day. The hastily-arranged and privately-run Hollywood Park venue in outer Sydney was banned by Fairfield Council on the eve of the opening, and the council was only thwarted by a last-minute injunction. The State then banned private bus services to the park and in a Dunkirklike miracle, the EYL organised private cars, trucks and lorries to shuttle the thousands back and forth.

Deery discovered that ASIO, in its "Operation Handshake", had two men and a woman in the Carnival headquarters and (probably) used agents to intimidate anyone offering Carnival services.

A Hobart ASIO man, J.J. Webberley, was flown to Sydney specifically to monitor Tasmanian attendees by trailing cars and identifying people in photographs. He even trailed himself into Taronga Zoo and Paddington Town Hall dances. He reported, "While at Sydney I was able to obtain the names and addresses of a large number of Tasmanians who have communist interests and will report on them accordingly on the following form."

The Menzies government couldn't ban the Carnival per se as the Liberals had just lost the referendum to ban the Communist Party and its ilk. But scores of Russian, Chinese, Czechs, Malayans and Americans were denied visas and had to stay home. Only New Zealanders got in. The 'international' flavour was from local ethnic groups.

Somehow the organisers created a panoply of sporting, dance, musical, art and literary events, many with handsome prizes of 200-250 pounds. We kids were offered prizes for plasticine models, drawings and costumes.

Literary sponsors included Gavin Casey, Eleanor Dark, Dame Mary Gilmore, Eric Lambert, Alan Marshall, John Morrison, Walter Murdoch and Katherine Susannah Pritchard. Colin Simpson signed on but then signed himself out.

Cultural groups were transported to factories to do their stuff. On a single morning, seven groups got to seven sites, each group with chairman, a presenter, and sound equipment. Knowing what a hassle sound gear is even today, I feel respect for those organisers of 1952.

ASIO's list of participating bodies in the Carnival runs to six pages, including the Atlas Greek Club, the NSW Ballroom Dancing Academy, the Melbourne Camera Club, and Geelong Choristers.

Individuals generously housed out-of-towners, including a Mrs Edwards of Fitzroy Street, Killara, who offered to billet two same-sex delegates in her spare room. She probably got the 2 pounds per person subsidy for costs.

As suggested by the Pathe newsreel, the wireless and the SMH, Tele and Sun ran a news blackout on the carnival. Deery says that the carnival's EYL news-sheet Challenge had daily print runs of tens of thousands and issue No 10 involved 500,000 copies.

Deery then broadens his canvas to ask why Menzies, fresh from his referendum defeat, went all-out to disrupt the Carnival. Apart from obvious reasons such as the Korean war outbreak and the supposedly-imminent World War 111, Menzies viewed the Carnival as part of a Soviet phony 'peace offensive' via the World Peace Council. As External Affairs had advised him, "Like shady night club proprietors the Communist promoters are no sooner put out of business by exposure in one place, than they are busy organising a fresh venture under entirely new management."

Deery puts the case that the Carnival none-the-less involved a genuine effort by young activists to connect with other youth through culture, sport and a bit of non-sectarian politics. "And it was, in the words of the woman who conceived the carnival, 'an attempt to break through to a whole new section of the working class movement, we were trying something new and it was terribly exciting…we hoped it would be a new start.' "

I was chatting on the phone the other day to Joe Lane in Adelaide about his archival research on South Australian Aborigines . He mentioned that he too had attended the Youth Carnival, at an even younger age, 9, than myself. He also thought he spotted himself on the kids' truck. Cue scepticism. Joe's parents named him after Joseph Vissarionovich Stalin, about which he's a bit embarrassed today. I said, "At least I'm not called Joe Thomas."

Despite my unusual childhood, I grew up to be a model citizen.

Quadrant OnLine, 31 March 2014

How The Truth Went Begging

They made a pathetic sight, the rag-clad Aborigines who tugged travellers' heartstrings at dusty stops along the trans-Nullarbor rail line – so pathetic very few of those reaching for their wallets realised they were being conned.

⬦⬦⬦

Some memories get 'burned in'. Though the events were 65 years ago, I was haunted by the spectacle of miserable Aborigines begging and trying to sell souvenirs to passengers on the eastbound Trans-Australian train at Ooldea, SA, on the eastern fringe of the Nullarbor Plain. The Aborigines were clad in rags, and mothers carried infants and toddlers, also in rags.

I was on that train from Kalgoorlie twice, as an 11- and 12-year-old in early and late 1952. On one of those trips I bought from an old Aborigine a kangaroo carved from a forked piece of soft white wood. It bore a singed pattern made with a hot stick or wire. It must have been cheap as my spending money was meagre indeed. This became a treasured possession for several years.

I have a vague memory of the consternation among the train passengers, seeing the pitiable state of the Aborigines. People leant out and put not just money but food and lollies into pleading black hands.

On the March, 1952, trip I was the youngest WA delegate to Sydney's pink-tinged Youth Carnival for Peace and Friendship. I can imagine, if not recollect, the indignation of my fellow delegates on the train at this iconic indictment of an unjust and uncaring capitalist society.

Well, I'm sure you're with me so far. But things are not always what they seem, and in this case, especially not.

My acquaintances Joe Lane and Alistair Crooks are working through the records of the South Australian Chief Protector of Aborigines from the1840s to 1950s and associated documents.

From these documents, it is clear that humbugging passengers on the Trans-Australian train had been a relaxed and lucrative past-time since 1917 when the line opened. It was done not just by local Aboriginals settled at the sidings but by groups wandering in from hundreds of kilometres, even a thousand kilometres.

As soon as the line's construction finished, a couple of hundred tribalised Aborigines from the WA/NT border hurried down to see the sights, a bit like how we white tourists now go to see the sights down in Antarctica.

The SA Chief Protector W.G. South wrote at the time that the line's visitors "were not giving the white residents any trouble and will no doubt return to their own country later on" – but he was wrong.

Mr South was soon lamenting:

> There is no necessity for them to [beg], as their natural food is plentiful in their own country, and several ration depots exist in the district where the old and infirm may obtain supplies…
>
> The able-bodied natives can find plenty of employment amongst the settlers, but as long as they are encouraged by sympathetic people to beg they will naturally refuse to work. In other parts of the north country, away from the railway line, all the aborigines find employment and earn good wages.

The WA and SA governments were thereafter bombarded with criticisms from well-meaning passengers about the importunate clusters on the line, with letters to editors getting published as far afield as London. An irony was that, as normally happens, being charitable only encouraged more begging.

Leftist historian Stuart Macintyre (2011) in his biography of Sir Ernest Scott (1867-1939), a doyen of early Australian historians, quotes a private letter Scott wrote to Scott's wife in 1926 mentioning the Aborigines begging from the passengers. 'They are the ugliest, most wretched creatures imaginable, hideous, dirty and skinny … The gins all smoke pipes,' Scott's letter says.

In 1937 there was a conference in Canberra of States' Chief Protectors. The South Australian Chief Protector M.T. McLean told them:

> We issue them with clothes so that they may appear more or less respectable, but we find that they hang their clothes on a tree, and present themselves in their rags before the passengers so as to excite sympathy. The only solution I can see is to have permanent police officers on duty to turn the natives back from the railway.

Worse luck for the Protectors, the Trans-Australian's Commonwealth owners themselves were marketing the trip as an opportunity to see picturesque Aborigines en route. Similarly, missionaries were doing their best to succour the Aborigines with the result that even more drifted in to the line.

Among the earliest well-wishers for Aborigines on 'the line' was Daisy Bates, serial bigamist, one-time "spouse" of Breaker Morant, and for all that, a dedicated recorder of Aboriginal ways. She set up at Ooldea in 1919 on a quest to civilise the Aborigines, not getting far with the project during 16 years.

Her accounts are colourful and not suitable for today's cossetted schoolchildren, given she reports common infanticide and occasional cannibalism. Her general veracity is subject to on-going controversy, with various academics writing her off as a fabulist. Others, such as anthropologist and editor Isobel White, were impressed by her extensive and painstaking notes and her willingness to put in the hard yards and years living among Aborigines in conditions remote from civilisation's benefits.

From Ooldea, Bates wrote:

> Just as I was buttoning the men into their first trousers, a thunder came from the Plain. All rose in terror to watch, wild-eyed, the monster of Nullarbor, the ganba [snake] coming to devour them [i.e. the train]. I needed all my tact and wisdom to prevent their flight. Two of the women were heavily pregnant. One of these, in spite of the abundant food bestowed on her, later gave birth to a girl baby in a hidden spot in the bush, and killed and ate the little creature. The other woman reared her child for a year or so, and then, giving birth to a half-caste at some siding, took both along the line and disposed of them either by neglect or design. One of the men … contracted venereal disease, and returned to Ooldea only to die…We buried him near my tent, with Inyiga, a woman who, after killing her diseased half-cast child, succumbed to pneumonia.

She went to great lengths to collect evidence of cannibal episodes. One set of bones she sent to Adelaide for analysis proved to be mere cat bones, but others were human. To be blunt, there are plenty of accounts by respected anthropologists about Aboriginal cannibalism, e.g. Elkin, Roth, and the two Berndts (under whom I studied in 1961). Even historian Manning Clark attested to the practice. [A colleague of mine, the late Dr C.G. von Brandenstein, who learnt at least four Pilbara languages, told me once that in hard times, dead infants would routinely go 'into the pot'].

As for infanticide, this has been estimated at up to 30% of babies before white contact, and close to 20% of babies even in 1966-67 in Pitjantjatjara country, the source country of many of the Aborigines on 'the line'.

Getting back to our train, WA's pre-war Chief Protector A.O. Neville had a lot to say about it. He is today infamous for wanting assimilation of half-castes – but he also wanted preservation of full-blood communities and their culture. Those twin policies were in fact the unanimous desire of all Protectors from all States and the Commonwealth, as expressed at that 1937 conference in Canberra. The policy, however much reviled today, compared favourably with apartheid and segregation in South Africa and the US at the time.

For Neville, the begging on the WA side of the line was a thorn in his side for many years. He told the 1937 conference, in the sometimes uncouth language of the times:

> I absolutely deny that the natives along the Western Australian section of the line are living in miserable conditions. .... I do not want to criticise the South Australian control in any way, and in a sense, the natives cannot be blamed for coming to the train. I merely want to place the facts before the Conference. When these natives approach the train, they are received with extraordinary sympathy by the passengers, who give them money, fruit, cake and many other things, and in every way possible encourage them.
>
> At Immarna about 100 very dirty natives of all sorts and conditions, dressed in filthy rags, crowded to the train. I have never seen such a collection. I should have been ashamed to have had anything to do with them. The train stopped at that station for nearly twenty minutes and these natives swarmed round it like flies.
>
> One extraordinary feature of this business is that although, ten years ago, there was hardly a child to be seen among the natives along the line, there must have been from 30 to 40 children from ten years of age downwards in that company. Knowing the natives as I do, I am quite satisfied that those children were bred for the purpose of begging, The mothers carried them along the train on their backs, and the little children held out their hands to the passengers who gave them shillings and sixpences and other coins. Their pathetic appeal

could not be resisted by the passengers.

It seems to me that only two things can be done to remedy this state of affairs. They must be taken away from the line altogether, which would involve the expenditure of considerably more money than Western Australia or South Australia can spare for the purpose, or the passengers must, in some way, be prevented from making gifts to them.

It is not charity to these people to give them money. It is actually pauperising them. On our end of the line they are already properly fed and clothed, and they do not really want for anything. As things are, it is difficult to keep them from contact with the passengers.

He went on that Aborigines were allowed free travel on the weekly tea and sugar train taking rations between Kalgoorlie and Port Augusta. But they used it as what we would now see as a hop-on hop-off exercise, waiting at remote sidings for the next Trans-Continental and plying their begging skills afresh.

Neville told his peers that provision of rations and supplies to needy Aboriginals was standard policy in WA, but it was always a problem working out if the poverty was actually due to gambling or work-shy lifestyles. He had no sympathy for handouts to able-bodied Aboriginals. For example, it was common for Aboriginals to get free trips to Adelaide, where they spent all their money and expected the government to pay their trip home. He said:

... (I)t is very difficult to do anything with them. I suppose it would cost £3,000 or £4,000 in capital expenditure to provide adequate quarters for them away from the line, and it would probably cost £1,000 a year to maintain them. This must be done, or the Commonwealth Government must request passengers to cease making gifts to them.

Both WA and SA Protectors felt their hands were tied legally from doing much to fix the problem. SA Protector McLean in his 1936-37 annual report said:

Even if a large reserve were proclaimed for these natives they would in all probability leave the reserve and continue to visit the line. The only method of punishing them if they did leave the reserve would be by prosecution in a court of law and sending them to prison, which, with such people would be quite ridiculous and unsatisfactory.

He also considered imprisonment counter-productive. The

traditional men enjoyed the excursion to the Port Augusta jail, and it was an incentive rather than a deterrent, he wrote.

What emerges from the accounts of the time is officials' honest desire to support Aborigines in their traditional lifestyle. The Protectors struggled to stem the pernicious creep of hand-outs, whether privately or government sponsored. They also, being good public servants, were highly conscious of both the limits to their legal powers, and a vigilant public ever ready to haul them over the coals for sins of omission and commission. As today, we can look back and criticise them, just as – who knows? – we too will be criticised from a 2070 perspective.

Quadrant OnLine, 10 January 2014

OK, how I missed that story

Our contributor wasn't always the serious, sober scribe *Quadrant* readers know and respect. Once, long ago, there was a young reporter with rather more on his mind than covering long and windy speeches…

I had an Oedipus Rex moment in 1963. If you recall the play, Oedipus goes looking for the man who killed his father and married his mother. On discovering the man is himself, he is so horrified he stabs out his eyes. (Incidentally, Oedipus killed his father in a prehistoric fit of road rage, involving chariots at an intersection).

I was an earnest but wayward reporter, aged 23, on *The West Australian*. My editor Griff Richards was troubled. A very illustrious gent called General Sir John Hackett had visited Perth. He was the son of an even grander Winthrop Hackett, who co-founded, edited and later owned *The West Australian* itself. Griff's problem was that he had picked up rumors that he, Griff, had seriously and deliberately snubbed General Hackett. I assume Griff had heard some elliptical references to the matter at the Weld Club in Barrack Street.

Griff had misplaced a lot of faith in me, and hence assigned me to get to the bottom of these rumors. They involved something about a magnificent speech Sir John Hackett had made where he had used his coat as a prop and declaimed about the sleeves. That didn't sound very poetic but I got the drift. Rather thrilled to have been given this unusual detective-like assignment, I began my investigations.

To put all this in context, I intend to inflict on you some excessive detail about the Hacketts.

Winthrop Hackett, at times in league with Premier John Forrest, virtually ran WA for the decades straddling 1900. With his immense wealth and influence, he created most of Perth's institutions, including the free-of-fees and female-friendly WA University, the State Library and Museum, Kings Park, the Zoo, even Karrakatta Cemetery. Under his regime, *The West* was a 'paper of record' – it used to report verbatim the entire Sunday sermons of Bishop Riley at St George's Cathedral, for example.

For all that, Winthrop must have had a certain gleam in his eye. At the age of 57, the bachelor magnate married in 1905 the 18-year-old Deborah Vernon Brockman, from WA's pioneer landed gentry. At one stage she ran a tantalum mine in the deserts of the Northern Territory. The tantalum became a crucial input to Britain's development of radar in World War II.

How and why Winthrop decided so late in life to wed a teenager is unclear (he did have a lifelong and probably innocent friendship with a chap named Leeper).

He wrote a fortnight before the marriage: "The place is so dull, and life so monotonous that I absolutely must have a new experience. Hence this determination. It seems to me as good a reason as most men have for marrying. What do you think? This is in the strictest sense a 'marriage de convenience' " [Pardon his French].

After marriage, he wrote querulously: "Did you find that marriage took at least a couple of hours out of your working day? It is my experience." This is very close to my favorite joke: When a tradie got married, he told a mate, "It's great, but long hours."

Winthrop even tried to run Deb's life from beyond the grave, putting a clause in his will that her inheritance would cease if she re-married. Deb not only re-married, twice, but became rich anyway, despite foregoing vast Hackett wealth.

Deb, sincerely or not, described her marriage as 'blissfully happy'. She was one hell of a snob too. She had to shift her *bric a brac* from Adelaide to Toorak, when she embarking on her third marriage. The job took 12 pantechnicons. At the time, it was the largest family consignment ever to go by road in Australia.

She was also loathe to relinquish her title-by-marriage of "Lady", which she had enjoyed since her teen years. Her second husband, Frank Moulden, was plain "Mr" but Deb continued to call herself "Lady Hackett". One cheeky social reporter wrote that Lady Hackett and Mr Frank Moulden "were sharing a room at the Menzies Hotel". Mercifully, Frank got a knighthood later, so Deb could call herself Lady Moulden. Her third husband lacked a title so thereafter she called herself "Dr" Buller-Murphy, trading on an honorary doctorate she got from UWA. This used to be considered pretentious, but now a lot of Honorary Doctors adopt the title.

The Hacketts' only son John, amid four daughters is the subject of my story and discomfiture.

Sir John, like his mother and father, had an astounding career. He joined the British Army after a not-so-good start in art and in the classics at Oxford. In every campaign, he did acts of heroism, accumulating war wounds and war medals at an equal rate. In Syria he was wounded and won the Military Cross. In North Africa he was in a tank blown up during an attack and he was seriously burnt climbing out of it. He won a DSO.

In 1944 he raised and commanded a parachute brigade, getting wounded again in Italy. Then he led the brigade into the airdrop on Arnhem, the celebrated Dutch 'bridge too far' which became an Allied disaster. He was severely wounded in the stomach and a German doctor was going to give him a mercy-killing injection, but a second doctor stepped in and saved his life surgically.

Hackett escaped with the Dutch resistance during a hospital transfer, after adorning himself with extra-bloody bandages. He won a second DSO for Arnhem.

After the war he rose to top ranks, including Palestine in 1947 and running the Northern Ireland campaign in 1961, both rather messy fields of conflict. His job from 1965 was as commander of the British Army of the Rhine and NATO's Northern Army Group but he was too abrasive politically to win the ultimate top job, chief of the defence staff.

After the army he became Principal of King's College London, where he liked to join student marches for improved study grants, to the horror of other Dons.

After his years on the front line of the nuclear Cold War, he wrote in 1978 a fictional and best-selling scenario of World War III based on a Soviet invasion of West Germany seven years into the future (1985).

This big man came to Perth in 1963, a year or two before the zenith of his military career. This year was the 50th anniversary of the first courses of the WA University and the uni Senate marked the occasion by conferring honorary doctorates on 15 alumni and bigshots, some with only tenuous WA connections.

As a further preliminary to my Oedipus moment, I will now describe my love life as at late 1963.

A young woman, "Libby", and I were magnificently in love and eager to neck in secluded places. This was long before typical young couples could hope for privacy in flats. My home was too inconvenient for trysts. Libby was still living with her mother, who made a point of never leaving us alone in her house, i.e., she was not stupid. At one point I tried a double-cross. I announced to Libby's mother that Libby and I would spend the evening at the pictures. Mother then felt it safe to organise a social outing of her own. At the last minute I announced that our movie was off and Libby and I would just have to entertain ourselves at home somehow. Mother showed such suppressed fury that Libby pulled the carpet from under me by discovering there was another movie she badly wanted to see.

The degree-conferring night found me seething with testosterone and fuming at the tedium of the ceremony. I had expected it would be all over by 9pm or so and that Libby and I could rendezvous and head down to the Crawley lover's lane in my car. But the uni felt that each conferee would want equal time and plaudits. Think 15 x 10 minutes, plus extras.

The chancellor, Sir Alex Reid, was in his peacock robes, along with all the Senators and profs. Each nominee got a speech about his accomplishments and was then presented with his doctorate.

None of the speeches so far were at all interesting, and of the 15, there were still three or four to go. The best to date was Fred Schonell, author of the famous *Schonell Speller*, lists of words which we as primary schoolers had chanted and spelled day after day, resulting in pretty good spelling ability, compared to today's slack brats. Some recipients seemed to have no connection at all with UWA or Perth, such as Sir Charles Blackburn, chancellor of Sydney Uni, who by the time he retired the following year, had himself conferred 31,194 degrees (true). Another was Freddie Alexander, a historian who had managed to bulk out his 50th anniversary history of the UWA to nearly 1000 pages. I had reported some other historian remarking bitchily that a 1000-year history of Oxford University had been a much smaller volume. I hadn't given Fred any right of reply, and Fred carpeted me over it, with justice.

I decided cut and run to Libby. Anyway, I reasoned, by the time the official ceremony finished, there would be little time to write the story, phone it through and still meet deadlines. Late night stories had to be particularly thrilling to justify the reworking of pages.

Libby and I managed to steam up my car windows and I thought no more about honorary doctors of laws and letters…

Until my editor asked me to discover what those rumors were about concerning our 'snub' to Sir John Hackett.

I began by checking our library files – nothing there.

I asked around, using my meagre list of Perth bigshots. Nothing much.

Finally, a uni contact said someone had told him something about a speech by Sir John. Maybe even at UWA.

An administrator confirmed, to my growing dismay, that the speech was at the Honorary Degree ceremony. "But wasn't all that just formal stuff?" I asked imploringly.

"No, I was there. It was terribly moving. You know that his father had also got an honorary degree? Sir John must have been wearing his own father's gown with all the academic stripes and trimmings, and he took it off and addressed it as though it was his father, still alive. We were all moved to tears, just about."

Well, that's cleared THAT up. All I needed to do now was break the news to my editor, Griff Richards. I'd just say…what would I say?

I could think of two precedents similar to this for breaking of bad news. As a boy I had once been caught by my stepfather, Vic, doing target practice with our chooks, using small stones. Reluctant to discipline me himself (although when I was about six he gave me a sudden slap on the bare bottom when he caught me peeing in the bathroom basin), Vic directed me to report my crime to Mum and take condign punishment at her hands.

I began by remarking to Mum on the smallness of the chook pen and the chooks' need for more exercise. Mum abstractedly agreed. In a few subtle steps I came to mention that I had even encouraged them to run around by tossing a few things at them. Mum abstractedly agreed…

The other occasion was when the local grocer-store owner caught me red-handed shoplifting a Cherry Ripe bar. Again, unwilling to discipline me and lose the family account, the grocer told me to report my crime to my mother. I trudged home, to find a serious Communist Party seminar in progress on the back lawn. Was this the right time for a general strike? How should we educate the masses (sometimes pronounced 'them asses') about the US war bases in the Indian Ocean?

As kids do (or used to do), I hung around Mum's skirts waiting for a break in the conversation. "Mum, I've got something I need to tell you," I whined. Mum was not interested. She was focused on the mood of the masses and the split with Tito of Yugoslavia. "Mum? Mum?" "Get out and leave us alone, we're busy!" I went off to play, with a clear conscience.

I couldn't visualise any comparable solutions for my present dilemma. Remarkably I decided to go the hang-out road, as Richard Nixon once put it, and do full disclosure.

Griff, by the standards of many modern-day editors, lived a remote existence in a paneled office off the reporters' hall. As I saw it, his senior people went in to report and came out to instruct. I never could reconcile this persona with the student Griff who was suspended from UWA over allegedly lewd material he published in the student newspaper *Sruss Sruss*. So "lewd" that the Student Guild had to literally burn the undistributed copies. ("*Sruss Sruss*" was onomatopoeia involving the rustle of female underwear).

I entered Griff's sanctum, apprehensively noting the subdued lighting and the important-looking desk.

"Mr Richards, Hackett made a big speech at the uni ceremony and I was there but it was getting really late. I'd been working long shifts and I was pretty tired and left a bit early and missed it."

Griff dismissed me from the office. He was not the emotional sort and I didn't know how annoyed he was.

But it so happened that he checked the time sheets and for one reason or another (perhaps I had done a day shift and then done a play review as well that evening), I did appear to have been over-worked. Very nicely, Griff gave me the benefit of the doubt and rounded on the chief of staff, Viv Goldsmith, for slave-driving his young reporter. Viv and I had never got on, but his hands were tied by the time sheets and he had to eat crow. I'm sure he liked me even less after that.

Quadrant OnLine, 20 May 2013

Taken from the wild

One day Tony Thomas was a lovestruck cadet journalist, the next he was sentenced to six months of rest and pills in the TB ward of Sir Charles Gairdner Hospital, Perth.

At the age of 22 I was motoring round Perth's Crawley foreshore in my souped-up but expensively clapped-out Austin A40. I saw a caravan parked on the verge near the newly-opened Narrows Bridge, offering free X-rays for tuberculosis screening. I stopped and had a chest X-ray. A fortnight later I got a letter inviting me to have a repeat. A day or two after that I was invited to see a doctor at Sir Charles Gairdner Hospital in Shenton Park for an interview. He pointed at my X-ray, indicated a 'spot' and said I would be a patient until my spot was under control.

"How long would that take?" I asked.

"Three months."

"*THREE MONTHS!*" I was dumbfounded.

"We want you settled in here next Saturday. Here's a sheet about what to bring."

(To shimmy my narrative forward, I was actually in hospital for SIX months. I'm sure the doctor bloody-well-knew).

I had never been seriously ill. The prospect of hospital overwhelmed every thought in my brain. My work? My uni studies? And top of the list, my girlfriend Stephanie (name changed), the most desirable young lady I had ever known, not that I had known a great many.

"Let's get married?" I had asked her a month previously (people married young in those days – it was like a mass race to the altar). "Yes!" she said as we necked ardently in the A40 in a lovers' lane in Crawley, in company with 12 other cars-full of couples, plus pedestrian voyeurs who shone torches through the car windows, pretending to be police.

The next day she had changed her mind. Sorry, but no marriage. Did she love me? Yes of course. But when she had announced our engagement to her parents, they had not been over-keen.

As for the TB, my next issue was to inform my employers that they would have to get by without me. My boss took the news with sang-froid (from the French: cold blood). "Sorry to hear it, let's know when you get out," he said distractedly.

Sick pay? "One month on full pay, one month on half pay, one month on quarter pay and after that, not our concern."

Well, I thought, at least I will get a sentimental send-off from my workmates. I had been to many of these, usually when a senior chap was quitting the company for greener pastures. In my mind's eye I saw a little stopwork called, and an admiring but concerned circle of colleagues would surround me. Speeches would be made, praising my talents and character, with hopes for my quick recovery. I would be handed a briefcase or boxed fountain pen, financed from a whipround among staff.

It was my last day at work before Ward 2B. I needed to depart the office early to clean up my affairs, but it would look silly for workmates to organise the send-off when I was no longer there. I dropped hints to the cadet counselor that I would be leaving a couple of hours prematurely.

He didn't seem to understand. I skirted the subject in various ways, until he indicated that he had something urgent to attend to. I slunk off…

Mum transferred me to my new surrogate mother, the hospital. I was in a two-bed room, my companion being a chap, Bill, who was devastated by his loss of occupation. He couldn't meet his family responsibilities. We were friendly but I couldn't identify with him.

The doctor briefed me: The more I rested and the most completely I rested, the quicker the TB spot would go away. Every exertion must be shunned.

Meanwhile, I would get three separate drugs daily - 30 PAS and Inah tablets, and a strep jab in the bum. (I soon perfected a trick of swallowing the 30 pills in a single mouthful).

The doctor mentioned there was a lad, Stephen Orgles, in my ward, a few years younger. The doctor hoped I would strike up a big-brotherly friendship with Stephen, passing on to him my more mature insights.

Bill drew the curtain around himself. I curled on the bed, mooning over Stephanie.

Stephen trotted in, eager to make acquaintance. He was about 17, strongly built, and evinced a quizzical expression, caused by scrunching up his eyes (which he always referred to as 'beadies') to take in the details of me and my room. He was on for mischief and adventure. I explained that, sadly, my treatment required absolute rest. Disturbances of any kind would retard my all-important cure.

Stephen cocked his head and looked at me appraisingly, as a slaughterman might look at a bullock. Snickering, he pulled back the bedclothes while I gazed at him, pyjama-clad, in mute distress.

My bed was next to the window, which had slat blinds pulled up with cords dangling. Stephen expertly tied my ankles together with one cord and my wrists with another. I was half amused, half indignant but conscientiously passive.

Then he tightened the cords to lift my legs and arms half way up the window pane, while my body was still on the bed and my head raised off the pillow. I think Stephen had farming experience and was used to trussing sheep. He stepped back, surveyed his handiwork, and said, "Well, I'm off! Tell me what Sister McGuiness says when she finds you."

Bill poked his head out of his curtains. He was familiar with Stephen's ways, and observing me trussed to the window, his depression lifted and he too waited expectantly for Sister's inspection. "Tell her you're tied up at the moment," he suggested.

Stephen's plan misfired to the extent that several junior nurses happened by, untrussed me and lowered me gently down. (The scene should have been painted by Raphael, "Descent from the Double-Cross"). I was so relieved from the overall stress of the day that I fell asleep. I don't know how the nurses described their spectacular find in the blanks of a ward-report template. But they had a good story for nurses' quarters that night…

The episode broke any mis-trussed with the younger nurses, some of whom found a 22-year-old student more personable than their regular clients, incontinent old alcoholics. But I was unavailable romantically. Memories of necking with Stephanie would bite me like a bull-ant.

In the evening I would hear her high heels tapping down the corridor, click-clack click-clack, the rhythm of love. But once at my bedside, although verbally she was mine, she avoided tactile moments. I checked: "You do still love me?"

"Oh yes, I do." She radiated sincerity.

A bit of a mystery. As the weeks turned into a month, I asked yet again, "Do you love me?" This time she replied, "Please don't ask me that!"

I twigged that she was no longer all that into me, as modern people would say. It was only pity and good-heartedness that kept her visiting me.

I told her morosely not to come any more. As she now loved a parent-approved suitor, an accountant for God's sake! - whom she later married, she was doubtless relieved to get me out of her hair.

Keep in mind that hospitals are crawling with boyfriend-less nurses. Various of them wasted no time in filling the vacancy left by Stephanie.

The harassment of the nursing body (no pun intended) by Stephen and me was reciprocated. I suffered one practical joke that went way too far - but who am I to complain?

One morning I noticed two sores on each side of my groin. The doctors suspected a reaction to the drugs. The sores evolved to circular rings, like coral atolls. A sister suggested the correct diagnosis – ringworm.

The treatment involved painting the sores with ointment and a tea-bag-like soaking of my dangling regions each evening in a red-purple mercurochrome bath. This event was delegated to nurses, not being high-tech medicine. Nurses and I were thus inducted into the Fellowship of the Rings.

After a few days, I developed startling side effects. My scrotum changed color from healthy pink to an angry red and began peeling as if from severe sunburn. The doctor discontinued the red baths and my scrotum normalised, thankfully before I became eligible to join a castrati chorus.

The adverse reaction to standard treatment mystified the medicos.

Maybe it was written up in the literature. But one of my friendly nurses tipped me off that a rival nurse had added a supplement to the bath intended to cause me itchy annoyance. It seemed like she had added a damn sight too much of it…

One day my guardian devil, Steve, had an inspiration. Someone had left a trolley idle in the corridor. "I'll dress up as a doc and wheel you round on the trolley," he suggested. A *tour d'horizon* sounded good.

But we over-did it. After passing through several wards, I decided to become a dead patient rather than just a bogus one. Steve pulled the sheet over my head, with my big nose forming an apex. He set off for the mortuary. (There were such departures even from our own TB ward, of older guys, mostly dead-beats, who contracted TB in the pre-antibiotic era).

Under the sheet I tuned in to the changing sounds as we clattered mortuary-wards. Steve later explained that as we entered a corridor, a doctor popped out, with his bevy of students and sisters. I heard Steve hiss: "Back to the ward, quick!"

Steve was wearing a surgical mask and gown as part of his medico get-up, so he was unrecognisable. Even as I sat up with the sheet still over my head, I heard Stephen's footsteps thudding away from me towards Ward 2B. I flung off the sheet and leapt backwards after him, the trolley ricocheting forwards.

We never heard of any repercussions. It must have been a surreal moment for the medical team…

Quadrant OnLine, 8 January 2013

How I Returned to the Wild

A young Tony Thomas is declared officially sane, although readers sharing his memories of six months in the TB ward may have their doubts.

There was a tragic episode in my hospital stay. At primary school we all liked our classmate Annie, who was short and cute. She was a bundle of good humor and impish charm.

I heard from a visitor that Annie was in hospital too. I didn't really know her and a decade had elapsed. But my gregarious self decided to pay her a visit.

When I came into her room, she was not the lively kid I remembered. Her parents and other family members were there too. They were surprised at my arrival, in my dressing gown, but we all made small talk around the bedside. I asked Annie, "What are your plans when you get out of here?"

"I'll be doing physiotherapy."

"What's up with you?"

"I was playing tennis and got a big headache. They've put me here to check up on it."

I'm a great talker but eventually I intuited, from meaningful glances, that I had outworn my welcome.

Next day a sister dropped by my bed and said, "By the way, don't visit Annie again. She just wants her family."

Oh well, fair enough, I thought.

She died a few weeks later from her brain tumor. I kicked myself for having spoiled that evening with her family…

I was now in love with a small dark nurse, Vicky, who had a squeaky voice. Her other charms more than compensated. How angry I would get when my sister imitated her as Donald Duck!

All our meetings depended on when she was rostered to Ward 2B. One late evening other nurses, vicariously excited by our romantic goings-on, told me that Vicky was rostered on the same floor, on 2D among the women patients.

I decided to wander over. I didn't really have a plan.

Just as I got to 2D a sister accosted me: "What are you doing here?"

"Isn't this the bank?" I replied.

These days, with banks consisting of a box in the wall, my query might be answered with, "Yes, autoteller around the corner to the right". But in those days, a "bank" was a substantial building you went into between 10am and 4pm. I just happened to blurt out my "bank" bit, not wanting to dob in Vicky.

"Stay right there," said sister, and phoned for reinforcements.

I elaborated on the bank story to what was now two concerned sisters.

They escorted me back to bed and departed, conferring in low tones.

"They've gone to get matron," said one of my nurses. "They think you've gone crazy."

People do go crazy in hospitals. I might indeed have become a touch hyper, excited by the gallantry of my conduct. Well let's do the crazy thing, I thought. When no-one was nearby, I hopped out of bed and dived under it, concealed by the overhangs.

A bustle outside, and the two sisters arrived, plus Matron.

I could see their six white shoes. I got a fit of the giggles and the bed twitched. Matron stooped and peered in at me.

She barely paused. *Patient gone crazy. Follow-up required.*

A nurse put me back into bed. As she tucked me up, she hissed: "Matron has gone to get the Registrar. He'll send you off to Heathcote (a mental hospital across the Swan River). Stop this fooling around or you'll be in big trouble!"

It was a shock like a smack in the face. How would I convince the Registrar that I was sane? Acting crazy is easy, but acting 'sane'? What do 'sane' people say, what do they do? If they talk a lot or don't say a lot, would it suggest sanity or insanity?

My 'look sane' solution was to haul out my chess set. I started playing a scripted game from my chess book, Alekhine vs Nimzowitsch 1930. (I had overlooked that many great chess players, like Bobby Fischer, were stir-crazy).

When Registrar arrived, I was deep in chessly analysis.

"I'm told you've been acting strangely."

"I suppose so, but there could well be rational explanations."

"Like what?"

"Well I'd rather not say, just take my word for it. There was a lady involved."

Registrar glanced at my chess board. "That rook's in trouble," he said.

As they left the ward, he was speaking sharply to the Matron. Probably: "You mean you interrupted my work on next year's budget cuts, to check out this *insanity* case?"

I assume that Matron rounded on the sisters, with similar irritation. Sisters probably gave nurses a hard time that night.

I finished the chess exercise and went to sleep…

From somewhere I acquired a do-it-yourself stereo amplifier kit, but only managed to achieve a rat's-nest effect with my bedside soldering iron. A near-stranger, husband of a remote cousin, took it off me and brought it back a week later looking kosher with all the wiring as disciplined as a traffic grid. I had also acquired for some reason a used 3-disk 12in stereo opera set, *Il Trovatore* (1959) with Mario del Monaco, he of the clarion voice. I plugged in my stereo earphones and lowered the stylus onto the turntable. At that time stereo music was a novelty and stereo over earphones even more so a novelty.

I couldn't believe what I heard. It was like the vault of the sky with each star beaming at me an instrument, a voice, a delight. The chorus – especially that anvil number – wrapped around my brain like the Milky Way. I lay back on my pillow, as ravished as St Teresa of Avila. Half way through the platter, a non-musical voice intruded into my first opera experience. It was Bill in the bed alongside: "Tony, you're stuff's on fire!" I opened my eyes: brown smoke was curling from the amplifier. I flung off the earphones and switched off the power. The transformer had shorted. No more heavenly music for me, I grieved. But my cousin's husband re-emerged and swapped in a new, non-faulty transformer. A half-century later I am still hooked on opera. But what if my first random choices had been, say, Richard Strauss's *Elektra* or some pot-boiler by Massenet? Was it just a fluke that my first pick, *Trovatore*, was the most tuneful of all operas, or is there a divinity that shapes our ends?

One evening we were assembled for a meeting, modestly attired in our dressing gowns. We came with a wide variety of health defects and a skewing towards the lower tiers of the social spectrum. For modesty's sake, we were sex-segregated – male invalids seated left, females to the right. The Registrar and a small troupe of his assistants came in and one began taking notes on a clipboard. The minutes were read from the previous annual meeting, 1961. Not many of us were at the previous meeting, because we were either cured or deceased. Regardless, the "minutes" (whatever that meant) were "adopted" and the Treasurer's report approved – we owned some trivial bank account somewhere. The bigshots raced through the rest of the agenda and came to general business. Questions? A lady, whom I viewed then as old, began rabbitting on about how her son never visited because her daughter-in-law was an evil influence. The bigshots managed to shut her up and closed the meeting. They filed out briskly, and we patients shuffled back to our wards, none-the-wiser.

What was it all about? Looking back, I speculate that some years earlier than 1962, there had been a scandal of neglect or worse, and the health minister had demanded a mechanism by which inmates could ventilate their concerns, a "patients' association" or some such. The formal charade of an annual meeting resulted, and the hospital bigshots could include the all-clear from the meeting in their annual report to the minister. For all I know, those annual meetings continue to this day, and the aforementioned bank balance has by now swelled to $80.23 or similar…

After three months I was all a-twitter because my sentence in the hospital was up. But when I inquired about my departure day, they told me, "Not yet." (The Russian word *'nyet'* gets the flavor even better).

It was three more months until I finally got the OK to exit.

I was gladness from tip to toe. I packed up my bedside possessions, and Mum collected me in my A40.

We arrived back in Willagee; there was the pine forest stretching across the valley, my home, my sleepout, freedom.

It was what my ego wanted, but my *id* had other ideas. I came down with my first migraine-style headache. Even now, at 75, I've never had another.

Mum rang the hospital, they sent a cab to get me, and back I went into Ward 2B, with people getting my meals, taking my temperature, and feeding me pills.

I stayed in 2B another week, and they released me again back into the wild. No migraine this time.

Mum had been driving my car for six months, ignoring the front wheels' vibrations. That first day, I drove it to a garage, cursing Mum as the steering wheel danced in my hands. The foreman said he'd do a four-wheel balance. He took off the right front wheel, and saw the entire problem: that tyre was misaligned. But he insisted I pay for the whole four-wheel balancing job. Back in the wild, one must be wary of predators.

I sort-of hated my hospital stay. But looking back, that youngster had some fun and maybe learnt a few things in Ward 2B.

Quadrant OnLine, 9 January 2013

An old hand recalls the first digital revolution

Dorothy Parker called her canary Onan because it cast its seed upon the ground. As journalist Mungo MacCallum was given to reminding readers of the long-defunct *Nation Review*, no one ever had to sweep up after *The Age*'s former economics writer.

Curse you, orgasmologist Shere Hite! I wish my (verbal) intercourse with you at Canberra's National Press Club had never occurred! But regrets are vain: someone long ago did a poem about the "moving finger" moving on, and nothing can lure it back.

At the time I was a Canberra Press Gallery-based reporter, aged 38. I had a title: "Economics Writer" for *The Age*.

A title is a precious thing. Later, I was an "Associate Editor" at *BRW Magazine*, but no-one knew why or what it meant. The reality was that another reporter was promoted to associate editor and I was awarded the same title in case I felt miffed.

At *The Age*, my title was often mis-stated by sub-editors as "Economic Writer", as though I was a bargain or – implausibly – sparing with words.

In fact I was just a poor-man's Kenneth Davidson, he being *The Age*'s (drum-roll!) current "Economics Editor".

We can't all be top dog. I did feel my title "Economics Writer" had gravitas.

Imagine my annoyance when gonzo journalist Mungo MacCallum began referring to me in the now-extinct tabloid *Nation Review* as "Tony Thomas, *The Age*'s non-masturbating Economics Writer". You may say, "What's wrong with that? It could be worse." Well, yes it could. But when I predicted a half-percent rise in official interest rates, I didn't want this portentous forecast marred by gratuitous, albeit complimentary, personal detail. Worse, I had no-one to thank but myself for Mungo's soubriquet.

The years have rolled by, but I still owe readers of both the *Nation Review* and *The Age* this explanation...

I was treasurer of the Press Club for several years (another title with gravitas, although I seldom got spending and receipts to balance). Our main activity was organising big-shot lunchtime speakers every few weeks, giving celebs the benefit of a national forum.

I felt an obligation to enliven the question times, which were often ponderous, with some pre-planned witticisms. In any event I enjoyed showing off, especially in high-level company such as the Shahanshah of Iran, Maggie Thatcher and sad-sack Labor luminary Jim Cairns.

To give you the idea, man-of-the-world Peter Ustinov was one of our speakers, and I went to some care to feed him a good question:

> *Me*: When I was about 11, I went to see *Quo Vadis*, in which you played Nero, very brilliantly. I loved the scene where Deborah Kerr was tied to the stake, clad in diaphanous garments, and all set to be gored by a big black bull. Then, as you in Rome fiddled, so in the cinema seat did one small boy…
>
> *Ustinov* (before I could even ask my pro forma question): My dear boy, you were the only person who really understood that scene!

He added that he had asked the director of *Quo Vadis*, Mervyn LeRoy, for any special insights into Nero's motivations.

"Nero," replied Mervyn, "The way I see him …"

"Yes?"

"He's a guy plays with himself nights."

Ustinov went on to explain that the "bull" from which the hulking slave Ursus saved Deborah Kerr, was actually a chloroformed cow, filmed so as to keep the udder out of shot.[1] Ursus had to twist the cow's neck, which woke the cow: "Every time Ursus put his foot on the carcass to symbolise his victory, the cow would look up and moo pathetically."[2]

Someone asked him about the lions. He said there were 120 of them on the cast list, but they refused to act their parts as Christian-killers, something to do with their dislike of bright lighting. Eventually the lion-tamers organised human dummies stuffed with meat, which the lions did get stuck into, but too horrifically to make the final edit, he said.

I came away realising that Peter Ustinov was not easily upstaged.

None of the above clarifies why I became "*The Age*'s non-masturbating Economics Writer"; it may even raise more questions than it answers. Am I unconsciously dodging proper disclosure? Let me screw my courage to the sticking place and try harder.

---

1 "Ursus" is Latin for bear. The actor playing Ursus was Buddy Baer. Spooky!

2 This was before the politically correct apologia, *"No animals were hurt in the making of this film"*, began appearing in end-credits.

Someone lined up Shere Hite as our Press Club speaker for April 19, 1978. She is often described as a "clitorologist". She argues that direct stimulus to that organ beats penile intercourse as a route (or should I say, "highway") to orgasm.[3]

While talk about some aspects of sex in the 1970s was fairly liberated, Hite's take on it was confronting stuff for an audience unaccustomed to female masturbation as a lunch topic.

As Hite got down to the nitty-gritty, people either forgot their roast chicken or subjected it to minute inspection and small forkfuls. The unease was palpable, especially when Hite began gesturing elaborately with her right middle finger to indicate her favorite style of clitoral stimulation.

Ms Hite finished to polite applause. She took a few innocuous questions, then I got the call: "Ms Hite, a good thing about masturbation is that you don't have to look your best.[4] I wouldn't know. I don't masturbate and never have…"

For form's sake, I began a question on female fantasies, but it was drowned out in the roar of mirth from the room. People had been way out of their comfort zone. The tensions of the past half hour's tutorial on ladies' solo fulfillment now dissolved into ribald laughter.

When the racket died down, Shere responded, in character:

"Well, I think when I'm masturbating I DO look my best."

In the audience was Mungo MacCallum, who specialised in outrageous prose (now many do, but he was a local pioneer).

I had caused him recent offence over a silly incident, the insolence of office, when I was wearing my 'Treasurer' hat. He came into *The Age*'s gallery cubby-hole to put himself down as a "maybe" for a Press Club lunch. Since I had to manage the numbers and capacity, I told him he couldn't register as a "maybe", only as "yes". I was cranky about too many "maybe" applicants and ended his expostulations by physically pushing him out the door. I should have apologised but life moved on, so I apologise now, 40 years in arrears.

Anyway, Mungo then pinned on me the descriptor: "Tony Thomas,

---

3 As her official website biog puts it: "In 1976, a young grad student from Missouri dropped a bombshell into the bedrooms of the world, and blew apart our preconceptions about women's sexuality."

4 I had picked up this bon mot from our worldly bureau chief, the late Allan Barnes, in a less-erudite context.

The Age's non-masturbating Economics Writer…"

I rang Mungo this week to see if anyone had ever asked why he had referred to me that way.

"As opposed to [name of famed *Age* colleague deleted]?"[5]

"Yes".

"Well I'd forgotten the whole thing. It disappeared into the mists of time. No, I don't think anyone ever asked."

An ugly thought crosses my mind: maybe no-one was reading me OR Mungo.

Quadrant OnLine, 31 December 2012

The big sleep

It was time. Fourteen years after he entered our lives, an old dog drifts gently into memory…

Although we'd agreed, my spouse had to keep up the pressure. I dialed the surgery: "Our Maltese, Percy, can you put him down today please?"

"Judith [name changed] is free at 4.15."

Percy was near-deaf, near-blind, and arthritic. That day a line had been crossed: two carpet puddles and one carpet poo.

I took Percy and Kara (our daughter's resident spaniel) for another walk along the creek. Percy, strangely shedding his years, scampered down the embankment and even scrambled up again.

With Percy sitting on the car's back seat – he was used to trips to the vet to be clipped – I surreptitiously put a green towel and a chaff-bag in the boot.

During what seemed a long wait in the back surgery, I didn't fuss over Percy (hypocritical). But I did dwell on how our enraptured kids first brought him home as a powderpuff puppy. They made him his first bed inside my bike helmet.

Judith put Percy on a blanket on the table. I felt less guilty as he turned to me with milky eyes and discolored little teeth.

Judith shaved his right front shin with clippers as I stroked him. He didn't flinch as she inserted a catheter and squeezed in some fluid. Within

---

5 Even then, it was a wide field.

seconds his four legs folded. He was now a white heap asleep, but alive, on the blue blanket. Judith squeezed in another fluid, and listened through a stethoscope. "He's gone now," she said. "Fifteen years, we had him," I said, adding: "Er, how do I pay you?" "Don't worry, I'll post the bill."

Percy hung like a slack sausage out of the towel. "Take the blanket," she said. "Don't you want it back?" "No, that's fine." I exited with my parcel by the rear door.

I put the parcel on our side garden, then went in to collect Kara to give Percy a final sniff, for "closure". Kara always runs to me to get her chin and ears rubbed. This time, she was on the decking and ran inside, away from me. I went inside, she ran out. She showed real fear. My wife had to capture her via an ambush behind the dog-door. Kara took a sniff at Percy but then showed more interest in the blanket (smells of other dogs, I'd guess).

My all-knowing tennis mates had said, "Three feet deep or rats dig 'em up." Percy nose-dived awkwardly out of his blanket into the hole. I quickly back-filled, planted an azalea and watered it in. My wife added two rose blooms.

Now there are no more carpet puddles – imagine if Kara had been the secret culprit! But Kara avoids us (I don't blame her) and lies in her basket looking nowhere through half-shut eyes. As her comforters, I've added two socks and a pair of used underpants to the basket.

Already my wife and I have separate, secret plans for a puppy.

Quadrant OnLine, 16 August 2012

Pretty Perth: Pity About the "Perverts"

Anyone who opposes same-sex marriage, or merely supports a plebiscite on the matter, is apt to be pilloried by Mardi Gras paraders and the like. How today's activists would have coped with the homophobic Perth of my youth is anyone's guess.

What a nice town my hometown of Perth was in 1968! Optimism in the air as the Pilbara development got under way. Pretty Swan River, friendly tolerant folks. Classy intellectuals at the University of Western Australia.

I mean, Perth was a nice place for heterosexuals. For homosexual males, not so benign. Public or private sodomy earned you a maximum 14 years hard labor plus a whipping. Masturbation with another man, "gross indecency", attracted a milder maximum of only three years hard labor, plus a whipping. Nor was the legal threat an empty one. About 25 convictions had occurred from 1960-68, with three offenders currently doing time.

The Police Minister in 1968 was Jim Craig. He wasn't all that homosexual-tolerant, in fact he told me that personally, "I'd have their b's out!"

Today of course, we celebrate homosexuality (plus LGBTI etceteras) and from primary school onwards, the rainbow banner proudly waves. Using Perth 1968 as a case study, it's amazing how social mores have changed in 50 years.

Perth's police style, 1968, was not to go hunting down homosexuals but if someone complained to the Criminal Investigations Bureau (CIB), then detectives had to follow-up and prosecute if evidence went that way.

At the time, Dr E.R. Csillag was senior lecturer in psychiatry at WA University, and he sought to 'cure' homosexuals via aversion therapy. This involved showing his client erotic homosexual pictures and texts followed by an electric shock and then showing an erotic female picture with no shock. "Dr Csillag tried the shock on himself once," I reported, and I quoted him, "I swore like hell!"

A consulting clinical psychologist, Mrs A. Creed, sought to correct "faulty attitudes towards women" through counseling. She told me, "To the homosexual I am the safe but warm mother-figure who cares, and all the sexual deviates I have helped have said that aspect was the most potent factor in their recovery." Good for Mrs Creed!

By now you may be wondering how and why I was getting up close and personal with Perth's homosexual set. You doubtless suppose that reporter Tony Thomas wrote a feature on the topic and my employer *The West Australian* published it. No, no such revelations ever surfaced in that conservative, dull newspaper.

So the back-story is worth telling. The features editor of The West was an old stick-in-the-mud who only wanted stock-standard mainstream matter. But I liked writing odd stuff. These pieces, comprising a little pad of paragraphs (one para per A5 triple-sandwich wad) would usually come back to me with the simple word "No" on the front of it, plus Feature Editor's initials.

Two miles to the west was WA University where I was doing Australian literature part-time. The Arts Faculty had a monthly journal called *The Critic* and I discovered *The Critic* was happy to run, without fee, my rejected pieces from *The West*. (Given that a 12- month sub to *The Critic* was only $1.75, *The Critic*'s non-payment for work was understandable).

I was always a bit nervous when my pieces appeared in Crawley's publication, wondering if my paymasters at *The West* would view it as *lese majeste*.

A typical piece rejected by *The West* and run by *The Critic* involved my research into liqueur chocolates on sale around town, and my discovery that nearly all of them were devoid of actual liqueur. I noted that serious liqueur-chocolate eaters knew how to get hold of imported chocolates with real 2% proof liqueur in them.

This caught the attention of Fremantle's Customs officials, who intended to enforce the existing ban on 2%-proof imported chocs. The ban was designed to protect innocent children from the ravages of chocolate-coated alcohol. Customs demanded that I disclose who was doing the importing. "Never!" I shouted. "I'd go to gaol first." Anyway, that's all off-topic except that The West spiked my story and The Critic ran it.

It was investigating homosexuality that got me into big trouble at *The West*. My feature was rejected with fury and sanctions. If I hadn't slipped the piece to *The Critic*, an important slice of Perth life ca 1968 would have gone unrecorded.

To that date, May 1968, I confidently reported there had been no surveys or public analysis of the Perth homosexual community whatsoever. A cone of silence enveloped the topic. The only mentions of homosexuality in *The West* were occasional Magistrate's Court reports of a conviction. In polite company and the press, the topic was unspeakable.

During my high school years (1953-57) at Perth Modern, there was one lad "Geoff " in my year who showed no fear of girls and had louche habits like removing a false tooth and menacing you with it. Geoff wound up in *The West* as a library assistant so we saw each other often.

In 1962, when I was in hospital with TB, I saw an item in *The West* to the effect that police had raided a party at a suburban house, arrested numbers of men dressed as nuns, and secured sodomy-type convictions. Geoff was among those convicted and hence was named and shamed to the world. I think he was fined. I wondered about this small-town tragedy, and felt I should contact Geoff in a friendly way. But I had no idea how to express my condolences, and never called.

A few years later I acquired a girlfriend "Trish" with a very conventional family that included Trish's older brother "Clive", a bachelor. Clive had a very close male friend "Ted" but the family tip-toed round the issue and assured each other that one day Clive would find Miss Right and settle down. Even though Clive and Ted behaved like a couple, Ted was always dubbed Clive's "best friend".

I felt motivated to lift the cone of silence by doing a solid feature on the topic. I suspected *The West* would disapprove, so I did all the work "off the books" between normal jobs. I thought that when I presented the Editor with my finished article, he would be impressed enough to give it an OK.

My first task was to locate and interview homosexuals ("gay" in those days meant cheerful). Easier said than done. First, I was unworldly and never involved in night-life, drinking circles and other places where people acquire sophisticated know-how. Second, I could hardly ask a question like, "Are you homosexual? If so, may I interview you?" Might as well ask, "Are you a burglar? Done any jobs lately?"

I wandered around in the evenings keeping an eye out for any two or more men behaving unnaturally with each other, and even accosted groups of men in pubs and asked if they knew any homosexuals for my interview-fodder. No success: indeed looking back I suspect I myself was viewed as a shy homosexual trying to line up a rendezvous.

Finally someone told me about a night club involving cross-dressers and libidinous goings-on. I turned up and joined a table of rough-looking males, after explaining to them my reportorial mission. They were non-committal – but made frequent side-trips to the toilet or adjacent lane and discoursed in a coded way about incomprehensible (to me) activities. I departed none-the-wiser.

Word got out around Newspaper House about my project. A few colleagues dropped by, ostensibly to chat but really to try to sniff out what my line was. For all they knew, I could be preparing to "out" them or otherwise draw attention to matters hitherto undisturbed by media scrutiny.

I then did the rounds of some Perth professionals who dealt with homosexuals. They mostly viewed homosexuality as a pathological condition.

Only one of them, WA's Director of Mental Health, Dr A. Ellis, had a view then which has stood the test of time. He told me the law against homosexual acts was medieval and capable of making criminals out of a third of the male population (i.e. who according to Kinsey, had a same-sex experience at least once in their lives). The main problem was not the condition but the draconian laws and their potential for blackmailers, he said. A government solicitor opined that Perth would not be ready for any legal change to homosexual laws for ten years to come.

A Law Reform Committee had recently been appointed in Perth but it deliberately ignored the homosexual laws, saying those were for the State government to decide on.

I got an interview with the then Police Minister Craig, a Country Party stalwart, whose views would not be described today as "enlightened".

I wrote in the piece that Police Minister Craig had read some of the recent UK Wolfenden report proposing UK reforms, "but (he) considered the British eagerness to legalise evils like drug-taking, prostitution and homosexuality was largely responsible for the state of morals in Britain today."

The danger with legalising homosexuals was that they could start preying on youths, he said. I wrote, "Basically, he considered homosexuality unnatural. This was on personal grounds, not religious ones. Homosexuals were perverts, he said, and he had no intention of legalising their behavior."

My punchline went: *"One cabinet minister said the government had an open mind on the laws. Another said bluntly: 'I'd have their [testicles] out!' "*

Feeling pleased with my draft feature, I dropped it in my Feature Editor's in-tray. Next morning I was summoned to the presence of the Editor himself, Griff Richards, who inspected me as if I was a blowfly on his blotter: "We are a family paper and this – [smacking my wad of copy against his desk] – is not what our readers want to read over the breakfast table!"

He followed up with some strictures to the Chief of Staff, Viv Goldsmith, to keep a closer eye on me, to keep me productively occupied and to ensure that no repeat offences of this nature occurred.

I certainly took a risk handing my manuscript to *The Critic* for publication. Luckily no-one in Newspaper House was a *Critic* reader.

Perth no longer gaols and whips homosexuals, I'm glad to say. Attitudes have changed in the past 50 years, but I rather wonder what Perth social norms will be 50 years hence.

Quadrant OnLine, 8 March 2016

Expletive not deleted

Obscenities have become common in the pages of *The Age*, a paper whose naked partisanship and post-adolescent groupthink have brought it to the grave's edge. Our correspondent explains how he started the rot.

In July, 1978, I happened to be in Brisbane, reporting an economics conference for *The Age*. The Friday session was dull and the Saturday program looked no better. On the Saturday morning I suspected my Brisbane trip was a waste of time.

From my hotel room, however, I noticed in a side street something more interesting than economics academics bolstering their research citations. The side street was head to tail with police buses, and the buses were packed with Queensland police. What's all this about?

I went outside and followed people to nearby King George Square. There a women's rights rally was warming up. About 100 women were active in the square, watched by an audience of 100-200. The surprising thing was the extent of the police presence – I estimated well over 300 of them, outnumbering the meeting itself. The other police in the buses were in reserve.

I recalled how Brisbane for more than a year had been embroiled in controversy over the right to march in the street. Premier Joh Bjelke-Petersen had banned street protest marches in Brisbane, although he did not ban peaceful meetings in St George's Square. "Protest groups need not bother applying for permits to stage marches – because they won't be granted," he said. He steamrollered the legislation through the State Parliament in less than one day.

Subsequently, more than 1,700 people were arrested for demonstrating or marching (or being in the wrong place at the wrong time). It was nothing unusual for 1000 police to be mustered for a day to maintain vigilance against a prospective march or protest. Further south, in Sydney and Melbourne, political marches continued to be a normal aspect of city life, usually with the good-humored cooperation of traffic and other police.

So here I was in Brisbane, in the eye of the cyclone. No, scrub that metaphor – the eye of a cyclone is calm. I was, well, in Brisbane, which was then an alien land where a Premier and his police commissioner ran the show. (The commissioner, Sir Terry Lewis, was later de-Sir-ed and gaoled, but I'm getting ahead of my story).

The meeting in the square was not a 'march', and technically it was not breaking any Queensland law. To entertain the onlookers, some of the women activists were staging a street-theatre. Six women each adopted the role of a female virtue and stood in a rubbish bin reciting some doggerel or song.

One of the women, playing "Prudence", recited a ditty that included the word "f***". Brisbane police were so shocked that they barged into the group and hauled Prudence out of her rubbish bin and carted her across to a paddy wagon parked half a block away. In this way they showed their sensitivity to coarse language.

The arrest of Prudence inspired her sisterhood to have another go. They sang a song that also included the word "f***", and the police again waded in for the arrests. As I described it for *The Age*:

> Big men barging through the crowd…Amplifier wires cut. Women dragged out, wriggling, fighting and screaming. Friends pulling at police. Friends also being arrested. Neat uniformed women police using their judo grips. Fear, pain, indignity.
>
> I followed one arrested girl to the paddy wagon. The policeman had her right arm in some sort of lock as he marched her away, and he kept the lock on while queueing for the charge sheet and photograph.

"He's twisting my arm! He's hurting me!" she kept crying, while
he kept repeating, "What's your name? What's your name?"

She gave what my notes record as a 'real scream of pain'...

The women speakers were in high dudgeon about the arrests over
the word "f***". One speaker said the police had called her a whore
and a slut. Another said she had been called a black bitch; she wasn't
black but it made her ashamed to be white, she said stoutly. Another
young woman took the mike and made what I considered to be the
speech of the day:

"One of my friends was just arrested, maybe because she looked
a bit butch. But if she's in jail, that's where I want to be." She paused,
amid cheers. "They should do something about their f***ing system."

They came in and got her. But the atmosphere became humorous.
She walked off grinning, with just a police hand on her arm, and
at the paddy wagon a policeman said, "You got your wish" and she
laughed. When they photographed her, she raised her fist...

What I didn't say in my *Age* piece, was that shortly after, a big high-
ranking policeman approached me and threatened to arrest me for
'obstructing police'. I was amazed. I was standing 30 metres down
the street from the paddy wagon, and the nearest police person was
20 metres or so distant. I was not communicating with anyone, just
watching on a near deserted bit of street, listening and taking notes.
I wondered, if I were to be arrested, what tall tales would the police
witness tell the magistrate to justify my conviction. Nonetheless, it was
not my job to get arrested, rightly or wrongly, so I moved out of view
of the paddy wagon and back to the meeting.

I finished my article with:

There's nothing funny about Mr Bjelke-Petersen and the police force
he uses. Democracy in Queensland is less safe than the average citizen
down South would imagine.

There was plenty more back-story to my Saturday in Brisbane than
what I wrote for *The Age*. Here goes: The police kept arresting the women
on one charge or another, till only a rump of players and audience was
left. This rump then decided to walk to the city watch-house and give
some moral support to their sisters within it.

I was still smarting from the way the police had tried to frame me. I couldn't help identifying with the women, rather than with the police, or neither. (I suspect that in reporting civil disobedience, reporters sometimes implicitly identify with the police, hob-nobbing with the police spokesperson and hurrying along to any press conference the police call during the day. Other times they identify with protesters, as when they write breathless copy like "Hundreds of thousands of angry protestors made a sea of color as they flooded down Bourke Street. Mothers wheeling prams shook their fists exultantly in support of (the politically-correct cause of the day)."

My case was unusual. I was in the capital city of a democratic but corrupt state government. This government was undemocratically suppressing dissent by arresting citizens for no good reason, and threatening to arrest a completely law-abiding reporter who was not obeying the unwritten rules about how to report events in Brisbane.

I figured that the best way to witness any police violence or misbehavior was to be as close to the demonstrators as possible. When they sat down on the grass outside the watch-house, I sat down with them, chatting and taking notes. They were singing songs of solidarity with the women inside the walls. Eventually the drama petered out.

I went back to the hotel and composed and filed my story for Monday's *Age*, leaving out how the police had threatened me. It was a difficult article to write, partly because I had no access to research (this was long before Google), partly because I was trying to be objective and indignant at the same time, and particularly because The Age was definitely not prone to printing the word "F***" except as, maybe, f–k.

Yet "f***" was central to the whole story. So I wrote it in full.

Next day in Brisbane I got a call from the night editor, Peter Cole-Adams. He wanted to print the story but had already received a call from a senior Brisbane police executive (I think a deputy to the Commissioner, or the media liaison person) warning that anything I wrote should be viewed by *The Age* with suspicion because the author Tony Thomas had himself been taking part in the demonstration he was writing about. And the police had photos to prove it.

It was the 'photos to prove it' that spooked night-editor Peter. He hadn't seen them, and if they were produced after the article appeared, and incriminated me, *The Age*'s reputation would suffer. So he asked me,

"Were you taking part or doing anything the police could photograph and embarrass us? Think carefully because if you mislead us about this, your employment is at stake."

I gulped. What photos? No, there could be nothing incriminating. I had just done my job. But being media-savvy, I knew that photos can often lie. Maybe they had a photo of me about to pick my nose, and it looked as though I was giving the finger to the police? I had to take that risk. No, I said, there was nothing I did that constituted taking part in the demo. "Well," Peter said, "you'd better be right, and by the way, we're going to print the word "F***" where you've written it."

I wondered for years about the police photos of me. By a coincidence, our chief political reporter, Michelle Grattan, one day remarked to me that she had some photos I would be interested in. She had been handed them by the Queensland police media person. They were of good professional quality, blown up to about A4 size, and they showed me sitting on the lawn outside the watch-house, in company with the protestors. It had been taken when I was interviewing them and waiting for any police violence or provocation to occur. I was not displaying any activist tendencies.

Among the readership of my feature was my own father, Pete, who excerpted it in his own 60-page political booklet on the street-march ban, titled "No! No! to Joh!" Pending a trip to the State Library to look up *The Age* original, I've been drawing on Pete's booklet myself, creating a son-father-son loop.

Regarding Sir Joh, I was quite surprised to find my experience was not uncommon. Wiki has a section on Joh and the media: "Journalists covering industrial disputes and picketing, were afraid of arrest. Some journalists experienced police harassment."

Joh's classic quotes include:

> The greatest thing that could happen to the state and nation is when we get rid of all the media… then we could live in peace and tranquility and no one would know anything.

Perhaps he was joking.

Commissioner Sir Terry Lewis eventually got his come-uppance but Joh didn't.

Lewis in August, 1991, was convicted on 15 counts of corruption.

The jury found that Lewis had accepted bribes totalling more than $600,000 to protect brothels, SP bookmakers, illegal casinos and operators of illegal gambling machines. Judge Tony Healy gave him the maximum 14 years and Lewis was released, minus knighthood, in 2002 after serving ten years.

During Joh's 1991 trial for perjury (he was acquitted), his former police Special Branch bodyguard, Sergeant Bob Carter, claimed that in 1986 he (Carter) had been given two packages of cash totalling $210,000 in Joh's office from a property developer.

Joh died in 2005 at 94.

Quadrant OnLine, 3 November 2013

Fool's gold on Rue de la Folie Regnault

This a true story, perhaps soon to be a major movie starring Penelope Cruz as the tormented Margaret, legally yoked to the brutish and unscrupulous Tony Thomas (Russell Crowe and Eric Bana are vying for that role).

Marg and I lobbed into our latest apartment in Paris, delighted to find it well fitted out. Previous apartments were stocked with items left over from the owners' attics after all the relatives and local gypsies had picked them over for anything of value. Next morning, I explored the bookcase in the bedroom while Marg washed up, swept the floor and went off to check the local laundromat.

Most books were in French, one of the few languages I have difficulty with. I opened an old paperback called '*Fontainebleu*' and – *oh ciel!* – banknotes began to pour out of it like beautiful pressed flowers.

They were Euro (€) notes, which meant they had been hidden there in recent history. As to the amount…a couple of hundreds, a fifty, a fistful of 20s, they just kept coming. Still unbelieving, I counted them out. €380 in total, that is, about $A600. I speculated that some previous traveler hid the funds, departed in a hurry or half-blotto, and for some reason never followed up to reclaim the money, or maybe thought it had been lost to pickpockets on the subway.

I was sitting there, eyes glazed over, when a sepulchurous inner voice began chanting, "Do not tell Margaret…do not tell Margaret." When I hear this voice, I am instantly in its power, fight it though I may.

In any case, I reasoned, if I did tell Marg, any of the following would happen:

1. She would tell the apartment agent to come and get it, or
2. She would spend it on essentials, or
3. She would insist we celebrate with a snack, coffee and cake for two at the friendly and picturesque French café down the street with its red-striped awnings, after which there would be nothing left of $600 but small change.

The sinister voice then commanded me, "Re-hide it in case Marg opens the book by coincidence. Put all the notes between the two baseball caps on the top of the wardrobe." This I did, robot-like.

But my higher faculties cut in. Would my actions, however involuntary, meet the four-way test of the Central Melbourne-Sunrise Rotary Club, of which I am a much-loved member and wannabe President? *Grrr*, probably not even meet a *two*-way test. But I could email the apartment owner in Adelaide and alert him that some money had been found, that it was held in trust by myself, and would be given to anyone who could correctly state the amount, hiding place and my mother's maiden name.

That left the ethical dilemma. Would Marg find out, e.g. through her snap audits of my wallet or her spooky intuition, that has felled me so often in the past?

Previously I could launder amounts I overspent (above my meagre weekly allowance) in the Bermuda Triangle between our bank and Visacard accounts, as per rogue forex dealers. But that has become dangerous since Marg took a course in forensic accounting, apparently as a hobby.

I remembered I shortly had a two-week window traveling solo in UK, where I could "disappear" quite a lot of funds on opera tickets, "presents", the odd book and CD etc.

Another option is the *fait accompli*. I would come home to Melbourne with the funds. Soon after that, I buy the computer I have long craved, and march through the front door with it, saying, "I'm home! By the way, I've just bought an iMac!" The *fait accompli* really separates the men from the boys. Although the initial explosion can be large, things usually settle down after three or four months.

Best thing for now, I thought, would be to let the matter ferment for 24 hours, in the expectation that a safe and honorable plan would emerge.

So, time now for our daily expedition. We headed off for Chateau de Vincennes. I walked with a slight swagger, as per a Lachlan Murdoch, youthful, virile and very rich. The subway trip was enlivened by some French plainclothes police collaring a small gang of teenagers from our train and banging their heads against the wall, as in excessively violent cop movies.

The chateau was wonderful and so was I, treating Marg to a coffee, buying her a CD (*Cavalry Fanfares of the Republican Guard*), and arranging a trip for her that afternoon to the Musee de l'Armee. On the way home she begged a second stopover at a French café. Instead of having the usual ugly scene, we sat on the pavement table sipping beer and watching the sun set on a perfect Paris spring day, while the café proprietor could hardly believe his luck. Certainly, Romance was in the air.

So much so that your hero began to re-examine his plans on the $600. Surely Marg deserved better treatment than this? I should come clean. But how to cover my grimy tracks?

I would seize a moment while she was peeling spuds or sorting washing. I would retrieve the hoard from the baseball caps, put it in my wallet, and leave the wallet conspicuously on the table. And it all went like clockwork. Marg looked out from the kitchen (not hard to do as it is the size of a phone box) and said, "Have we any money left over from today?"

Myself, on derelict sofa, engrossed in *The Guardian*: "Probably something. {Casually} Why don't you check my wallet, it's on the table."

The wallet is opened. I peer over the newspaper to enjoy Marg's expression. Her eyes widen. She starts pulling out high denomination notes, instead of the tatty €5 note or two she had expected. They pile up on the table. Of course, she wears an expression of deep suspicion. This I had allowed for.

Marg {deeply suspicious}: You have been to the autoteller and got money
    without checking with me!

Me {smugly}: No I haven't.

Marg: Yes you have! You promised me you wouldn't do that!

Me: No, I haven't been to any autoteller.

Marg: Yes you have. You're lying, as usual.

Me: No I'm not. I haven't been to the autoteller.

Several cyclical repetitions of this exchange, with a rising inflection, are
    omitted here to save space.

Marg: Well, where has it come from?

Me {triumphantly}: I found it!

Marg carefully counts the money and gets close to the tally of €380: What
    do you mean, you found it?!

Me {delightedly}: I found it in the bookcase!

At this point, I sensed from Marg's darkening expression that my
scenario was running off the rails. I felt I was out on a lonely plain, with
a bolt of lightning hissing down and a thunderclap to follow. What had
come unstuck?

Even my thickest reader, yourself probably, has by now worked it
out.

Marg made a tiger-like spring to the bookcase and I sat dumbfounded
as she grabbed that very same book, *Fontainebleu*, and shook it like a
brown bear with a salmon.

Marg {through gritted teeth}: Great. GrrATE! That just happens to be
    the rent money for the agent. I hid it in the book. She's coming in a
    couple of days for it.

Unable to find words, I essay a small fake laugh.

Marg: When did you find it?

Me: {unable to find words}

Marg: Where has the money been all today?

Me: {unable to find words}

Marg: Why didn't you tell me you'd {heavy sarcasm} 'found it' in the first
    place?

Me: {unable to find words}

In stage comedies, eg by David Williamson, the hero generates a wry,
self-deprecating line, the heroine responds with an angry put-down,
but then her eyes twinkle and we know that, actually, she has forgiven
him. She giggles, throws herself at him and they collapse helplessly on
the divan in a tangle of limbs, while the audience breaks into delighted
applause.

But I was in another screenplay altogether. Many husbands may have been in situations like this (perhaps even worse ones, although that's drawing the long bow) so there is no need for a verbatim account of the next half hour. I did all I could to show I was genuinely contrite, including a failed whipped-puppy impersonation.

When the counseling was over, we had a quiet dinner, characterised by rapid and somewhat noisy and theatrical table service. After that, I watched French TV.

Certainly, Romance was off the agenda. I would be a stupid man if I failed to draw any lesson from this trauma. I mentally reviewed the events phase by phase, and concluded, "Well, tomorrow night is another day."

Quadrant OnLine, 7 December 2012

A blight at the opera

Perhaps, if the Marx Brothers had been involved, that remarkable performance of *Turandot* might have been just a little stranger. But not by much.

There's nothing like a disaster: Captain Coward upending the Costa Concordia; Canberra race riots on Australia Day, 2012; the National Broadband Network; my first marriage…

In such a hideous catalogue, I should include the two performances of Puccini's *Turandot* at the Palais, St Kilda, December 14 and 18, 2004. For my $120 ticket, I got even more drama than I paid for.

In scale, *Turandot* is like *Aida*, minus elephants. In coordination of resources, think Normandy landings. *Turandot*, after all, killed Puccini, half-way through the third Act. Someone else had to finish the score.

This Palais performance hinged on an imported Italian soprano we'll call Ms 'Z'. The diva was interviewed for the Melbourne production:

> The soprano, who has sung the role at Torre del Lago in Tuscany where the open-air Puccini Festival is held, says she is carrying on the tradition of singing exemplified by Maria Callas and Joan Sutherland.

As is usually the case, a lot was riding on the success of this. Victoria's Premier Steve Bracks, along with Lord Mayor John So and

Dame Elisabeth Murdoch, were invited to the Palais, but not out of mere politeness. Melbourne Opera's chairman, Peter Donnelly, and Lady Primrose Potter had buttonholed Bracks wanting $2.3m a year for the company, and *Turandot* "shows we can back up what we are saying", Donnelly told him.

The production – sets, costumes, supervisors and the two principal singers, Ms 'Z' and Spanish tenor Antonio Ordonez – was shipped to Melbourne from Tuscany. This volatile mix was supplemented in Melbourne by an unpaid (volunteer) chorus, ballet dancers from the Victorian College of the Arts, a children's chorus from Carey Baptist Grammar, a troupe of body-builders as the opera's burly executioners, and an 80-piece paid orchestra. Local diva Rosemary Illing was the tortured and ill-fated slave girl, Liu, though not as tortured and ill-fated as the audience.

This *Turandot* had a rough ride from the outset. Supposed to open in November, it was delayed a month, requiring a vast phone-around to alert the myriad ticket-holders.

The ticketing and attendants system ran rough (the Palais, in all its faded grandeur, seats more than 2000). On Tuesday the show started 30 minutes late. (A scheduled Thursday performance disappeared).

Between the Tuesday and the Saturday, someone discovered that the two imported principals lacked work visas. The Palais itself was a nightmare for performers, with its backstage passageways and stairwells airless and so narrow that the cast of 120 suffered grid-lock en route to their entrances. Costumes could not be washed: the plus for the cast was that by Saturday all smelt equally bad.

'Z' made a big impact at her first rehearsal. A chorus member, also a Melbourne University employee, provided this account:

> She looks about my age or a little older, has a dramatic Italianate face and this tumbling mane of black hair. And she's a size 20 easy and dressed dramatically in black and white. She walks from her face down – that is, her head and face go first and the body sails around underneath it. Very Dame Joan although without the lantern jaw.
>
> She started to sing and we all thought "oh bugger" because none of the parts of this HUUUUGE voice seemed to be connecting and she's supposedly this big international star. But then she went right

up the top and did a NOTE of extreme loudness and bigness and made-my-ears-go-blat-and-ringness and KAPOW! There it was. This big, big, big dramatic soprano voice which one could use as a blunt instrument in a riot. She sort of picks it up and launches it into the music, like a bowler hefting a bowling ball. In her lower ranges it's almost a growl, it's so feral, and it doesn't get any less feral as it goes up, just more intense. It's an extraordinary, exhilarating, exciting sort of sound.

But it's just a little too much for indoor use. Having that sort of thing shot at one from 10 feet away in a dusty, echoing church hall was an experience neither I nor my eardrums will ever forget.

Others have remarked on Z's voice. I noticed one comment on a youtube about 'Z' in the role of Amina, the lyrically vulnerable Swiss village maiden, in Bellini's *La sonnambula*:

She is mistress of the Art of Can Belto! She attacked that air with gusto and wrestled it to the floor. . . and Bellini and his Amina definitely were the losers here.

How bad was Thursday's opening of *Turandot*? The Australian's Martin Ball wrote:

Maria 'Z''s singing as Turandot was completely inadequate. She was out of time, out of tune, out of breath – in a word, terrible. What is more, she appeared to be aware of this, and her bravery in going for the high notes was almost poignant but for the fact it was largely in vain. Her curtain call was greeted with muscled boos....

One of the boo-ers later outed himself as a 'Philip Murphy', who wrote:

Aside from the planning bungles, Z in the title role was quite atrocious. So much so that I felt compelled to bring some Continental realism to the proceedings and, much to the shock of my companion that evening, threw out some raucous 'boos' at the curtain call.

The Age's critic John Slavin concluded: "I could not discern whether she had a bad cold (why not alert the audience beforehand if this was the case?) or the voice had passed its use-by date, but her *tessitura* was crumbling at the edges and she sang flat...One of the greatest soprano roles was reduced to a case for an ear-and-throat specialist."

Slavin also conjured up a titillating description of the set: "Pietro Cascella's art nouveau set design is evocative of the 'female' principle. A semi-abstract egg embraced by a crescent moon strains to drop into the narrow slit of a throne that represents the female yoni."

Insert your puns at will. Slavin must have a highly-charged imagination – I just couldn't put the alleged yoni pieces into any anatomical order.

Audience members were traumatised to varying degrees. For example, a University of the Third Age class member, apparently as therapy, turned his recollections of the performance into an essay on Schadenfreude, after changing the name of the soprano and the opera. Another audience member, "Bertie", blogged that if an opera is not over until the fat lady sings, the show must be still going on.

My spy in the chorus was wearing a wig resembling, she said, a dead marmoset. She put the debacle of the first night down to a bad case of pride, self-delusion or "plain old terror". She wrote:

> "We were all happily excited, and ready to strike a few blows for The Re-Establishment of Opera in Victoria."
>
> Come 8pm and the audience was pouring in STILL and we were all backstage ready to go and suffering through an excruciating half an hour of "can't we start yet?".
>
> Finally – the oboe note in the orchestra – the signal for tuning up and we got to go on and start.
>
> First act: it went well. They clapped. We tried not to be too excited.
>
> Second act: it goes well. Until the arrival of The Soprano as Turandot. Let me say that this is a bugger of a role and it starts with an absolute bugger of an aria "In Questa Reggia" which is an Olympic-class aria and it needs to be sung by a big dramatic voice in full command of its faculties ... lots of top Cs and bated breath all round for this act to work.
>
> And Jesus Mary Joseph and Ethel Merman, her voice went PHUT on only about the second page of the aria. She squeaked, she missed a note, and it went PHUT again.
>
> As one, the chorus froze and then broke out into a hot-and-cold sweat. We were guilty of murmuring: 'She isn't'; 'No she IS'; 'I thought she was better'; 'You know she's always awful the first 10

minutes'; 'No, this is something worse, there's something wrong with then middle voice'; 'Oh BUGGER'.

The look upon Richard Divall's [the conductor's] face was scary to behold.

She limped through the aria. Limped? She CRAWLED. The middle voice was just not working.

Just to attempt "In questa reggia" shows true self-delusion. Maria 'Z''s voice is so freaky anyway, that we really didn't know what would happen next at rehearsals. But usually it got better.

Not this time. The bit where she gives him curry was more sort of a Maggi Hot-Pot (with soggy sultanas) than the beef vindaloo (with extra chilli) that it needed to be.

We were in agonies and although they clapped again at the end of the second act we were now knocked sideways, unsure of everything....and bloody ANGRY. Here we had toiled away for months and months and this …ITALIAN PERSON had just scuttled it with her DRAMA.

I seem to have a knack for being in the right place at the right time backstage because I got to hear the conductor go past muttering 'I can get any singer through ANYTHING but first they have to tell me that there's a PROBLEM'. I also had a chat to a couple of our chorus tenors who are bloody knowledgeable and they assured me the third act would be fine because it was all in the upper part of the soprano's voice.

And lo, it came to pass that we got through the third act in fine style and she got through it and at the end we all got a rousing reception and much applause and love from the good people of Melbourne, bless them.

So we were much cheered: Saturday was days away, her voice must surely get better, and, Gods-dammit, we had just sung a grand opera in full traditional style to a full house at the Palais theatre!!

As for the Saturday's grand finale, a full picture can be drawn, thanks to my own note-taking from the stalls and the brilliant account of my back-stage informant. (The newspaper critics had had enough after Tuesday, and Saturday's catastrophe went unreported). My account:

In 'Z''s first big scene she was wobbly, her voice broke, she tried singing lower, and crumbled on every big note. When singing softly she was thin and feeble, and then she started breaking down altogether. Poor hero Calaf (Antonio Ordonez, from Spain) was trying to sing his part of the passionate duet to a vacuum and getting thrown, with a 'where am I, what is going on?' manner.

Midway through the piece, 'Z' stopped and clutched her throat. She called across the stage to the conductor in Italian, saying 'I can't go on', and the prompt and the conductor (Richard Divall) were gee-ing her up to get through the scene.

This short debate continued while the orchestra paused in wonderment. The audience was agog. Divall struck up the band again and mercifully the second act finished soon after.

As lights dimmed again for the third act, Divall strode alone to the front of the stage and said, as near as I can recall:

"The soprano (he didn't use her name) is having great difficulty, she is suffering from a serious allergy. During interval I suggested to her that we had several choices. We could stop the performance at the death of (Calaf's loyal servant) Liu (Rosemary Illing), which often occurs by tradition marking the point where Puccini's own death cut short his composition of the opera. However, in loyalty to the fellow cast members, the soloists, the chorus, the dancers, the producers... who have worked so hard for the performance, she said they should have the opportunity to take it through to the end. My wish is to minimise the strain on her. We have other choices including that she sing at times an octave lower, or that I do something I have never done in my career and that is deliberately have the orchestra drown her out. You are attending a wonderful production and you are a very special audience. This whole episode is an event I have never faced before, and I hope you will give the performers your best support."

The audience applauded. The third act went forward with 'Z' managing to hold her role together, though singing in a very restrained way and not attempting any peaks.

At curtain call the cast all got a good ovation but 'Z' didn't show until the last (we initially thought she was opting out) . She got some sympathetic applause and no boo-ing, as occurred on the first night.

Now let's go to the backstage version with our articulate chorine:

Saturday afternoon: open the stage door and descend into the Stageworld again. I breathed deeply of excitement, sweat, adrenaline and the Funny Smell. We waited for half an hour for the audience (ANOTHER full house – bless the people of Melbourne) and we did a bloody good first act. They really clapped!

Gazelle-like tenors (pranced) again in the dressing rooms.

Second act: Yes! it's all good. And here comes Maria! Who was WORSE. She actually STOPPED in the middle of the effing aria!!

I didn't think it was possible to feel even more panicked and hot-and-cold-sweaty than opening night. But it seems the body has endless reserves of adrenaline overload.

Antonio was magnificent – supported her all the way through the damned aria, sang over the top of her where possible – but if someone does a Sally Robbins and STOPS, even to apologise – no no no no NO! It was so all WRONG.

We came off and again I sat in the right place just off in the wings with other despondent chorines. We might as well have been furniture. We were incidental to the DRAMA, you see.

Maria had fled in tears (yeah – you SHOULD cry, you nutsoid soprano) to her dressing room and locked herself in, all so DRAMATIC. Oh the scurryings! The director, the director's assistant, the other director's assistant, the stage manager, the repetiteur, the chorusmaster, the producer and finally the conductor. Back and forth, many many tight conversations in Italian and broken English.

Rampant speculation all over backstage: Would she go on for the third act?? Would we continue?? What about Nessun Dorma? if Antonio didn't sing that we'd get lynched!

More scurryings. More conversations. Finally, Richard Divall (who should get a knighthood or something) went past metaphorically pushing his sleeves up and saying "Right". Then nothing for a while.

Finally Richard came back. And he leaned over to me and another chorine and said "I should have been a mother."

By which – loud cheers! – I took to mean that we were going ahead. I'd already spotted the orchestra coming back in and they only turn up when there's a paying gig, so I was confident.

Richard went out and made The Announcement and he was

brilliant – in a few short phrases he turned the audience around to cheering for the stupid woman who Had Bravely Decided to Battle On. Berloody Hell! I was fascinated. I thanked him later for doing this and he said "That's called Showing Leadership". What is more, it absolutely was.

We zoomed through the third act and got another rousing ovation (the chorus got loud cheers – yay for our claque!). But victory was overlaid by the bitterness of the mismanagement of the whole Maria thing – her mismanagement of her voice and her inexplicable decision to go ahead without knowing how to deal with an Australian audience (ie let them know you're struggling they'll be with you every note of the way – treat them like idiots and you deserve everything you get) – and the mismanagement by the producers of the situation. No understudy, no backup – how did this blind spot happen??

I leave the final words on the matter to my dear friend Elley.

As we were wandering along Acland Street looking for coffee afterwards I said "Well, she won't ever work in this town ever again."

And Elley said "What are you talking about? She hasn't worked in this town YET.

However, to all this came a happy ending. There was no disaster, Madam 'Z' triumphed, and the audience was in raptures over her performance, or so the Italians in Italy were informed.

In faraway Livorno, Italy, the local newspaper *(Stampa)* carried a review, which I have rendered for you (via google-translate) in English.

"MELBOURNE. Ten minutes of applause for Turandot in Melbourne before the 2,800 spectators at the Palais Theatre…

"Many personalities attended this highly anticipated event.

"The performance ended with a standing ovation and bestowed a special tribute to the soprano Maria 'Z'…Huge success for the interpretation by soprano Maria 'Z'…"

I have no idea whether this auspicious production inspired Premier Bracks to decant millions of taxpayer dollars onto the Melbourne Opera Company. I'd certainly hope so.

Tony Thomas enjoys opera. Hang the taxpayers.

Quadrant OnLine, 2 February 2013

Ratepayers and Ratbaggery

Catastropharian David Spratt came to my home turf Moonee Ponds, near Melbourne, to tell the faithful why Victorians must turf out the government of Liberal Premier Denis Napthine. His audience loved the show, but why is the municipality putting ratepayer funds and facilities at the service of a fact-averse and nakedly partisan preacher from the outer limits of the loony left?

><><><><><><><><><><><><><><><><><><><><><><><><><><><><><><><><><><><><><><><><><><

The Labor-dominated, but notionally non-partisan, Moonee Valley City Council kindly provided a public platform on a Wednesday evening for far-left activist David Spratt to advise on how to get rid of Victoria's coalition government. Spratt summed up, "At the 2010 (State) election, five to six bayside seats, from Brighton to Frankston, fell from Labor to conservatives, basically because the train line didn't work."

Warming to his theme, Spratt continued: "A group called Environment Victoria has spent two years and is starting a third, talking to people there, setting up a shopfront, street stalls, door-to-door knocking, phone-banking, asking people to commit when they vote to put the environment first.

"If, across Victoria, by that process they can change 2000 votes in half a dozen seats, that will probably make the difference to the election. So there are a lot of things that can be done, and are being done, at a concrete level to make a difference, and here are my contact details for anyone wanting to continue the conversation at another time."

The free, two-hour event was meant to be "an information session" on climate change, but the only speakers invited were Spratt and the Australian Youth Climate Coalition's national co-director, Kirsty Albion, who spoke with youthful passion on how to subvert and, hopefully, destroy the Australian coal industry. Mayor Jan Chantry (Labor) opened the show with the council's tribute to spirits and ancestors and said, "Moonee Valley is proud of its diverse community and acknowledges the contribution that all people make to this diverse, vibrant and inclusive municipality."

She had somehow overlooked the biggest minority group in the Valley – conservative voters like myself, who comprise about 40% of her ratepayers. A rate notice for $2358 the same week augmented my pain. I judged that I was the only conservative voter in the audience of 60.

The tone wasn't set by accident. The promotional brochure says that Spratt's work "focuses on climate science, communications and climate-movement politics, drawing on experiences that include the peace, anti-uranium and solidarity social movements."

The mayor left early to go to a Rotary meeting but Councillor Jim Cusack (Labor) stayed for the duration.

The council is comprised of four Labor people, three independents and two Liberals. It is pretty clean by the standards of north-west councils. Only two of the nine councilors have pleaded guilty to a criminal offence in the past two years, one being a left-leaning independent and the other (whoops!) a Liberal.

Spratt began his talk by painting a terrifying picture of climate change turning the communities of Point Nepean, Point Lonsdale, Altona and Albert Park into vast lakes brought about by 2m sea level rises (even the IPCC only talks about 60cm rises by 2100). Spratt said, "With three-degree warming we get 20-30 metre rises in sea level. We are drowning human civilisation on the coastal fringe – Cairo, Manila, Bangkok, Florida…" Temperate Dubbo would change to a climate like Tom Price or Hermannsburg, agriculture would cease west of the Dividing Range, the Murray River system would go dry, and Melbourne would have to get used to "yucky" 50-degree days. "Our addiction to fossil fuels is killing us," he said, to the visible and audible horror of his audience.

His solution to civilisation's near-term collapse? We should intensify community efforts to get rid of the state and federal coalition governments, which he accused of putting economic and vested interests ahead of CO_2 safety. PM Tony Abbott for example, was "sacking all the researchers" – which would be news to our vast academic climate-change industry. Spratt recommended we all join groups like Yarraville's Climate for Change, Moreland and Northcote activists, and Brunswick's door-knocking pests.

Sandra Mack, one of the council's three sustainability officers whose salaries are underwritten by residents' rates, arranged the event. She thanked Spratt for his talk and said, "David showed us the impacts and urgency to act. When David and I had a chat before, about what he would be presenting on, I asked him, 'David can you please present on climate change without trying to make people depressed'. I feel glad that you gave a very positive spin at the end by showing us what can be done. There's also a climate petition here for people to sign."

I went over to get a hot cup of tea in one of the council's "Biovene" degradable plastic cups (not Styrofoam, of course) but found the tureen water had somehow lost its electric heat during Spratt's talk. Could the council's 'zero-emission electricity efforts' be to blame?

Mack had told me earlier that she had picked Spratt as speaker because she thought his 2008 book *Climate Code Red* was terrific. (It claims climate catastrophes will be far worse than governments say, which seems inherently difficult). She had picked Albion after being 'blown away' (an apt phrase) by her inspirational talk at another meeting. I asked Mack if it was appropriate for the council to be allowing Spratt to run a public anti-government rally under the council's roof, but she denied Spratt had been party-political. She explained that the evening was about sustainability issues for the citizenry, e.g. light bulbs and solar panels.

I said Spratt's politicking was undeniable and asked why, if she was selecting two speakers, she didn't choose one of them from the government side of the argument, as a sop to us conservative ratepayers. She repeated that it was not a political meeting.

However, she saw fit to make a nervous announcement late in the evening: "I emphasise that we [the council] are not in favor of any political party here. Tonight is a non-political event about community action getting Moonee Valley toward zero emissions. It is all about community action."

She also disclosed that Spratt and Albion had volunteered their time, but I'm still sore that my rates paid for all these lefties' and greenies' pastries and cake.

Mack was kind enough to give me first question in the miserly ten minutes allocated to question time. I asked Spratt if the measured 18 year halt to warming made his predictions of death and disaster "a little bit ridiculous". To murmured approval from the audience, he replied that the heating had continued but, as always, the great bulk of it had gone into the oceans, which were warming. "Because tomorrow's colder than today doesn't mean it's autumn," he said.

He continued, "Climate denial is not about science. What interests me is that very few young people are deniers and very few women are. Very few are under 60, they are just grumpy old men."

Me: "That's a bit ageist."

Spratt: "It is true, many deniers are geologists and meteorologists struggling to deal with changes in their professions that have surpassed the knowledge they were brought up with. Knowledge has changed, their professional lives are over and it is too difficult for them to deal with. Grumpy old men."

Me: "How old are you?" [I'd guess about 60].

Spratt: "I am a grumpy old bloke, too."

And I certainly am, after last night.

Quadrant OnLine, 22 August 2014

Even this mob can't hold a candle to Gough & Co.

It is a live issue whether the federal Labor government circa 2010-13 is crazier than Gough Whitlam's lot in 1972-75. Is the National Broadband Network, for example, crazier than Rex Connor's planned national gas pipeline grid? Is Treasurer Wayne Swan's deficit-laden legacy crazier than Whitlam's economic management which involved, among other things, a planned 46% increase in government outlays in 1974-75?

I was sort-of present at the creation of the national pipeline grid by Rex Connor, then Labor Minister for Minerals & Energy. He called me to his office in early 1973, looking for a bit of favorable press, and produced a map of the Australian continent similar to one found in a primary school geography text book. He had a thick pencil and joined up the North-West Shelf gas field with the Palm Valley gas field in the Centre, via the Gibson Desert, and the Bass Strait gasfield in the south. Spur lines radiated to Perth, Adelaide, Sydney and Brisbane.

Rex's clever plan was that if one gas field was knocked out or dried up, the other fields would combine to keep our capitals' supply safe. Apparently the grid would also permit uniform national gas prices.

He also planned to site our very own uranium-enrichment plant at the head of Spencer Gulf, South Australia, where it would be "safe from enemy submarines". (You don't believe me? I'd give you the Hansard reference, except I'm in Budapest at the moment).

On this craziness comparison, I conclude that today's federal Labor government, while very dysfunctional, is not in the Whitlam league of "please call the men in white coats and take the ministers away to a safe place where they cannot harm either themselves or others."

The federal government is profligate with the money we pay in taxes – that's very bad. But even Julia and Wayne never suggested, nor does Mr Rudd, that we do away with money altogether and revert, for social justice reasons, to the sort of barter or ritual economy pre-dating the Sumerians and Babylonians.

That reversion was the plan of Dr Jim Cairns, Whitlam's deputy prime minister and minister for trade. Of course, he was love-struck at the time and maybe didn't actually intend to get this great project endorsed by cabinet and implemented.

You won't find any record of this speech in the media, and that's my fault. I should have filed a report for *The Age* on it, but figured my bosses at *The Age* would not merely spike the copy, but conclude their Economics Writer in Canberra was deranged, rather than Jim Cairns being deranged.

It all happened like this: In 1974, Jim was riding high. He had his status as prior leader of the anti-Vietnam marches, and he had his PhD credentials (in economic history, mind you, not economics). He was our philosopher-king, peddling a soppy version of Marxism.

I picked up that he was scheduled to address students at the Australian National University – I had noticed the flyers pasted up as I went to my economics lectures and tutorials. It wasn't a normal press occasion but I decided to check it out.

The venue was in one of the medium-sized lecture theatres and about 60 students were waiting. Jim arrived, accompanied by his assistant Junie Morosi, clad in swami-style robes.

As for the date, it must have been around August-October, 1974. It had to be during the uni year, and before December, 1974, when he moved to appoint Junie Morosi as his principal private secretary. At that point Junie became a big news story. Before then there was no "public interest" hook and his married status made discussion of Junie dangerous from a libel point of view.

Jim treated the uni event as informal. Junie gathered her robes with a graceful gesture and sat on the floor in front of him. Jim was an accomplished public speaker and was relaxed and chatty. He just talked to the students, sans microphone and sans any notes or structure.

We all took this living tableau in our stride – if a deputy prime minister has a seriously glamorous assistant who sits at his feet in exotic robes, well that's how things were in 1974.

Jim got onto the theme of choosing between materialism and brotherly/sisterly love. It became more an impromptu sermon than a speech. Relations between people should be based on lovingness; material things don't make you happy, blah blah. I figured this was all well and good but Jim-as-preacher/philosopher wasn't going to make a story in next day's Age. It was just, well, mushy. I stopped taking notes – to get all this pap down in shorthand seemed ridiculous.

Jim drifted onto a new theme. Money transactions epitomised the soul-less state of relations between people. Money put barriers between us, money made us selfish. In fact, he said, it would be a better world if money were abolished. We would give and take, based on a better style of relationship between individuals. Strife would subside. Harmony would reign. The world would become a better place, he concluded.

It was familiar to me as a riff on the Communist notion that once the class basis of society dissolves, the world would see a New Man arise (and, we hope, 'new Woman'). Society would operate as "from each according to his ability, to each according to his need." Jim had once applied to join the Communist Party but was sent packing by party boss Lance Sharkey, who thought Jim (an ex-policeman) was a secret agent.

Jim finished his spiel, and took a few lame questions from the students. They applauded politely. Junie gathered herself up from the floor and the pair headed off to the waiting Comcar to be driven back across the lake to Jim's parliamentary offices.

I was seriously non-plussed. I tried to imagine my story, headlined: "Trade Minister seeks abolition of money". The body copy would read:

"The Deputy Prime Minister and Minister for Trade, Dr Jim Cairns, yesterday proposed that money cease to be used in transactions.

Addressing 60 students at the ANU, he said a superior system would involve inter-personal relationships based on love and kindness.

The use of money was degrading, he told students. Without money, international relations would become more harmonious and a source of global conflict and wars would be removed..."

If my bosses in Melbourne took this story seriously, it would have to be a Page 1 screamer. Given Australia's role as a world trader of mineral and food commodities, it would also be a story of major international significance.

Note that I said "if" my story were taken seriously. I had a few shorthand notes, but this was one occasion where notes needed to be comprehensive and, preferably, a tape-recording available (in that era, tape recorders were the size of Gladstone bags).

I also had a bit of a reputation for being too eager to rubbish the Labor government. A year later, when the government's craziness was broadly acknowledged, my story might have been taken seriously, but at the time of Jim's speech, the consensus Gallery view was that Gough was leading us all into those broad sunlit uplands, against the worst endeavours of assorted conservative gargoyles and goblins.

Like it or not, the Press has agendas and fashions as to what is "news" and what isn't. A report of Jim's proposal to abolish money didn't fit the current paradigm of "news", I decided.

What next to do? We had daily columnists whose job on *The Age* was to assemble half a dozen faintly amusing snippets about politics and events. Maybe I could place a few paras about Jim's speech there. I wrote a sample. It just looked horrible in that context, as though I was sneering and lying about one of our nation's admired leaders.

Meanwhile, that afternoon, I had to start my usual serious work of digesting the daily statistics and following up government/bureaucratic announcements on the economics and resources fronts. I was behind schedule and it would soon be 5pm, when public service contacts became hard to telephone.

"Arrgghh, damn it!" I said. Exactly as actors do in movies when playing reporters, I crumpled up my story about the Deputy Prime Minister wanting to abolish money, and threw it in the bin.

By the Christmas break, Jim was the hero of Cyclone Tracy in Darwin, and there was a bit of a push for Jim to supplant Gough as Prime Minister. By February, 1975, he was confessing to a "kind of love" for Junie.

Jim was chucked out of the ministry in July 1975 for having offered his dentist George Harris a potential $50m commission for a potential $2b loan-raising from Arab sheiks. (For someone wanting to abolish money, Jim was somewhat free with other people's money).

Jim kept Junie on as his research assistant, and they organised alternative lifestyles festivals outside Canberra, a sort of poor person's Woodstock. Despite Jim's views on the non-utilitarian nature of money, issues concerning money kept the Jim-Junie nexus in the media spotlight for several decades.[6] The alternative lifestyles movement they kick-started post-1975 dissolved in the 1980s amid acrimony and lawsuits over finance.

Did Jim ever go public elsewhere about his dreams for a non-monetary society? In 1998 he tape-recorded a very long interview for *Australian Biography* that included these thoughts, going not quite as far as in that uni talk I overheard:

> I used to think being acquisitive was simply a result of life experience in capitalism… And I thought acquisitiveness was learned by experience in capitalism. Then in about 1975, when the other change came in my way of seeing things, I could see that it went further back than that. I could see that acquisitiveness was a cultural product, a product of the way we are treated psychologically, emotionally, and not just with money, not just goods and services: much deeper.
>
> So if you're going to change acquisitiveness in capitalism, you can't simply change it by trying to persuade people to become co-operative and generous within capitalism. That hardly works at all. You have to see what are the sources of their character and behaviour, and you have to try to implement ways of changing that into something else.

(Tony Thomas is available for any vacancies as a Professor of Journalism.)

---

6 Junie won a total $27,000 damages from Radio 2GB and the now-defunct tabloid *Mirror* in 1977 and 1978 over their allegation that she had a sexual relationship with Jim. Jim put his foot in it in 2002 by remarking that they had indeed gone to bed, although he had sworn otherwise in 1982 in one of Junie's damages claims involving *The National Times*.

A Letter From Naples

A trio of vandals deface a crowded train platform, raising neither eyebrow nor protest from the Italian commuters who watch them do it. Australians have reason to admire Italian culture -- the museums, the history, the gilded palaces – but let us hope such indifference is one aspect we choose not to ape.

Yesterday I was returning to our nice flat in a very run-down part of Naples near Garibaldi Square, after half a day at the Naples National Archaeology Museum. I decided to detour via the subway system to Montesanto because my map insisted there were some nice palaces there. This detour proved a damp squib because those palaces had disappeared centuries ago, although their names remained.

Eventually, I arrived at the right Montesanto platform for the trip home. It was packed with commuters, as it was about 5pm, and the subway trains are not at all frequent – every 20 minutes or so. The platforms on both sides were clean, but youths were using my platform edge as seating, dangling their legs above the tracks. After a while one of them, in his late teens and with red hair, pale skin, a New York University sweater and baggy pants, stood up and joined two mates. One was thin but very tall, the other swarthy and clad in a camouflage top. They were all only a metre or two from me.

The redhead was clutching some tubes, about half the size of a relay runner's baton. One tube was giving him trouble as he tried to do something with the lid. Was something edible inside? Apparently not, as I next noticed a wad of cotton fall to the platform. He put it back in the tube. I was standing against the station's light-green Perspex-style wall. There were dozens of other would-be commuters around me, some standing and others filling seats against the wall.

Still struggling with the cap, the redhead moved to a rubbish bin inches from where I stood and ground the top of the tube against it. He looked pleased when something blue came out. He took two steps towards the wall, between the bin and the first row of seated commuters. This was a wall gap of only a metre.

With practised movements, he waved his arm at the wall (I couldn't quite see what he was doing), stepped back, admired the wall, and took a few steps to the left to rejoin his two friends. They all seemed quite merry and animated.

Someone moved and I could see the wall. Previously pristine for the whole length of the platform, on it now was one of those mindless 'tags' – the scribbled letters P,W and C, in a squiggly pattern about half-a-metre square. I now saw that at least two of the trio were carrying handfuls of these tubes, king-sized felt-tip markers. They made no attempt to conceal them.

I looked at the commuters to see how they were reacting to the wall being defaced at peak-hour right next to them. They would all be fully aware of what had happened but they studiously minded their own business, and acted as though the trio of graffitists was invisible. The trio was clearly on a graffiti mission, and my surmise was that they had been active for an hour or two. Surely, I thought, some of those studying their smartphones would tap out an alert to the station police? Obviously this wasn't happening.

At that moment the train arrived and those still sitting on the platform edge pulled up their legs.

I found myself sandwiched among the three graffiti youths as we boarded. Thankfully they moved down-carriage a bit. From there they kept up a loud banter. I tried unsuccessfully to work out from their talk if they were native Napoli citizens or just visiting. I did make out some variant on *'chi uccide'* – croaker, killer, zaps or some other unpleasant jargon.

When I stood up to get out at Central Station, once again I was sandwiched among the trio. They ignored me and formed a knot in the crowds heading for the stairs.

Even now, at Naples' main station, they flourished their graffiti tools of trade. They moved purposefully, I guessed to some other line where they would continue their evening's fun. Whatever police or officialdom was present, the trio obviously had no fear of them.

I wonder about it all. They did not seem particularly tough or threatening, although that's not to say the other train-goers weren't intimidated: who knows what else besides giant Textas they were armed with? Or were my fellow train-riders utterly indifferent to vandalism on their subway, in broad daylight among crowds?

Melbourne also has its train graffiti vandals, daubing their horrid tags on platforms and carriages and rigorously scratching train windows into an opaque mess. I recall a case a year or two ago where three such vandals were caught and prosecuted – they had come from Adelaide on a spree – and in a week or two, had vandalised hundreds of places on our train system.

They had operated late at night. Let's hope Melbourne never gets to the pass where graffiti vandals do their work openly.

Quadrant OnLine, 21 June 2014

An Ozzie on Constitution Avenue, 4 July 2012

What luck! To be in Washington on Independence Day. To be able to watch the big parade down Constitution Avenue, flanked by so many majestic and classical buildings as a backdrop. This is the capital-C celebration of the Declaration of Independence.

I may be burned at the stake at Moonee Ponds Junction for saying this, but the experience made me feel good about America. So many thousands of patriotic families celebrating their country's founding and progress, a sea of red, white and blue.

All morning small troops of families, oldsters and youngsters ambled towards the Mall, in palpable excitement. Stars and stripes were everywhere, on toddlers, pushers, hats, banners, and T-shirts. Most groups carried a forest of small flags. In patriotism, there was no distinction between the accoutrements of blacks, whites and in-betweens of Asian and Latino stock.

Washington is in the grip of a heat-wave, with centuries (Fahrenheit of course) more or less daily for the past fortnight and forecast for a further week. This is a muggy heat and to skip ahead a bit, water-carriers went with every marching group. Some marchers even incorporated a dangling water bottle into their Ruritanian uniforms.

For some reason I expected a sterner tone to the march, perhaps because of Anzac Days. In fact it's a march largely of elaborately costumed high school bands and novelty groups. Very small contingents, maybe 30 each, represented the Army, Navy and Air Force, and the only military equipment involved was their rifles. Here and there through the parade, a rank of four flag-carriers would have a rifleman on each side. Some school displays involved rifle-twirling but the rifles were unashamedly bits of white-painted wood.

There were two other military reminders: several black-painted floats honouring the Missing in Action & Prisoners of War (who were treated as a special case in the parade), and a tableau of the Iwo Jima flag-raising photo, the tableau I think being about the flag rather than the victory.

I happened to get a spot at the precise start of the parade, under a shady tree. There was no pushing and shoving, and elderly people who had brought picnic chairs were tacitly permitted clear sight-lines, resulting in unoccupied territory which I initially found perplexing. In fact I invited some short kids at the back to make use of the spots, but the assertive sitters ordered them out again, to the approval of others around.

Given the long wait before the parade, I struck up a conversation with a young executive from out-of-state. He made polite but rather dispiriting comments on all my stories, either "That's cool" or "That's too bad".

The show was led off by a pack of no-nonsense coppers on Harley-Davidsons. Behind was a police car that was boarded by some senior police, including a tall athletic blond woman about 40 years old.

"That's Cathy, she's Chief of Police," people said proudly.

Googling later, I found Cathy Lanier had been a high school dropout and unwed mother at 15, but became a crime-fighter and at one stage ran the District of Columbia narcotics and gang-busting unit. Her MA was not in organisational design or similar, but "Preventing terror attacks on the homeland." I couldn't help make a mental contrast with Victoria's ex-commissioner Christine Nixon. Her US counterpart could definitely run down and tackle a malefactor in an alley.

Each arriving contingent was met with tireless whoops and cheers. The only sombre note was the expression on the face of the policewoman assigned to watch our 10m section of the crowd. Her gaze never lifted from us in two hours; it was frightening in its intensity.

To get in the parade, high schools and community groups undergo a competitive selection process, followed by nomination from a state governor. The overall goal is for each state to be represented. Each school sought to out-do in splendour of uniform, with lashings of gold braid, contrasting colours and cockaded hat-wear. None of the bands, fife or drum corps that I saw used music sheets, they kept good formation, and heaven only knows how much practice and discipline had been needed to reach such standards.

Some schools used other formulas. For example, one group was all on unicycles, ranging from nearly 2m high to little unicycles for kids of 6 or 8. They all managed to carry the flag in one hand.

Giant balloons (and I meant 'giant') were *de rigueur*, in the shapes of Uncle Sam, the flag (of course), bald eagles, Yogi Bear and other kids' icons. There was a hot wind down the avenue and it took around 30 rope-handlers to keep each towering balloon somewhat under control.

There was only one float a feminist could object to – featuring the winners of some sort of Miss Teenager contest.

A number of floats and groups celebrated ex-immigrants, especially Vietnamese, and some ethnic groups such as Pueblo Indians were clearly there for their folk talent and enthusiasm rather than polish. Which interest groups got the nod for the parade was arbitrary – there was no attempt at giving any sectoral claimants equal time. In fact, the only overtly religious-type groups represented were Hari Krishnas and Falun Dafa.

The main commercial activity permitted was selling bottled water. Throughout the march, people with sacks would patrol the crowd and bystanders would toss them their empties. I had the impression that at parade's end, the avenue would be rubbish-free.

As soon as the parade ended, most people hot-footed it to the nearby shady parks and ornamental pools, police vigilantly keeping revellers out of the water itself. I was amazed to find the museums and galleries along the mall were open – they appear to shut for only two days per year, a practice that would send any Australian counterpart broke.

To sum up my impressions:

- Overt pride in one's country and flag is not something to be denigrated
- There is an impressive level of public-spiritedness among American high-schoolers, with those represented here having made enormous sacrifices of their leisure time to put on a good show
- The politically-correct element yesterday was positive – concern for the aged and handicapped, a genuine blindness to ethnicities, and a determination to celebrate progress and hard-won freedoms.

I could draw some parallels with contemporary Australian culture, but prefer not to be a whingeing Ozzie.

Quadrant OnLine, 7 July 2012

Freedom ride 'round the Potomac

Washington DC, July 9: The Americans are a bit in-your-face with all this free speech/freedom-of-the-press stuff. Back in Australia we're over that.

[At the time of writing this essay, Australia had (and still has) a Racial Anti-Discrimination law against public use of words that can offend, insult, humiliate or intimidate. The federal Labor government was also proposing to create a "Public Interest Media Advocate" to enforce "fairness in reporting". After outcry, that plan was shelved].

The American obsession is at its most blatant at the Washington DC "Newseum" (i.e. News Museum) on Pennsylvania Avenue, where there's a marble tablet 74 feet tall engraved with nothing more than the 45 words of the First Amendment. The bit that the Newseum is most interested in is: "Congress shall make no law ... abridging the freedom of speech, or of the press."

My landlady's place is in M-Street South-West. This morning, starting early to escape yet another century, I took a public bike from across the road and set off around the Tidal Basin of the Potomac, barely a mile away. Goal: to study this American free-speech idiosyncrasy.

First stop was the Thomas Jefferson memorial. This is one of the many neo-classical efforts in this town, all pillars and porticos and rotundas and domes. In yesteryear the monument was damned as a "tired architectural lie" but it's dignified all the same, especially as it looks directly north across the water to the White House.

Among the engraved excerpts inside from Jefferson's works is this:

> Almighty God hath created the mind free ... All attempts to influence
> it by temporal punishments or burthens ... are a departure from the
> plan of the Holy Author of our religion.

Jefferson was quite obsessive. In the Newseum there's another of his *bon mots*: "If it were left to me to decide whether we should have a government without a free press or a free press without a government, I would prefer the latter." Ridiculous! In the real world, who could object to our own government's plans for a fair and balanced press?

My bike tour continued clockwise through the cherry trees to the Roosevelt Memorial, a modern work covering a huge 7.5 acres. It has four "outdoor rooms" of imagery and symbolism involving his four terms. The main statue has him shrouded in a cloak so you can't tell that he's in his wheelchair. This got the lobbies for the handicapped so annoyed that another statue of him, definitely in a wheelchair, was added a few years later.

One of the focal points here is a granite block, with the Four Freedoms chiselled into it. Freedoms 2, 3 and 4 are freedoms of worship, freedom from want, and freedom from fear. The first freedom listed is "Freedom of Speech."

My next monument around the basin was a surprise, because it was opened only a year ago and it's not even on my map. This is the Martin Luther King memorial – a no-bike zone but I took a chance that it only meant no-bike-riding. I wheeled my bike through the gap in the two big rocks comprising the "Mountain of Despair" and came to the carving of King representing the "Stone of Hope". The mountain and stone references are from King's "I have a dream" speech: "Out of a mountain of despair, a stone of hope."

There were a lot of blacks there – Black Pride is manifest everywhere in Obama's capital – and they didn't seem to mind my bike.

There's nothing on the long wall of King's quotations that involves freedom of speech and the press, but I did notice his "passionate desire to see our beloved country stand as a moral example to the world."

From there I got lost among the loops around the Washington obelisk, the incredible 555ft stone spire that's the icon of this capital. Eventually I found myself in the sunken "V" constituting the Vietnam Memorial Wall, which I can't really fit into my story. But as a by-the-way, the ranger on duty told me that Maya Ying Lin, who designed this memorial as an 21-year-old undergraduate at Yale, got a B grade from her architecture professor because the design was too simple. Like most good stories (except mine), that one may not be true.

From there I pedalled down the Mall to the Newseum, experiencing first-hand an "urban heat island" effect as the city centre cooked up.

The seven-level $US450m Newseum, opened in 2008, has about the same prominence as the Smithsonian museums along the mall, and its mission is "educating the public about the value of a free press in a free society."

The main funder, tipping in $US100m, was the Freedom Forum, "a non-partisan foundation that champions the First Amendment as a cornerstone of democracy." It is some sort of descendant of a foundation set up pre-war by publisher tycoon Frank E. Gannett. A sinister co-funder ($US10m) was News Corporation. In horrid capitalist mode, the Newseum charged me $US20 admission (the Smithsonians are free).

It displays the history of the press and media, has a whole gallery on just the First Amendment, and special displays on things like FBI/Press relationships, Pulitzer-winning sport pictures, TV and radio coverage of the Twin Towers disaster (which had me choking off tears), and the Berlin Wall.

As background activity, it highlights events bearing on press freedom. The latest is somewhat prosaic: Last June 29, the Supreme Court said CBS television wouldn't have to pay the $US550,000 fine levied by the Federal Communications Commission over the wardrobe malfunction of Janet Jackson at the 2004 Super Bowl (no relation to our Prime Minister Gillard's Hyper Bowl, that's how she pronounces 'hyperbole'). The court's reasoning was that the nipple only peeped momentarily. But it warned that any future wardrobe malfunctions on TV can be and should be dealt with by the full majesty of the law.

One point made by the Newseum concerns bias in the media. It says that under the First Amendment, newspapers and magazines "can publish information as they see fit, biased or not. If published information is libellous, the publication can be sued by the person claiming to be libelled. But the Federal Government does not and can not regulate newspaper content." Another tablet records how US television stations used to have a government-imposed "fairness doctrine" requiring balanced coverage, but this was repealed in 1987 to give them the same freedom to be biased that the US press has always had.

My freedom ride took me home without incident, other than a near-miss and imprecations at 7th and M streets. Note to self: ride on the right.

Obviously, it's a good thing we don't have anything comparable to America's First Amendment. Instead we have the government prescribing 'fair and balanced' reporting. Perhaps in 2030 our next Labor Prime Minister will commission a white marble building between the National Library and the High Court, "The Newseum of Fair & Balanced Journalism".

Quadrant OnLine, 13 July 2012

How I snubbed Bill Gates (sorry Bill!)

In early 1986 Microsoft' co-founder Bill Gates got an appointment to see me at the BRW office at 469 Latrobe St. It was not a successful interview, because I forgot he was coming and went out to lunch. I was habituated to a circuit around the block to stretch my legs after a morning at the computer, with a time-consuming stop at JB Hi-Fi on Elizabeth St to browse the cut-price classical CDs.

I returned to the office to find an indignant Pictures Editor, Tom Brentnall, who had to baby-sit Bill Gates to cover my absence.

My lapse was so egregious that it featured in ex-Editor Jeff Penberthy's 25th anniversary essay on BRW's history (Issue of August 24, 2006). He wrote:

> When Bill Gates walked into the old BRW offices on Little Collins Street in Melbourne [actually we'd moved by then to Latrobe St. TT], there was no-one on hand to greet him. The young Microsoft founder had called to see senior writer Tony Thomas – but Thomas was a busy man. He was out to lunch, and he deserved it. Among the first owners of a personal computer in Australia [Eh? I don't think so! TT], Thomas was writing a sponsored page that answered questions for the few PC users, but the magazine was ahead of its time.
>
> In almost a year there had only ever been one genuine question come in from a reader. Week after week, Thomas wrestled to pose intriguing questions to himself, typically sourcing them from the reaches of Adelaide or Brisbane, and you could bank on his answers. Incredibly, then, some nark had written in to say he had checked the electoral rolls, and there was no person named Samson living in Willagee, which happened to be Tony Thomas's old Perth home suburb.
>
> Such is the price of exigencies. God knows what Bill Gates thought of us – Bill probably told Him when they talked that night. Tom Brentnall sat the geek from California down and gave him our latest issue to read while he rustled up a photographer...

Gates was in early 1986 just a 31yo in the geeky personal computer world. Microsoft was then just a private company on the verge of floating on the stockmarket. (The offering raised a modest $US61m from the public).

It took me quite some research even to establish when Gates visit to BRW happened. It was when Gates was doing overseas PR for the float.

Most IBM-style personal computers were still running the clunky MS-DOS operating system. Windows 1.0 involving mouse-pointing and clicking at the screen, was only a few months old. Bill Gates was not then famous, nor a model employer (he used to memorise staff licence plates so he could check who left the carpark early). But anyway, I now apologise to him over my inadvertent snub.

Microsoft, with its 118,000 workers, is now valued at $US400b, while Gates personal wealth is $US75b. BRW in contrast ceased as a printed magazine in 2013 after 32 years. Then on March 4, 2016, the on-line vestige of the magazine also disappeared. It was never the same – perhaps better – after my retirement in 2001.

11 March 2016

2

THE COLD WAR

Brezhnev: My Part in his Downfall

I once found myself being courted by an oily Soviet diplomat, who somewhat ineptly pursued what he mistakenly hoped would be a valuable intelligence source by plying my children with storybooks featuring anatomically correct puppy dogs. No need for me to worry, ASIO was on the case.

On a limpid autumn day in 1977, my phone rang in the *Age*'s office in the Canberra press gallery. We were in the rabbit warren of second-floor rooms in what is now the Old Parliament House. A heavily accented voice said, "Good afternoon, Mr Thomas. My name is Oleg Petrovich Tsitsarkin. I am with the Soviet embassy."

"Well, hi, Oleg Petrovich! What can I do for you?"

"I would say first, that at the embassy we think highly of your economics writing."

That was nice, I love compliments. I had been Economics Writer for the *Age* for seven years.

"Thanks. I do my best."

Mr Tsitsarkin continued, "I must tell you I have a problem. My boss Mr Shilin sends a monthly briefing on economic policy back to Moscow, and he has gone on leave and these briefings I now have to write. But I do not know much about your economics and my reports will be criticised. Perhaps you can help me with advice?"

"Sure! CPI, GDP, SRDs, whatever. I'm a walking encyclopaedia."

"Mr Thomas, let us have lunch and a talk. You can explain about Mr Howard's Treasury policies perhaps. May I suggest next Monday, the 19th Hole at the golf club?"

I don't know about other journalists but I would sell my grandmother for a swanky lunch. Plus I had been angling unsuccessfully for an exclusive interview with the reclusive Soviet Ambassador Mr A.V. Basov, and Mr Tsitsarkin could be a useful lever.

The Royal Canberra Golf Club's restaurant is no longer called the 19th Hole, but it's still a ritzy joint for "a memorable and enjoyable experience". That's what I got, four decades ago.

I gathered for Mr Tsitsarkin some economic bumph that cascaded across my *Age* desk, and a speech or two by the Treasurer.

He was a slim and nervous chap about my age (then thirty-seven). The restaurant had glossy panels and pretty views of the links. I ordered a rare steak and breezily selected a shiraz. Mr Tsitsarkin gallantly approved my choice. He was full of bonhomie and seized upon my "Treasury Round-Ups" with gratitude. I impressed him with the finer points of fiscal and monetary settings.

I mentioned my desire to interview the ambassador. A great idea! He would talk to the first secretary, Mr Pavlov, this very afternoon on my behalf.

By the end of the bottle I was full of goodwill. Poor Mr Tsitsarkin, he didn't get out much, literally, holed up in the Soviet residential compound. His wife Ekaterina would get out even less. He was a guy just trying to do a difficult job. We had things in common.

"Tell you what, Oleg," I said brightly. "Grab your wife and have dinner at our place in Dominion Circuit. What about next Thursday?"

That was only a few days ahead. I was taking a real risk here, not because I was dealing with sinister Russians but because my then wife did not like being sprung with dinner guests at short notice.

Oleg gave a startled response. Sure, thank you, he said, he would ring me back to confirm. He seemed to have come by taxi so I offered to drop him back at his office in my Cortina. As we neared the embassy in Canberra Avenue, he suddenly remembered some dry-cleaning to collect at the local shops. I dropped him off there and returned to Parliament.

I waited for his acceptance to dine with Mr and Mrs Thomas. Days passed, Thursday came and went. I was curious about this breach of good manners, but spared a row with Mrs Thomas, so I didn't think much more about it.

A couple of months passed and the phone rang again. It was Oleg, as if he'd never stood me up. How about lunch? Well, why not.

His new choice of restaurant was a budget-priced Chinese at Belconnen about fifteen kilometres out. When we met, he was at a table at the edge of the room. (Interjection from John le Carré—"So he can check out anyone else entering!"). Oleg had a few things to discuss and I was happy to enlighten him: the press secretary to the Minister for Resources was so-and-so, the private secretary was so-and-so, to get an appointment you would go through the chief-of-staff.

My interview with the ambassador? Oh, he's been travelling, no opportunity. Expect an invitation any day now.

We parted amicably. He didn't need a lift home.

He would ring now and then with inane questions. All my calls back to the embassy, I later realised, were three-way, with ASIO listening in and keeping an eye (ear?) on things.

The embassy now seemed lukewarm about my value. The next Oleg invitation, in early 1979, was for lunch – at McDonald's! – to talk more economics. I liked getting tidbits about the diplomatic circuit. This time I showed up with my three-year-old daughter, who loved Maccas and chips, and I again handed over a few economics bulletins in an A4 envelope.

He looked a bit surprised to find we had a threesome. In fact it was a fivesome. ASIO, I later learned, had assigned a young man and woman, ostensibly courting or skirting domesticity, to join us at Maccas. Sadly for them, the racket in the store made conversation too hard for them to record.

Oleg accepted my envelope of bumph somewhat nervously. The ASIO couple took careful note. Technically it was a "live drop", much inferior to the favoured "dead drop" in the espionage world.

Oleg fobbed me off again on the ambassadorial interview. I still thought it would be nice to meet the friendly Tsitsarkin couple at home over dinner, and this time he accepted for lunch. But Mrs Tsitsarkin didn't speak good English and he would come solo, he said.

Mrs Thomas was far from pleased but turned on some chicken and salad. Oleg arrived bearing children's books for our three-year-old. They were dowdy but nice and the Russian illustrators ignored the Western convention (to this day) that puppy dogs lack an anus. All the rear views of the Russian puppy dogs included a small black dot.

At the table, the awkward atmosphere got worse when Mrs Thomas, who had never wanted this socialising, abruptly turned the conversation to Aleksandr Solzhenitsyn, now in the USA. Why was the Soviet Union bad-mouthing him? she demanded.

Poor Oleg. Whatever he replied would have repercussions. He chose to give the party line on Solzhenitsyn, even if it meant hostilities with Mrs Thomas and loss of best-buddy status with me.

Solzhenitsyn was a dishonest person who had cheated in his high school exams, he said, and became an army coward and was now in someone's pay to blacken the good name of Soviet society. Mrs Thomas revved up the dispute.

The rest of the lunch was frosty. Oleg decided he had little to lose, and made an announcement: "I wish to speak to Mr Thomas – alone!"

Mrs Thomas's face changed colour at being ordered out of her own dining room. She exited with bad grace. I sensed I was going to hear more about this later.

With her out of the way, Oleg came close and lowered his voice. "I want to ask you, will China invade North Vietnam?"

I was dumbstruck. Why ask me? I had an inspiration. "You know, the *Far East Economic Review* had a piece on this topic only yesterday. I'll find it."

I rummaged through the pile on the coffee table, found the magazine, flicked to the article, ripped it out, and handed it to him with a pleased expression. He took it, unimpressed, and soon after he departed. I never heard from him again. A month later, China invaded Vietnam.

Alert readers may wonder how I know ASIO was on my case. Here's how. A couple of years later I stayed the weekend in London with a friend, Ken, in the Australian public service. Also staying was another chap, Maurice. Ken mentioned that Maurice was with ASIO. I got chatting privately with Maurice and related my trysts with Tsitsarkin. We were interrupted and I never got to finish the story. We all went our separate ways.

Months later, back in Melbourne, Maurice phoned me and suggested lunch. Nothing loath, I agreed and over steak and shiraz, this time ASIO-financed, I gave him the full saga.

Maurice had done his homework and probed my inconsistencies. He seemed less interested in Oleg than in the Soviet embassy's press attaché, Mr Lev Koshliakov. "Tell me about your contacts with him," Maurice said.

I racked my brains. He was the chap I originally phoned for an interview with the ambassador. But I denied any other contact. Maurice kept at me. Eventually he disclosed his hand: they had logged me making a couple of calls I had forgotten about. Maybe Maurice was concerned I was using innocuous lines as code to Koshliakov. I hope I straightened him out. I also explained what was in the A4 envelopes I was handing over to the Soviets.

"Why so concerned about Koshliakov?" I asked.

"It's like this. Koshliakov was the senior KGB man in the embassy. The press attaché bit was his cover. Some of his stuff was illegal and we hoped to expel him back to Moscow.

"Now about Oleg. He wasn't that important but we like to know what they want to know. He was low-level GRU, that's the military intelligence. He was called third secretary. I don't know why he was cultivating you. Sometimes it's cloak-and-dagger but sometimes these guys are genuinely at sea and need a local's advice." I was relieved. I usually take people, even Russians, at face value.

What about that first dinner invitation to Oleg and his wife, that he ignored? Maurice laughed. "To him, entrapment. Same as you trying to drive him back to the embassy. Everyone knows that we have photographers across the road."

My economics help to Oleg? Useless, said Maurice. "Anything published, they already had. That's why you got downgraded to McDonald's." I flinched.

In Canberra a few years later, a Labor Party apparatchik, David Combe, formed a friendship with a Russian diplomat and KGB man, Valery Ivanov. It blew up, Bob Hawke expelled Ivanov, and Combe was severely punished – by being sent to Western Canada as senior trade commissioner. Why am I never punished like that?

I was stupid to have any truck with Russians. Or, and this is delicious, I should have rung ASIO to be "wired" for my meetings with Oleg. But how would this fit with my day job? Technically, I should also have asked my *Age* editor Greg Taylor if he wanted an agent on the payroll. (Probably not!)

As for my hopes of an interview with Ambassador Alexander Vasilievich Basov, he was most unlikely to have been beguiled into giving me a colorful, potentially Walkley-winning scoop. I now know from John Blaxland's Vol 11 ASIO history that Basov was a full member of the Soviet Communist Party's Central Committee (most unusual for an ambassador), and freshly arrived here from ministering to the ill-fated Marxist President of Chile, Salvador Allende, who shot himself while literally besieged by the CIA's minions. ASIO found Basov to be 'dogmatic, thrusting and difficult to deal with'. During his tenure in Canberra he flooded ASIO with work, from his 'political interference in local affairs' and 'recruitment of agents of influence' (ouch!).

The other day I acquired my ASIO file. It showed me tick-tacking with Tsitsarkin about a lunch at the Lotus restaurant (sounds plausible) on October 19, 1977. Then there were many pages about Tony Thomas doing rabid agitprop for the Palestinians against the Israelis – mistaken identity by ASIO, as that was a different "Tony Thomas".

Then nothing (time-travelling backwards) until December 1972, when I attended evening cocktails at the Soviet embassy in my capacity as National Press Club treasurer. This evening appeared uneventful to me but a Soviet official, Lazovic, kept calling in as Duty Officer to see if everything was "in order". It wasn't. Soviet official Morosov "was reported to be 'very drunk' at 2225 hours and was collected from the residence and taken home".

Geronty Lazovic, it emerged last year, went on to recruit a top agent inside ASIO or Defence and earned a medal for it. More satisfying than carting drunk Russians home from cocktail parties.

As for Koshliakov, he was rated Moscow's most dangerous agent in Australia, with more than 115 press contacts. I could have been number 116. He became KGB station chief in Norway, was busted for spying, and got handed a top job at Aeroflot where he remained until at least 2010, about his retirement age of sixty-five.

On the excitements of my briefings of Oleg Tsitsarkin, ASIO files were blank. Not blacked out, but blank. Yet according to my chats with Maurice, ASIO was seriously interested. A little mystery there!

As to my part in Brezhnev's downfall, well, sticking him for my steak and shiraz at the 19th Hole was another straw on the camel's back.

Quadrant OnLine, 7 January 2016

Australia's Civil War, Almost

At a distance of decades, the very idea of a secret army standing ready to thwart a Communist takeover of Australia seems laughable. In the years after WWII, however, the plots and paranoia came thick and fast.

◇◇

Last June [2012] I did a tour of the Gettysburg battlefield, marveling that such fratricidal slaughter had taken place on those now-tranquil Pennsylvanian paddocks. "Could a civil war ever have occurred in Australia?" I mused. "Unthinkable!"

However, the question nagged, and later I re-visited a passage in the memoirs of ex-WA Premier Sir Charles Court, a war-time Lt-Colonel.[7] He writes of the late 1940s:

> The Communist Party in Australia was strong, having built up tremendously during the war. A great number of men and women throughout Australia who had held positions in the armed forces and had the training, experience and understanding of what subversive elements meant, were very concerned that the Communist Party was seeking to undermine the elected government.
>
> A group of us came together. Most of us were politically conservative, but we were just as determined to do what we could to protect Ben Chifley as the elected Prime Minister as we would have been had it been Menzies...
>
> There were kindred groups in other States. We had clandestine meetings with people who were prepared to go to extreme lengths to defeat the Communists. We had reason to believe that Chifley knew what was going on and did nothing to stop our covert activities. In fact it was reported to us that he said, 'You know I can't condone it, but don't stop it'...
>
> Not all the people concerned about Communism were from the forces. Some were senior in industry and commerce and hadn't been able to go to the war. There were no paid positions. It was a watchdog type of organisation to make it clear that if the Communists moved in any way to upset the elected government, there were plenty of people

---

7 At war's end, with only 70 troops, Court took the surrender of 20,000 Japanese in Bougainville.

in Australia who would be prepared to go to the barricades to defend the right of the elected government to govern.[8]

This passage is elliptical, as if Charlie couldn't decide how much to disclose or to conceal. In fact, he was one member of a secret force called The Association, put by historians at 100,000 to even 130,000 men. The WA troop was led by Brigadier Eric McKenzie, concurrently WA's Chief Scout (Motto: Be Prepared).[9]

Was that national stand-off the civil war we almost had? I next came across this pregnant paragraph in Dr Frank Cain's *Terrorism & Intelligence*:

> On the day immediately following the passing of the [Communist Party] Dissolution Act...Menzies ordered the establishment of a secret organisation under military command, identified by the code name 'Alien', which would rally mainly civilian forces to counter the effects of possible industrial actions and demonstrations in protest against the banning legislation...."[10]

Curiouser and curiouser! Was there not just one secret army tolerated by Chifley, but another formally established by Menzies? Secret armies are, well, secret, so confusion is understandable.

As background to all this, Communist general secretary Lance Sharkey in March, 1949, had affirmed his support for any Soviet invaders of Australia; the Soviets exploded their first A-bomb in August, 1949; North Korea invaded South Korea in June, 1950; and in March, 1951 Menzies was warning the electorate that Australia had less than three years to prepare for World War III.

The point of the secrecy about the "armies" was to conceal from the Communists the opposing strength in planning, manpower, money, armaments including machine-guns, and leadership. Some indecent exposure occurred when William Morrow (Lab, Tas) rose in the Senate in June, 1950, to denounce a subversive and fascist secret group called "The Association". He said it had bought a large number of .303 rifles, and he correctly named Brigadier Frederick Hinton as a leader. Hinton

---

8 Charles Court, *Charles Court: the early years*. Fremantle Arts Centre Press, 1995, p277-78.
9 David Horner, Blamey: the Commander-in-Chief. Allen & Unwin, Sydney, 1998, p576-8
10 F. Cain, *Terrorism & Intelligence in Australia*. Australian Scholarly Publishing, North .Melbourne, 2008, p106

adroitly denied involvement in "fascist" activities.[11]

Even now, be careful what you say. A newspaper in 1989 paid up for defamation over an article on The Association. My own brave article here tries (Part 1) to elucidate "The Association", and then (Part 2) to look at Operation Alien and other plans to defeat Red "fifth-columnists".

Far from being unusual, secret right-wing armies have been part of the Australian landscape since 1910. The closest we came to a pre-war civil war was in May, 1932, when the Old Guard of anti-Bolshevists was within 24 hours of ordering its 30,000 members onto the streets.[12] This right-wing insurrection was headed off when Governor Sir Philip Game dismissed NSW Labor Premier Jack Lang and his ministers. (The New Guard was a 1931 breakaway from the long-standing Old Guard. In contrast, the New Guard gave little care to secrecy and hence is better known, especially after Captain de Groot's swording of the Harbour Bridge ribbon during the opening ceremony in 1932).

Post-war, General (later Field Marshal) Blamey was titular head of the revived right-wing army, The Association. When he fell terminally ill in 1950 Lt-General Sir Leslie Morshead, hero of Tobruk and second-Alamein, took charge of it.

According to historian Associate Professor Andrew Moore (University of Western Sydney), the Chifley government's Commonwealth Investigation Service (CIS), viewed The Association as a potential threat to the Labor government.

The Association's credo was honour the King, uphold the Constitution, and resist regimentation of the individual. But the CIS reported that there were some "real Nazis" within The Association's ranks who were "prepared for any sort of 'putsch'".[13]

Charles Spry, later head of ASIO, told Blamey biographer John Hetherington privately: "I tremble to think what would have happened in a crisis when I think of some of the odd people in it."

---

11 A. Moore, *The Secret Army and the Premier*. NSW University Press, Kensington, 1989, p245. Morrow's own credentials as a democrat were not all that flash. He supported the Nazi-Soviet pact of 1939 and left the Labor Party in 1953 to become a stalwart of the KGB-controlled World Peace Council. In 1961 the Soviets awarded him a Lenin Peace Prize and the ruble-equivalent of 5000 pounds.
12 C. Coulthard-Clark, *Soldiers in Politics*. Allen & Unwin, St Leonards, 1996, p172.
13 Andrew Moore, "Fascism Revived? The Association Stands Guard 1947-52". *Labour History*, 74/1998, p108.

The CIS, according to Blamey biographer David Horner, said The Association had up to 73,000 men in Victoria, 55,000 in NSW and 1,000 in SA. Its chief of staff was Major-General Colin Simpson. Other leaders included Brigadier Hinton (NSW); Colonel Charles Withy (Qld); and Lt-Col Alexander Pope (SA) All were retired officers.

Blamey got the Queensland wing going while ostensibly on a fishing trip there in 1948. It may even have had a Ladies Auxiliary. A somewhat over-excited CIS official reported that Blamey believed there were 200 Communist military officers in Australia backed by trained saboteurs. There were also, supposedly, two divisions of Sukarno's fully-equipped Indonesians ready to invade on 24-hours notice in support of an uprising.[14]

Hetherington lamented that his account is largely hearsay because the movement took care to not write anything down. Even its emergency battle orders were verbal and memorised.

Hetherington says "The Association", also known as "The White Army", had peak strength at 100,000 war veterans, including blue-collar and Labor men. They were prepared to hold the line against any coup d'etat by Communist irregulars, pending counter-attack by the slower-moving constitutional forces. Serving officers were excluded, but army intelligence was well aware of what was going on.

Administration devolved to State and then area and sub-area commands or secret cells, such that meetings were generally kept under 20 men. Even then, they parked their cars in scattered places and walked to their venue. Senior officers did not know their opposite numbers in other States, although they had the "keys" to communication channels in any emergency.[15] (This may explain Charlie Court's vagueness in his account).

Blamey's rationale was that a Red uprising would come in the wake of a general strike, coupled with a Red threat to vital community services. The "White Army" would be sworn-in at short notice as special constables and then counter-attack. Prime targets for both sides would be traffic junctions, water channels, bridges, power pylons, fuel stores,

---

14 Brigadier Hinton foresaw Stalin arranging a 'super Pearl Harbour' attack against the West using local Communist cadres. Locally, Red-run unions could initiate "H-Hour" – paralysing strikes followed by overnight seizure of vital infrastructure as prelude to a putsch.

15 J. Hetherington, *Blamey, Controversial Soldier*. Australian War Memorial, Canberra, 1973, pp. 389-92

phone and telegraph stations, arms stores including gun retailers, and newspaper offices.

"Well-trained combat teams would use all necessary force. Many of the members had rifles and shotguns, and knew they could get more firearms, including machine-guns if necessary," Hetherington wrote. Others would make do with pick-handles. Each man could respond to the command within minutes, knowing exactly what to do and where to go.

Hetherington's view was that the "army" originated from a conversation in about 1947 between Blamey and Melbourne's Lord Mayor Sir Raymond Connelly about the Communist threat. Blamey said he was hamstrung by lack of funds; Connelly then did a whip-round among wealthy businessmen and community leaders to produce the funding. (Dr Andrew Moore of University of Western Sydney puts the funding at 100,000 pounds, an astounding amount in 1949).

Blamey's job was to be top planner and also to satisfy members that their army was not a rightist subversive plot to seize power, Hetherington said.

According to historian Moore, the Communist-backed coal strike in June, 1949, brought The Association to the brink of mobilisation. Brigadier Hinton was initially cool-headed, but within days was acting as though a Red coup was imminent. Instructions went out to engineer battalions to safeguard infrastructure such as water and sewerage, and create barricades, trenches and barbed-wire barriers. Explosives, gelignite, and detonators were to be furnished. In the event of casualties, named replacement leaders were to be installed.

Hinton then visited the NSW Police Commissioner, Scott 'Nugget' MacKay, and NSW special branch chief Len Jones to inform them that The Association would be mobilising in two days.

Jones told Hinton to calm down as there was no evidence from agents within the Communist cells that an insurrection was pending. Hinton on June 29 backtracked and told his paramilitaries to stay quiet and beware of provocations. The same day, Chifley legislated his draconian response "Operation Kangaroo" against the striking miners. On August 1 regular troops began work in NSW open cuts.

Moore wonders if Chifley's response might have been related to The Association's latent threats. The head of the Commonwealth

Department of Transport, A.W. Paul, had gone to great lengths to warn Chifley personally of a planned paramilitary or 'fascist' takeover of infrastructure and possibly, of power. Chifley himself has left no records of his private thoughts on his coal-strike intervention.

On The Association's origins, Moore's view, based partly on a cache of Brigadier Hinton's documents that he discovered in western NSW, is that The Association was largely a re-birth from 1947 of the 1930s "Old Guard" paramilitaries of the 1930s. The Old Guard, like The Association, was led by Generals Blamey and Simpson (Vic) and Hinton (NSW). Former members, and sometimes their sons, were re-mobilised as leaders.

Moore also cites a CIS report claiming The Association was set up after Blamey had watched a group of 8,000 unionists moving off efficiently in 30 minutes. Blamey then wondered at the unionists' efficiency were they were fully armed: they could defeat the regular forces, the CIS report said.

Yet another CIS theory was that The Association was the antipodean spawn of a meeting of imperial defence chiefs in 1946, headed by Field Marshal Montgomery and calling for right-wing guerilla resisters in the event that the Soviets conquered Britain and Western Europe.

Moore believes that The Association started in 1947, led by a Lt-Colonel Penrose, a pre-war "New Guard" alumnus. The CIS noted that a high army informant described Penrose as "vicious with a cruel temperament which would suit him as an officer of Hitler's Gestapo."

While Brigadier Hinton in NSW professed that The Association would always obtain constitutional approval before acting, its country members were less fastidious. In Bairnsdale, Victoria, a member reported that because even the police force harbored Communists, an independent armed body was necessary to take control "in the best interests of the community".

The CIS, with its primary loyalty to the Chifley government, tracked and infiltrated the movement. CIS people staked out the Association's Melbourne headquarters in the not-so-aptly named Sunshine House in Bourke Street, and even prepared a floor plan of the offices used by the chief of staff, Major-General Simpson.

In Sydney, the CIS headquarters were in the Mercantile Mutual Building at 117 Pitt Street and the rival headquarters were directly opposite at 84 Pitt Street.[16] Because the 84 Pitt Street office was small, the White Army leaders would sometimes run their conferences in the board room of the Mercantile Mutual, to the delight of the CIS co-tenants.

The CIS was soon reporting that The Association, whatever it professed, was a danger to the Chifley government. It appeared to be answerable to no-one but its own leaders, who thought Chifley and Doc Evatt were undercover Communists. One CIS executive reported that The Association was "prepared for any sort of a 'putsch'". The Association responded with such mistrust of the CIS that one CIS infiltrator feared for his personal safety. (Conversely, The Association had infiltrated the CIS).

The Association's infrastructure allegedly included first aid posts to be run by the British Medical Association, and a trucking magnate's fleet, used to take members for rifle and drill training 60km out of Sydney.

The NSW police were thick with The Association. Commissioner MacKay wanted Association members as special constables in any emergency. He addressed a meeting of The Association in January, 1948, claiming he had dossiers on 45,000 Communists [total party membership at the time was only about 6000]. The Chief of the General Staff, Lt Gen Sturdee, said at the same meeting that he expected war with Russia in 18 months. Liberal politician Richard Casey (later Governor-General) was another bigwig lending The Association high-level support.

Among The Association's irregulars were schoolboys from Scotch College, Melbourne, who were enlisted in a "youth division" and one night assigned to guard the school cadets' armory against Communist onslaught.[17] Senior journalists, sympathetic to The Association, were prepared to assist through their reporting or non-reporting. The Association's Intelligence chief was a former Asian Airlines employee J.M. Burgoyne, assisted by J.M. Prentice, the former Director of Military

---

16 When Petrov's political seducer Michael Bialoguski visited the CIS premises on the sixth floor, "I found myself in a large empty-looking room. A counter opposite the door and a wooden bench near the entrance were the only pieces of furniture. Nobody was in the room. On the counter was a very much used sheet of blotting paper and an inkpot with a pen protruding from it … " *The Petrov Story,* p26-27.

17 School cadets also featured in September 1974, when the Defence Department confiscated 175 weapons from a school armoury to keep them from possible anti-Whitlam vigilantes.

Intelligence, Eastern Command.

Quality of the intelligence varied. For example, there was a chain of art deco coffee houses in Sydney called Repins Cafes, founded by a White Russian refugee Ivan Repin in the 1930s. An Association report claimed, implausibly, that the cafes were managed by imported trained men and the staff were all card-carrying Communists.

Perhaps the cafes' clientele of European-style roasted-coffee-lovers, such as Vienna-born journalist George Munster and Hungarian-born cartoonist George Molnar, aroused suspicion.[18]

The Sydney University economics faculty was another purported hotbed of revolutionaries, and the suspected top leader was the proprietor of the Coronet Chicken Grill.

Moore writes that The Association was frustrated by the CPA's failure to insurrect, and itself went in for some vigilante violence, although his only example is an elderly shearer who got bashed. His other examples are more of intimidation and vandalism. In Cowra, a Communist public meeting was under way about that hardy perennial "the coming depression". An Association mob arrived but found the audience was only six.

The Association lingered on after the Menzies government came to power, ready to assist Menzies with the internment of the thousands of Communists and fellow-travellers in camps. The detention process was even designated "Order No 1" by The Association.

Writer Martin Boyd recalled that at the 1950 Melbourne Cup, a senior member of the Association had told him that in the event of any "trouble", the secret army was ready to "rope in every shade of pink", which Boyd feared could even include himself.

The Association also re-channelled its energies into issues like civil defence mechanisms against nuclear strikes.

Its official demise was in late 1952, when ASIO seemed to have the Red threat under control. Some Association members joined ASIO. There is one indication that a Colonel Neil McArthur kept a Collins Street office going for the "White Army" until his death in 1961.

Dr Moore concludes his study:

---

18 The Association included anti-Semitic elements, and in Queensland, there was even an anti-Catholic undertow.

The secret army was an understandable response to the tensions of the period. But for all its links with formally constituted authority, it was a mendacious enterprise, a reminder of the extent to which liberal democratic freedoms were threatened during the Cold War in Australia. Having fought a world war in order to crush fascism, some soldiers remained ambiguous about the merits of liberal parliamentary democracy. In the final resort, powerful members of Australia's military and commercial elite threatened democratic values and practices far more than supporters of that detested 'foreign ideology', communism.

Quadrant OnLine, 15 October 2012

Australia's Civil War, Almost — Part II

Australia's Communists firmly believed the Menzies government had plans to lock up their leaders in the event of hostilities with Russia or China. They were wrong about that. Operation Alien envisioned not just a few Reds behinds barbed wire but thousands.

The strike-breaking "Operation Alien" (1950-55) was an official enterprise, albeit just as secret as The Association's secret army described in Part One. Operation Alien would break subversive strikes and maintain order, using combinations of civilians and troops.[19]

Prime Minister Robert Menzies launched Alien to ensure that essential services and industries continued after the Communist Party Dissolution Act came into force in October, 1950. One outcome of the Act would be the naming and banning of various union officials, and Menzies knew that the response would be strikes on the waterfront and in coal mines and transport.

Les Louis, a retired associate professor of history at the University of Canberra, says Alien was basically run by Department of Labour head Henry Bland, and ASIO had nothing to do with it. Alien had been the best kept official secret of all time. Louis interviewed Bland long after Bland retired, "and Bland still denied any knowledge of Alien, he denied to his dying breath that it ever existed. I got the facts from the archives," Louis told me.

---

19 Les Louis, "'Operation Alien' and the Cold War in Australia". *Labour History,* 62/1992

Top Alien leaders included Brigadier Eric Woodward, later deputy chief of the general staff and NSW governor; Brig. Leslie Binns; Brig. Augustine Wardell; Lewis Luxton, assistant general manager of Shell; and an ex-Navy captain as Commonwealth War Book Officer.

The initial plan was to use civilian strike-breakers, sworn in as special "Peace Officers", with troops to be used as last resort. But Henry Bland, Alien's dominant bureaucrat, convinced the politicians to use troops first. (The troops could carry their personal weapons to the concentration points but would go to the job sites unarmed and protected by police).

Louis says troops-before-civilians was a brilliant tactic by Bland and his fellow mandarins. During the war people had got used to seeing troops on the wharves; it was not a shocking sight. Volunteer labor would have been intensely provocative to wharfies. But Alien was on a scale far beyond the wharves. Use of troops became a routine part of anti-Communist planning, he says.

The view of Louis, a self-professed Marxist historian, is that Australia's key industries – wharves, coal and railways – were run-down after the Depression and the war, and were also in the hands of Communist union leaders. In addition, the late 1940s were a rare period when laborers had the upper hand in industrial bargaining. Hence, although the overt issue for the government was Communist imperialism, breaking the Communists' industrial power via Operation Alien was also the key to restructuring those inefficient industries, Louis told me.

Menzies gave Alien even higher priority than troop needs for the Korean War and the training of national servicemen. When US President Truman urged the government to send more troops to Korea, Menzies instead sent the aircraft carrier Sydney.

Application of Alien to Papua-New Guinea, for reasons unfathomable, involved the shipment of 2,300 .303 rifles and 200,000 rounds of ammunition. Another 20 .303 rifles, bayonets and accessories, labeled as "Merchandise", went to Nauru.[20]

On cue, Australian mining and waterfront stoppages began in early 1951, which the government interpreted as a Red conspiracy, rather than industrial disputes.

The government had some ground to fear the worst from Communist

20 Les Louis, "Guns for Nauru in the Cold War". The Hummer, 33/1992.

insurrectionists. In 1948, Queensland Communist leader Gilbert Burns had said that, in the event of any war between the Soviets and Australia, Australian Communists "would fight on the side of the Soviet Union".[21] Soviet defector Vladimir Petrov claimed that Moscow had provided $25,000 funding the party in the early 1950s. This was eventually verified when a receipt for $25,000 turned up from CPA general secretary Lance Sharkey for an alleged Soviet "purchase of wool" in 1953.[22]

According to the NSW south coast district secretary of the Communist Party, one of the central committee secretariat members had developed a strategy to use the coal strike to bring on revolution in Australia. The plan involved "surrounding" Sydney with the militant working-class districts of Newcastle, the South Coast and Lithgow.

Another group of CPA members planned to immobilise trains and dynamite the Hawkesbury railway tunnel to prevent "scab" coal from reaching Sydney. According to the Newcastle CPA district's then-secretary, a member of the central committee secretariat, J.C. Henry, had advocated this action on the grounds that it would concentrate the class struggle.

A former Communist recalled of party planning that during a tense point in the coal strike "some of the gunmen associated with the waterfront were called in".[23]

As late as 1961, Ted Hill, then Victorian State CPA secretary, was still arguing that "the party should start preparing for armed struggle, and should commence training people for it" according to his colleague Bernie Taft.[24]

Menzies first "Alien" mobilisation alert went out on March 2, 1951, with the army advised to ready "all troops practicable" for action on March 6. The press, unaware of Alien, merely reported that large numbers of troops appeared to be massing for the waterfront. The wharfies and miners, intimidated, called off their stoppages a few days later.

The re-elected Menzies government on May 25 again signaled the

---

21 David McKnight, *Australian Spies and their Secrets*. Allen & Unwin, St Leonards, p113

22 David McKnight, *Rethinking Cold War History*. Labour History, No. 95, November, 2008, p185-196.

23 Phillip Deery, "Communism, Security and the Cold War". Journal of Australian Studies, No. 54/55, 1997. p162-75, including footnote 66

24 Bernie Taft, *Crossing the Party Line*. Scribe, Newham, 1994, p127

military to activate the Alien plans, this time in response to industrial stoppages in solidarity with NZ unionists. Troops worked affected ports and the government threatened to deregister the Waterside Workers Federation, leading to WWF capitulation by June 12.

Alien came into further operation sporadically in the next few years, including an airlift by Skymasters and other commandeered aircraft of 220 armed troops to Bowen for sugar loading in late 1953.

Menzies terminated Alien in October, 1955, ending what Les Louis describes as an extraordinary period of troops being readied and used against unionists in strategic industries.

That is not quite the end of the story. Fossicking in the archives, Louis came across the Menzies government's detailed planning for detention of Communists and fellow-travellers in the event of war. Louis' article is provocatively titled, "Pig Iron Bob finds a further use for scrap iron: barbed wire for his cold war concentration camps".

Leftists had always claimed Menzies wanted to silence them by concentrating them in camps, while officialdom decried such talk as ludicrous fiction. But the Lefties weren't wrong, as Les Louis discovered during years of pestering ASIO for early documents.[25] Technically, internment needed to be preceded by some sort of declaration of war and activation of the Commonwealth War Book, but Louis believes the government and ASIO would have struck pre-emptively.

From July, 1950, ASIO head Colonel Spry embarked on urgent compilation of internment lists, and by December already had an interim list of "750 selected Communists" whose detention "would render the Party organisation innocuous" while the remaining enemies of the people were rounded up. By August, 1951, the list had grown to 1100 suspected party officials.

Arrests were to be by State police, and detainees handed over to the Army, which would run and guard the camps. WA and NT Reds would be transferred to SA camps, and Tasmanians to Victoria.

---

25 Louis found many important documents of the Victorian branch of the archives stored in a broken-down laundry and reading room in Brighton, Vic.

Intended Internees (excluding enemy aliens), April 1955

ARMY COMMAND	MEN	WOMEN & CHILDREN	TOTAL
Northern	130	390	520
Eastern	600	1800	2400
Southern	160	480	540
Central	50	150	200
Western	60	180	240
Tasmania	30	90	120
NT	10	30	40
TOTAL	1040	3120	4060

Criteria for detention included membership of the party's central committee; state committees; metropolitan district committees; branch officials; and "Communist paid journalists, organisers and other activists". Then there was prominence in the Eureka Youth League (did ASIO overlook the Junior Eureka Youth League, of which I was a member and inefficient goalie in Perth's JEYL soccer team?). The list also included Communists in suspect organisations, such as the Australia Peace Council, New Housewives' Association and New Theatre League.

Detention plans then moved on to Communist trade union officials, ditto "disrupters of industry", those in significant public service jobs and government science bodies, those in firms doing secret government work and those likely to be spying and sabotaging things.

A different category were enemy aliens (with a special category for "Asiatics"), who were aged 16-65 and associated with Soviet states, China, the east European bloc, and curiously, Finland. This involved, according to Louis, "two trusted immigration officials" in each State winnowing their files for ASIO's benefit.

The main safeguards were (assuming use of the WW11 template) that Ministerial approval of an ASIO brief was needed in each case, along with an appeal tribunal. "This involved ASIO in mountains of paperwork," Louis concluded, given that at April, 1955, there were 1040 Reds listed along with their 3120 women and children (Table One, above), along with 12,500 enemy aliens. By 1960 the total listees (including enemy aliens) had declined from 16,630 to a mere 1436.

Louis was unable to tell me what constituted "a war" (the Korean War, for example, was a "police action" or "peace enforcement mission"). "It was all I could do just to get the official figures," he confesses.

David McKnight published his book, *Australia's Spies and their Secrets*, a year after Louis' article. McKnight found that detention planning continued at least until the early 1970s.

Children were to be detained with their detained parents, although by 1956 ASIO became aware that this contravened the Geneva Convention. The "lists" were so sensitive that ASIO's Spry wanted them disclosed not to cabinet but only four top ministers.

McKnight also found that in 1960, the military and ASIO were speculating about internment policy for "a limited war" involving Vietnam or China – our Vietnam "war" got going five years later. He also says that ASIO almost drowned for a decade in the paperwork required for briefs on each individual – especially as ASIO made 16 copies of each person's brief.

Even the Communist Party wildly underestimated the detention planning, imagining it might involve detaining on Flinders Island a mere dozen leading Communists, rather than a thousand encamped in all States.

McKnight concludes: "Ultimately the problem was that in law, it was not a crime to be a Communist nor to espouse 'subversive' ideas. ASIO just acted as if it was."

Quadrant OnLine, 16 October 2012

Spy vs Spy: ASIO and the Reds

Moles, sleepers, double agents, clandestine printing presses, agents of influence in newsrooms and police squads -- the war between the comrades and intelligence agencies had it all, except desk drawers.

The scene: 9th Floor, headquarters of the Communist Party of Australia (Victorian branch), 49 Elizabeth Street, Melbourne.
Date: About 1952.
Victorian CPA Secretary Ted Hill presses an alarm button to signal through the party's rooms: An ASIO raid has commenced!

Party members know what to do.[26] State President Ralph Gibson empties his person of all useful documents, and eats them.

Party functionary Gwladys Bourke cannot work out how to get rid of her sensitive financial records. She prepares to dive out the 9th Floor window with them, a human sacrifice to the betterment of the working class.

Just in time, she discovers from Hill that the alarm was only a test.

Actually, I wonder about the efficacy of Gwladys' plan: had she simply scattered the documents out the window, she would not have needed to jump; but if she took the documents down with her, they could be recovered from the impact site.

A touch of paranoia in party offices was understandable. In July, 1949, the Commonwealth Investigation Service had used 24 operatives to raid Marx House, the NSW party's headquarters, but found little and suspected the party had been tipped off. The raid attracted a crowd of 3,000 passers-by and with considerable aplomb, two party women left Marx House and mingled with the crowd selling copies of "Tribune".

Life was never dull in the CPA (Vic). The Australian Security Intelligence Organisation had an office some floors below to listen in to the Reds upstairs. Party executive Bernie Taft worsened their workload by switching between French, German and Russian in any phone chats to cosmopolitan colleagues.

Party officials were confident they had the upper hand over ASIO (how wrong they were!) They had their own captain of security, the party's "control commission" leg-man Ernie O'Sullivan, a shuffling snoop who was dedicated, ignorant and paranoid. Like a toothless version of Stalin's "bloody dwarf", the later-executed Yezhov, O'Sullivan scribbled semi-literate "unmaskings" of loyal party members as spies and wreckers. After Hill got himself expelled in 1963, O'Sullivan's poison-pen tracts fell into the hands of the rival Bernie Taft faction. Pity no-one's published them yet!

One weekend O'Sullivan, on Hill's orders, came in and removed 100 drawers from party workers' desks, to check for security breaches. He parked 20 of the bulky drawers at Taft's Surrey Hills home, and to this day no-one knows where the other drawers went. Party workers arrived on

26 Bernie Taft, *Crossing the Party Line*. Scribe, Newham, 1994, p141

Monday and mourned their lost drawers. Over the years, observant visitors wondered why the party's desks were all drawerless. Taft writes: "I suppose O'Sullivan must have thought that, after the revolution, which he confidently expected, he might be able to put the drawers back in our desks."

Perhaps the most loyal and heroic of all the Victorian party people was the wife of Bernard Heinz Jr (Heinz Sr was assistant secretary with the Building Workers Industrial Union).

The party in the early 1950s decided to create, yet again, a secret wing that could carry on if the party got banned.[27] Bernard was nominated to become a 'sleeper'. He had to resign from the party and cut links with all his leftist friends. What's more, he was told to accommodate a senior party sleeper plus a printing press underground at his suburban home in outer-eastern Melbourne, where he had just settled in with his new wife. The new project meant laying a concrete slab and then digging a big hole below for the literally underground operations.

Initially, party members dropped by to assist in the dig. But not all the workers' friends have horny hands, and soon Bernard was left to dig unaided. He dug till the 1970s but his important guest and the printing press never turned up.

This was all very well for Bernard and the party, but what about Mrs Heinz? Did she mind? Apparently, she never complained, at least officially.

These true tales are all drawn from Bernie Taft's memoirs *Crossing the Party Line*. He was a one-time joint national secretary of the CPA and for decades on the state executive of the Victorian branch. He recounts his growing distaste for the party's Stalinists and Maoists. He left the party in 1984, and the party as a whole collapsed in 1991. Taft died in 2013. His son Mark Taft SC, after co-running the Socialist Forum with Julia Gillard as the paid staff in the mid-1980s, in 2008 became a Judge on the Victorian County Court.

Bernie Taft's memoirs haven't had much attention. One noticeable thing is how much overseas travel party leaders did, in an era when overseas trips were a rare prize. In 1968-69 Taft did five trips in 18 months. On one trip in 1968 to Moscow, he had an enjoyable dinner, as one does, with the British spy Donald Maclean, "an impressive person –

---

27 The same policies were implemented in 1939-40 and 1947, including the hiding of printing presses

pleasant, reasonable, and serious."

The memoirs get really interesting when Taft describes a pro-communist mole within ASIO who betrayed would-be infiltrators groomed by ASIO to enroll into the party.

For an equivalent mole in earlier times, one would have to go back to the war-time security service, when counter-intelligence on NSW communists was run by a police officer Alfred Hughes, a secret Communist code-named BEN by the Soviets. Hughes adroitly protected top Communist official, Wally Clayton, from scrutiny while Clayton and his group fed valuable documents to the Soviet Embassy. Hughes would sit for hours at the Special Branch HQ reading files about Communists and the party, to which he had unlimited access.[28] Apart from writing a predictably anodyne report on Clayton for the security director-general in 1945, he provided Clayton (Soviet code-name: KLOD) with Clayton's own security file, along with the security files on the Soviet embassy's senior spies Mikheev and Nosov. Hughes retired as Det Sgt 1st Class in 1960 and died in 1978.

Did the CPA really have an ASIO source? Bernie Taft writes that during the early 1950s, "we often knew the identity of ASIO agents who were about to infiltrate the party. [State party secretary] Ted Hill told a number of us that someone in ASIO would contact him every now and again, and give him the names of people whom ASIO had selected to infiltrate the party...weeks, sometimes up to two months, before they actually did."[29] Sometimes the party allowed them to join and then kept them under tight supervision. Others were rejected, to the indignation of sponsoring members impressed by the applicants' enthusiasm.

After the party expelled Hill in 1963, a man calling himself "Bluey" got in touch with party contacts and said that now Hill was out of the picture, he would keep sending notes about the incoming infiltrators. These notes naming new "plants" continued for a year and then suddenly stopped, Taft says.

Taft also describes the party's Melbourne double-agent in ASIO, Duncan Clarke, a bon vivant and serial annoyer of party women. Wesley-educated, Clarke worked as journalist on the *Sunraysia Daily*,

---

28 D. Ball and D. Horner, *Breaking the Codes*. Allen & Unwin, St Leonards, 1998, pp. 243-4.
29 Ted Hill's younger brother Jim Hill was identified by the Venona code-breakers as the important Canberra spy TOURIST.

the *Daily Telegraph* (Sydney), and then the *Herald* (Melbourne), where he was a favorite of Sir Keith Murdoch. Clarke then made an ungrateful departure to join the party's organ *Guardian*.

The Clarke affair was top secret until Taft's memoirs. Clarke was a double agent from 1951-53, on ASIO pay of ten pounds a week. He would meet ASIO handlers in the city and sometimes early on the beach near his Brighton home. He kept Ted Hill fully informed, and supplied ASIO with a regular flow of documents, unbeknownst to other party members. He wrote reports for ASIO on party policies and personalities; and about which journalists were sympathetic. He gave ASIO reports by party leaders before the leaders had even presented them to inner meetings. Clarke claimed that Hill ensured that all the material Clarke supplied would not actually damage the party.

ASIO'S plan was to boost Clarke's prospects in the party and even help him become State Secretary, where he could do wonders for ASIO.

Clarke said he had left ASIO with Hill's agreement, when ASIO pushed too far by asking for the keys to the *Guardian* office so it could be scoped out at night. (I thought ASIO could pick locks, especially as it employed "Leon", a former Chubb employee who was one of the best lock-pickers in the country. Apparently keyed-entry was preferred).

Clarke continued to meet ASIO contacts socially for months afterwards. "Apparently, I was all right with Security," he told Taft.

Clarke had become infected with Hill's paranoia, wondering if ASIO had a second undisclosed plant in the party. That agent could blow the whistle on Clarke to Clarke's ASIO handlers. Clarke also used to fret about whether party mishaps were accidents or successful wrecking exercises by ASIO plants.

Hill himself often labelled his inner colleagues as "security agents". Taft speculates that ASIO could have been stoking Hill's suspicions with disinformation. (Such tactics were used by Hoover's FBI from 1956-71 with great success against radical organisations).

Taft, who must have absorbed a lot without shuddering, writes,

> It makes one shudder to see how that sort of thing works – how 'evidence' of subversion, of deliberate damage to the party, is produced…They [party vigilantes] would argue, 'Clearly he is an enemy, or he wouldn't do that when the party is under attack.' (Of course, the party was always 'under attack').

Clarke wrote for Ted Hill a 200-page report on his ASIO dealings, which went into the snoop O'Sullivan's archives. The archives were accessed by the Taft faction after Hill, O'Sullivan and Clarke decamped in 1963 to set up the Maoist splinter group. Clarke died in 1991.

Taft says Hill must have had his own ASIO contact while master-minding Clarke as double-agent. Taft reserves judgment on Clarke and what his real activities and impacts were, pending release (unlikely) of ASIO files: "Only then will we know the name of Hill's source and how much he really knew." Taft hints that Clarke and Hill could have been using ASIO resources to damage their internal party rivals.

ASIO had mixed fortunes recruiting student agents. In 1975 it recruited a Lisa Walters to infiltrate the youth arm of the Socialist Workers' League (SYL). Nine months later she "came in from the cold" and denounced ASIO's machinations, and was re-admitted to the SYL as a bona fide member.[30]

In the late 1960s, ASIO recruited Monash engineering student Peter Higgins to report on Labor Club doings and student activism. He got annoyed about being asked to report on some students' sexual affairs, and about ASIO's complicity with Santamaria's National Civic Council, and told all to the student newspaper Lot's Wife.

In some of the Eastern bloc, security files became public after the fall of the Wall. Perhaps one day we will have a "Canberra Spring" and be able to read the real deal.

Quadrant OnLine, 25 September 2012

Spy vs Spy — ASIO's Supremacy

While Australian communists watched ASIO, the intelligence agency repaid the favour with a program of surveillance and penetration so thorough its unwitting moles often informed on each other.

◇◇

The mythology of the Communist Party of Australia (CPA) in the Cold War era includes the assertion that members could "smell out" agents from the security forces. In fact, the party was riddled with successful ASIO plants.

30 Philip Deery, "A Double Agent Down Under". http://vuir.vu.edu.au/15470/1/15470.pdf

In 1950, ASIO was employing 30 people just to look after the agents. That year it inserted 10 agents (in addition to those already inside the party). In 1951, new agents inserted were 27; in 1952, 43; and in 1954, 52.[31]

That's 132 new agents, milling around in a political party with only about 5,000 members. Little wonder that, by 1951, ASIO was reading insider accounts of five out of the six state party conferences. ASIO's released files even note that a lover of Ironworkers' Union boss Ernie Thornton had gold fillings in her teeth. When the party's political committee scolded Miners' Federation President Idris Williams for excessive drinking, ASIO heard about it straight away.

One agent appeared to be on the CPA's central committee. He reported on one of its meetings on October 16, 1953, even though, as a (failed) security measure, the party had called that meeting at such short notice that other members only just discovered it was on.[32]

At executive meetings of the Socialist Workers League (SWL), there would sometimes be two ASIO agents unwittingly represented, filing reports about each other. There was definitely overkill. By the 1960s, the Bendigo branch of the CPA still had its ASIO plant Phil Geri, even though the branch's total membership was three (or four, depending on how you count Geri).[33]

ASIO's snoopy coups were often ingenious — and illegal. In 1972, for example, ASIO specialists created a duplicate key to the Melbourne offices of an innocent accounting firm, W. Alexander Boag, in Goodwin Chambers, Flinders Lane. ASIO was then able to enter secretly at will for the next 18 months to photograph the tax and financial records of Boag client Ted Hill, head of the pro-Chinese CPA (Marxist-Leninist). To aid the exercise, ASIO had set up an office on the same floor for a front-company, Kalamunda Mineral Reserves.[34]

It is claimed "very likely" that leading Melbourne communist and

31 F. Cain, *Terrorism & Intelligence in Australia*. Australian Scholarly Publishing, North Melbourne 2008, p. 105.

32 Philip Deery, "Communism, Security and the Cold War". http://www.api-network.com/main/pdf/scholars/jas55_deery.pdf

33 Philip Deery, "ASIO and the Communist Party". www.historycooperative.org/proceedings/asslh2/deery.html

34 D. McKnight, "The New Left and the Old Moles". http://beyondrightandleft.com.au/archives/2006/07/the_new_left_an.html

president of the Australia-Soviet House, John Rodgers, was an ASIO worker. The party's own plant in ASIO, Duncan Clarke, was reporting on Rodgers, under the impression that ASIO viewed Rodgers as a person of interest.[35]

Bernie Taft, long-time Victorian state executive member of the party, claimed he could detect agents because of their faked emotions and ignorance about party mechanisms. He cites in particular a party member who wanted to become the office cleaner. Taft claimed that such people were easy to spot.

Yeah right! One ASIO agent, "Bosch", was Czech immigrant Max Wechsler, an Houdini of anti-communist espionage. He came (in); he saw; he reported. Indeed he furnished ASIO with 702 reports within two years, 1973-75, meeting his handlers initially thrice-weekly and then every weekday. He passed through Communist and Troskyist security barriers as if they didn't exist.

The Wechsler ASIO details became public after ASIO in 2006 released 10 normally redacted files to Professor Phillip Deery at Victoria University, much to Deery's surprise. Wechsler, a fitter, told our immigration officers in Vienna that he had been a resister to the Soviet invasion in 1968. ASIO liked the cut of his jib and he migrated in 1969.

In 1971 he was hospitalised in Queensland for six weeks with anxiety and neuroses. His wife, a nurse, was convicted in Brisbane in 1972 on 13 forgery and theft charges as a result of her infatuation with slow horses. ASIO was unaware of those matters when Max applied for a spy-ship in Melbourne in November, 1972. Peter Barbour, ASIO's then director-general, still viewed Wechsler as a dubious and implausible candidate, and was eventually proved right.

On February 21, 1973, during a single day, Wechsler, then 23, applied to join the CPA and Taft enthusiastically signed him on. Wechsler had hardly arrived inside the Victorian CPA before he was answering the phone on behalf of party president John Sendy. He also acquired the part-time office-cleaning job, contrary to Taft's memoirs.

His progress in the party, and then in Trot groups, was so rapid that his ASIO pay within two years shot from $10 a month (plus expenses) to $90. He was living better than he should as the party's cleaner on $18

---

35 B. Taft, *Crossing the Party Line*. Scribe, Newham, 1994, p. 140.

a week, and ASIO told him to stop taking taxis, for example. He was also instructed, being "impoverished", to badger the party for a pay rise.

He successfully conned ASIO into lending him $300 in June, 1973, to buy a motorbike "to improve his agent role", but he sold the bike for $200 in a fit of desperation over his wife's losses at the local TAB.

At one point the ASIO Assistant Director-General noted: "This file is becoming cluttered up with the financial dealings with [Wechsler]. I thought that when the last request was made, this would be the end." Wechsler's handlers, however, were sympathetic. For example, they "strongly" recommended an expense claim by the "extremely hard working" Wechsler, and noted that "Agents in other States who are [Socialist Workers' League] members receive far in excess of what this agent receives".

Wechsler's mystique included amazing ability to sell the party newspaper *Tribune*, despite its mind-numbing party jargon. As the party newsletter put it: 'A new member, Max, a migrant to this country, has energetically taken up selling on the city streets and at public meetings. In about six weeks he has sold some 260 papers. How about more comrades joining the sales drive?'

My suspicion is that he was actually dumping the newspapers and getting reimbursed by ASIO for the cover price. But top official Bernie Taft saw with his own eyes Wechsler selling 15 Tribunes in 90 minutes, which Taft surmised was "something of a record". Maybe I've been reading too much Le Carre, but could other ASIO operatives have been mustered to pose as Clarke's newspaper customers? Did ASIO have the resources for such a sophisticated operation? Was it coincidence that, when Wechsler later infiltrated the Trotsky-minded Socialist Workers' League (SWL) and Socialist Youth Alliance (SYA), he also won cred there for his ability to sell (or dump) *Direct Action*?[36]

Taft gave Wechsler (whose name translates as 'Changer') two Russian cameras for an extra role as party photographer. ASIO then had to rush Wechsler through a photographer's course, incidentally enabling Wechsler to take high-class portraits for ASIO's rogues' gallery of the CPA. ASIO files record that Taft and Victorian President John Sendy "value his work" and "seem to trust him without question". Taft was "pushing Agent as

---

36 Philip Deery, "A Double Agent Down Under". http://vuir.vu.edu.au/15470/1/15470.pdf

fast as he can into the industrial side of the C.P.A."

Wechsler's reports, according to Deery, ranged from briefings on AMWU faction meetings, the protest movement against US bases (especially the Omega station in Gippsland) and a planned demonstration against the Signals Intelligence Unit at Albert Park barracks, local travel arrangements of an Italian communist, Guiliano Pajetta, reports on the CPA State Committee Conference, the particulars of donors to the CPA's 'fighting fund' and subscribers to *Australian Left Review*, "the identities of all secretaries of CPA branches in the metropolitan area, a list of financial members of the Victorian Branch of the CPA and much of its financial and banking arrangements, details of the electoral campaign of a CPA candidate, George Zangalis, and additional profiles of Party leaders."

Wechsler's rise was so meteoric that ASIO began to worry that he might be a "push-in" to ASIO, i.e. a double agent. The Victorian ASIO office demurred: he was "a likeable little fellow who is proud of his Australian citizenship and simply wishes to assist the A.S.I.O." He moved into the Socialist Workers League in late 1973, and became a full-time activist, a State executive committee member and even its Minutes Secretary, a handy job.

In mid 1974, he helped arrange a demo against the visiting Shah of Iran. He persuaded the other members of the organising committee in the Trades Hall to concentrate the demo at a spot which happened to be the best focus point for hidden ASIO photographers in a building overlooking City Square. He also furnished keys to the Adelaide offices of the Trots, enabling ASIO to do "black bag" break-ins.

The Trots had rented and renovated premises in Peel Street, North Melbourne. Wechsler tipped off the real estate agent about the movement's nature and the agent cancelled the lease. Wechsler identified influential SWL members inside the Labor Party, which then proscribed the AWL and expelled its members.

Despite ASIO's solicitude, the Wechsler story ended in tears. On February 16, 1975, Wechsler went to journalist Chris Forsyth of the Sunday Observer to sell his story for $2,000, and a few days later gave his resignation to his ASIO minders in their official rented room at the Southern Cross Hotel. Wechsler's gripe was that the Whitlam government wasn't responsive enough to his reports.

When Forsyth's story ran in the Observer, the embarrassment of ASIO was matched only by the embarrassment of the CPA. The Whitlam government and the CPA both lied that Wechsler had not been their paid employee and each denied that they had awarded Wechsler the slightest credibility. Now that Wechsler was unfrocked, both government and CPA echoed the succinct and independent judgment of the Brunswick CIB that Wechsler was "a nut".

Wechsler, meanwhile, had unwisely been parked by the *Observer* in the Wrest Point hotel and casino, where he attracted attention for his lavish spending and gambling. Even journo Forsyth got his private parts caught in the Wechsler wringer. Someone successfully sued the *Observer* for libel and as proprietor Max Newton was bankrupt and overseas, Forsyth was eventually ordered personally to pay the $15,000 damages.

Wechsler ended up in Bangkok as a drug spy for Commonwealth police, where his successes included fingering Ananda Marga activists. In 2002 he made local news there as victim of a robbery of his 4 million baht in cash and three Rolexes. The cash at least was recovered.

The last reference I can find to Wechsler is in January 2010, where he pops up as a freelance journalist for *The Bangkok Post*, with a piece involving an interview with an Iranian intelligence defector forecasting the early downfall of President Ahmadinejad. At that time Wechsler would have been 59.[37]

The Trots in Melbourne made the best of a bad job and claimed that because of good party discipline, Wechsler had been unable to influence policy. Wechsler, despite his sterling service to ASIO, never got an OAM for it.

Tony Thomas was a member of the CPA from age 18 to 22, and became a leading pamphlet letter-boxer around Willagee, Fremantle. He left the party as part of a futile plan to improve his low success rate with women.

Quadrant OnLine, 26 September 2012

---

37 This piece is no longer on-line at the Bangkok Post but a copy is at http://tinyurl.com/8grlp9r

Stalin and the Melbourne Symphony Orchestra

Tony Thomas wonders why one of the cruelest modern tyrannies, and the cruelest of its leaders, got such an air-brushing from the Melbourne Symphony Orchestra. But he's glad the MSO now sees the light.

Call me obsessive (OK, I am) but I turned up at the Melbourne Concert Hall on June 20, 2009 to enjoy Prokofiev's 5th Symphony (1944), and nearly blew a fuse.

The MSO's free program notes were as if written by some hack from the Soviet era. The notes quoted Prokofiev praising the cultural freedom of Soviet artists.

Without any editorial comment from the MSO, Prokofiev in these notes swiped at the lack of 'freedom of the human spirit' in the US, in contrast to 'free and happy (Soviet) man'.

A Soviet-era music bigshot called Dmitri Kabalevsky (three times a Stalin Prize-winner) was also quoted about Prokofiev helping to run a war-time composers' commune, at which Prokofiev "encouraged the others to discuss their daily achievements in an atmosphere of mutual trust." (By coincidence, Prokofiev died on March 5, 1953, the same day that Stalin died).

Strangely for a 2009 performance, these notes by a "Graeme Skinner" were dated 1997 (six years after the Soviet Union's collapse).

Arriving home, I penned a letter to the MSO noting that Prokofiev had already suffered his wife Lena and two sons being held in Siberia as hostage for his good behavior, and for all I knew, his quotes could have been drafted by the NKVD for his signature at real or implied gunpoint.

"I can hardly believe MSO program notes could be so ill-informed and so keen to whitewash an era of hideous tyranny and murder in the now-unlamented Soviet Union," I wrote.

To defeat any normal bureaucratic reaction, I posted a copy of the letter not only to the MSO managing director Trevor Green and the MSO's publicity guy, but also to then chief conductor Oleg Caetani, who as a son of Russian conductor Igor Markevitch, doubtless knows a thing or two about Soviet musical history. (I am sure Oleg had not read those program notes).

You suppose my letter just got filed? Not so. One month later, MD Trevor Green replied:

> I agree with you that Prokofiev needs to be discussed more even-handedly. Accordingly, we will commission a new note for our next performance of this work, and will, when the budget allows, commission new annotations for other Soviet-era works that may be performed in future seasons.

Bravo, Trevor Green!

However (why is there always a 'however'?) on May 22, 2010 I was again in the Concert Hall, this time reading the notes for Prokofiev's 'Romeo & Juliet'.

Arriving home, I penned a further letter to the MSO. The notes, I wrote, were OK, but

> I was outraged by the illustration of Stalin…This is a propaganda photo/illustration from the height of the Stalin cult period. Yet the caption merely states that it is 'Joseph Stalin'. It is NOT Joseph Stalin, who was short, with a low forehead, and a swarthy pockmarked face. The illustration shows Stalin as handsome, wise and statesmanlike, a heroic war leader, avuncular, stern but with a hint of kindness. Using such a picture without describing it as a propaganda picture is an insult to all the many millions whom that man murdered, including at least a few hundred artists, writers and doubtless composers, along with their colleagues, family and friends.
>
> I am sure that in illustrating, say, a program note on Richard Strauss, you would not accompany it with an illustration such as the one I attach here [a war-time Nazi portrait of the all-conquering Der Fuehrer].
>
> I am sure that whoever selected the 'heroic Stalin' illustration did so merely from lack of sophistication and lack of historical perspective.[38]
>
> But I am surprised that someone of more maturity in a cosmopolitan city like Melbourne did not tell him/her that Stalin was a mass murderer and not a hero.

This letter was mailed to the new MD Matthew VanBesien, guest

---

38 One of my critics has made the reasonable point that non-propaganda pictures of Stalin are almost non-existent.

conductor Andrew Litton and the MSO's long-suffering PR guy.

A month later, Mr VanBesien replied, acknowledging that the choice of photograph could have been more discerning – "for which of course I apologise to you – but I am not convinced that the photograph automatically denies Stalin's atrocities."

VanBesien cited other music programs that had featured Jacques-Louis David's propaganda picture of Napoleon or official photos of Czar Nicholas II. "These men were responsible for thousands – if not millions- of deaths…None of this was wiped away for me by seeing Napoleon on a horse or Nicholas II looking statesmanlike. I will of course bring this issue to the attention of the staff responsible for production of printed programs."

So far so good. The MSO talks the talk but does it walk the walk?

Today (10 December 2011) I was in the Melbourne Town Hall reading the program notes for Shostakovich's Symphony No 5.

Text? All fine.

Illustration? Joe Stalin. Outfit: bemedalled uniform circa 1945. Build: tall and fit. Forehead: high. Expression: noble, but caring. Complexion: to die for.

Caption: "**Propaganda** portrait of Stalin." (My emphasis)

Bravo, MSO!

Commenters on Andrew Bolt's blog got confused about my position, so I clarified as follows:

> For all posters, could I please explain that my article above was not meant to be condemnatory of the MSO management. OK they stuffed up with their original pro-Soviet program notes to Prokofiev 5, but as I pointed out, instead of getting defensive about my complaint, they manfully admitted error and promised to do better next time.
>
> On the Prokofiev Romeo & Juliet program notes, they stuffed up again using a propaganda pic of Stalin without labelling it as such.
>
> Again they manfully apologised, and added an arguable point that it was no worse than using a propaganda pic of Napoleon.
>
> On the program notes for Shostakovich last Saturday, I was delighted to discover that they had this time correctly labelled the pic of Stalin as a 'Propaganda Portrait.' Hence my 'Bravo, MSO!'

The real point of my article is that we humble members of the public should always be assertive towards the powers-that-be when they get things wrong (for whatever reason). In this MSO case, they have been responsive and positive towards an admittedly cranky music lover, who takes anything to do with Stalin very seriously. (I have just been re-reading all volumes of the Gulag Archipelago).

Andrew Bolt's blog, *Herald-Sun,* Melbourne, 11 December 2011

Stalin's Daughter: an unlikely asylum-seeker

In the comedy "Children of the Revolution" (1996) Judy Davis's character bonked Joe Stalin in the 1950s and their love-child Joe gained a career in the Australian police union.

In the real world Australia came quite close to adopting Stalin's daughter Svetlana as a political refugee in 1967. Svetlana, then 41, was an unwelcome arrival by taxi at the US Embassy in New Delhi, demanding asylum. The US was trying to mend fences with the USSR, and Washington wanted her thrown back to the unforgiving Soviets.

Too late, they were told: she was already on Qantas to Rome. Actually the flight had been delayed two hours and Svetlana was still in the departure lounge.

The sequel is laconically described in John Blaxland's *The Protest Years – The Official History of ASIO* - Vol 2, 1963-75, published last October.

> Occasionally ASIO was approached by the Americans to consider resettling defectors. Generally, the Australian Government looked favourably on requests to resettle such people but there were instances when it objected.
>
> In 1967, for example, the Americans approached [ASIO director-general Charles] Spry to see if Australia would be prepared to grant asylum to Svetlana Iosifovna Stalin, the daughter of Soviet dictator Joseph Stalin. Spry advised the Minister for External Affairs, Sir Paul Hasluck, and the Secretary of the Prime Minister's Department, John Bunting, that a number of factors had to be taken into consideration before agreeing to the request, although 'the difficulties of looking after her would not be insuperable'. Australia had plenty of experience looking after the Petrovs.
>
> Hasluck acknowledged that the principal argument in favour

of granting the request was 'to please the Americans', but believed that acceding to the request would have significant repercussions on relations with the Soviet Union and South-East Asian countries. Hasluck saw more disadvantages than advantages, and Prime Minister Holt agreed. In the end, soon afterwards, she settled in the United States.

Svetlana defected on 6 March 1967. The flurry of memos began when Svetlana was holed up in secrecy and stateless in Rome. New Zealand turned down a concurrent US request to take her. South Africa offered residence but she refused.

Moving on to Switzerland, she had a US-organised disguise as "Fraulein Carlen", an Irish tourist. The cover was so weak that an ex-Soviet circus performer, now an Australian citizen, mailed her a marriage proposal.

Svetlana made it to New York on a six-month tourist visa. She'd been hiding her manuscript Twenty Letters to a Friend and US publishers offered $US1.5m royalties. This windfall meant she needed no official subsidies and could enter and live in the US as a private citizen.

Australian connections keep popping up. When Vladimir Petrov defected in 1954, two burly Soviet agents at Mascot frogmarched Mrs Petrov onto a plane to Moscow. In the famous tarmac photo, one Soviet minder was unidentified; the other was burly moustachioed Vasily Stanko.

The day before Svetlana got to New York, the same Vasily Stanko also also arrived, as "chauffeur" with the Soviet Mission to the UN. Svetlana's entourage hastily hired six minders from the "Fidelity Detective Bureau".

Stanko's failure had repercussions. Brezhnev fired KGB chairman Vladimir Semichastny over it three weeks later, and replaced him with Yuri Andropov, the next Soviet leader.

Svetlana and her brother Vasya were the offspring of Stalin's second marriage, to Nadya Alliluyeva. Nadya shot herself in 1932 after a dinner-party row when Stalin flirtatiously threw bread rolls at her rival. Svetlana was only six.

Stalin's son by his first marriage, Yakov, surrendered or was captured by the Germans within days of being sent to the Smolensk front in 1941. Stalin in 1943 refused to exchange him for Stalingrad's Field Marshal Paulus. Yakov suicided or was shot by guards at Sachsenhausen.

Stalin had an often affectionate relationship with "his little sparrow". All the same, he wiped out most of her mother's kin in purges. Not many girls grow up with the mass murderer of their own family.

Svetlana married four times. Her love-life began badly with her teen crush getting ten years in the Gulag. Marriage #1 to a Jewish co-student Grigori Morozov lasted three years. Stalin pushed her into marriage #2 to Yuri Zhdanov, son of Stalin's offsider Andrei Zhdanov. The latter's alcohol-fuelled demise became Stalin's pretext for the post-war "Doctor's Plot" pogrom.

Yuri himself got into trouble with Stalin by criticising the crackpot genetics of Trofim Lysenko, but grovelled his way to safety.

In 1962 Svetlana briefly married Johnik Svanidze, raised in an orphanage for children of executed parents.

From her teens she was disgusted with Soviet brutality and conformity and in 1966, shortly before her defection, supported openly the dissident writer (and one-night lover) Andrei Sinyavsky, who got seven years hard labor.

Her defection arose because of her de facto marriage in Moscow to Brajesh Singh, the son of the rajah of Kalakankah in Uttar Pradesh. They met when both were hospitalised in Moscow, but permission to marry was refused. When Singh died in 1967, the regime allowed Svetlana to go to India to scatter his ashes in the Ganges. She seriously overstayed her visa, and then tricked her minders into giving her back her passport, skipping to the US embassy. She abandoned a son, 22 and daughter, 17 in Russia.

In the US Svetlana denounced her late father as "a moral and spiritual monster" and likened the KGB to the Gestapo.

In 1970 she made her fourth marriage to architect Frank Lloyd Wright's offsider (and ex-son-in-law) Wesley Peters. The three-week courtship was orchestrated by Lloyd Wright's widow Olgivanna, who had a nose for Svetlana's royalties fortune. The pair had a daughter Olga before divorcing.

In 1984, when Olga was 13, Svetlana (now known as Lana Peters) decided to rejoin her adult offspring in Russia. In Moscow she denounced the tyrannical West. She regained Soviet citizenship but amazingly, was allowed to return to the US in 1986, and died a recluse in Wisconsin in

2011.

She had a distinguished career as writer and translator, despite her unfortunate paternity.

In a rare late interview, she said of Stalin, "He broke my life. Wherever I go, here, or Switzerland, or India, or wherever. Australia. Some island. I will always be a political prisoner of my father's name."

Rosemary Sullivan's excellent 700-page biography *Stalin's Daughter* (Fourth Estate, 2015) is the source for many of these details. Svetlana's reference to Australia is in the book's first paragraph.

Australian Spectator, 17 March 2016.

Quick-draw capers at a 1960s H-bomber base

RAF electrician Kevin Durney at the height of the Cold War used to work, eat and sleep in one-week stretches alongside two Canberra bombers, each loaded with a 1 megatonne American H-bomb. The planes were ready to go at 15 minutes' notice.

He and his older brother Blaise were at the RAF's 3 Squadron base at Geilenkirchen near the Dutch border. Kevin, now 73, did aircraft electrics there from 1963-66; Blaise 76, did ground electrics like equipment and runway lights (1962-65).

They're both retired, Kevin in Perth and Blaise at Gowanbrae Retirement Village near Essendon. I got their story because Blaise and I play social tennis nearby.

The Canberras were kept under adjoining huts like carports. "The B28 H-bomb filled the bomb bay. We could see the lower fin sticking out," says Kevin. "Only the Americans had the code to arm them."

Ten other Canberras in the squadron could in theory be loaded with an H-bomb within half an hour. During the Cuban crisis in October 1962, the regimental sergeant mustered the men. Blaise says, "He was 6ft 6in and he had a handlebar moustache and he could throw his voice right across the parade ground. He told us, 'All right you horrible lot! The VIPS are in their underground bunkers. You lot are unimportant. At any moment the Russians may lob missiles on this base. You will get no notice or chance to say goodbye to your families. You will all be dead.'" Blaise says he was annoyed because erks like himself had done all the electrical servicing of the equipment down below. The briefing didn't improve morale, but the sergeant was just being realistic.

Did they worry about the H-bombs? "Never gave it a second thought," the pair agreed. Kevin: "We were about 21. We just had a great time, the best time of our lives."

Blaise adds, "Of course, we remember the good times, not so much the RAF crap we had to put up with."

Kevin's real fear concerned the pairs of American guards, called "Custodians", who guarded the H-bomb on each Canberra.

The Custodians rotated in four-hour shifts. There was a painted white line at the entry to the bombers' huts. This marked the "No Lone Zone" boundary, meaning no single person could cross. If one did, a Custodian would use his sub-machine gun. Pairs of base workers could cross, but the guards would follow one pace behind.

The brothers agreed, "Those guys were crazy!" Bored and getting through piles of Playboys, the guards played a little game while doing escorts. They wore a loaded pistol on each hip, a la General Patton, in specially cut-down holsters. They practiced quick-draws on their escortees, making Kevin sweat. "At Brugges base near us, we heard they killed one of their own guys," he says.

"During alerts we'd be issued with .303s to protect the base, but the magazine was bandaged with Sellotape. It would have taken us five minutes to unwrap the bullets."

The base's three squadron commanders each happened to have female sounding names – Carroll, Adrian and Jean. Blaise says, "At monthly parades they'd greet each other with upright swords, 'Hello Carroll!' 'Good morning, Jean!' and we'd snicker. They never understood why.

"We hated Carroll, he was so vain. He had a little dog called Dudley. Dudley had a hard time because any chance we got, we'd give him a kick up the arse.

"One time Albert, one of our dog handlers, stopped Carroll for ID when he was walking down the tarmac smoking a pipe. 'God man! Don't you know me? All those planes are mine!' Carroll said.

"Albert said, 'Sorry, you'll have to get in the Landrover and I'll take you for identification.' Carroll went to get in the front seat and the German Shepherd was already there and went 'Grr!' at him, and made him leap into the back seat.

"Albert drove him to the flying officers' blockhouse which was a shambles – they were all fed up and boozing. They leapt up as if they were spring-loaded.

Carroll said, 'Tell this blithering idiot who I am!'

Albert said, 'Sorry sir, you had no ID. I was just doing my duty.' 'Corporal, if my men can be half as efficient as you are, I'll have a good squadron, but don't you ever cross me again!'"

Blaise's wife Shirley was also on the base, working as assistant to the commander and with a higher security clearance than Blaise. She knew when there would be a practice alert; he didn't. He might propose a romantic dinner out followed by the movies and she would go along with it, although aware of an alert scheduled for 8.30pm. However, Blaise says the Germans on the base somehow always got wind about the alerts and would tip him off.

The Canberra's huts were next to an entry guardhouse, a blockhouse for crew living quarters, and a surrounding pair of fences, with guard dogs trained to lope around between the fences. The inner one was electrified.

The area was floodlit all night. Ground crews lived on-call in the blockhouse for seven days straight, waiting for an alert. "We played cards and did silly things. Our sport was indoor croquet," Kevin says.

When a "Quick Readiness Alert" siren went off, ground crew would plug in the auxiliary starters, take the chocks away, and the planes would taxi 20m to the first runway gate. Kevin says, "I'd go out under escort with my key and open it. The plane would then sit between the gates idling. We knew that if someone else got the call to open the second gate, it was for real. We were always told to 'stand-down', then the Canberras got towed back."

The real thing would be a suicide mission for the pilots, because the H-blast would take the Canberra down with it. Kevin says, "They were supposed to use LABS – low altitude bombing system – flying in really low, and spiralling upwards at the target. A ram would push the bomb out sideways and they'd roll over and try to race away from the shock wave.

"For practice, our other ten Canberras would suddenly come down the strip and get ready to be loaded up with H-bombs from the armoury.

Each bomb weighed about a tonne."

The North Atlantic Treaty Organisation (NATO) had a line of bases from Turkey through Italy and France all the way up to Norway.

Blaise says, "We were just one British base. The other four were Wildenrath, Laarbruch, Bruggen, and Gutersloh, the same as ours, a couple of hundred miles away. And this was just the Brits. The Germans, the Italians, the Belgians, the Dutch, six squadrons of Canadians, even the Greeks, they all had planes on alert with the American H-bombs. The French had the same deal but de Gaulle later told the Americans to get all troops off French soil forthwith." [Secretary of State Dean Rusk made the famous reply, "'Does your order include the bodies of American soldiers in France's cemeteries?'"].

Blaise says, "The aircraft of the NATO countries would often drop in on our base. They were all compatible so I knew what to expect regarding power supplies, servicing, fuels and so on."

Both NATO and the Soviets teased each other with overflights, monitoring fighter responses, Kevin says. "Near us we had some little Pembroke twin-engine prop planes. They would cut an engine and accidentally wander into East German space taking photos. A couple of fighters would arrive and the pilot would re-start the engine and scamper back."

The Geilenkirchen base had 12 Canberras (3 Squadron) and two squadrons (5 & 11) of Gloster Javelins, comprising 24 delta-winged fighters billed as "all-weather interceptors". In reality, they were the biggest rubbish in British aviation – in heavy rain they couldn't even take off, Blaise says. "Our response time was pathetic, but the Americans were right on the ball."

One morning a Javelin ran off the runway on landing, skidded through the crash barriers and up-ended itself on the Dutch side of the border – while carrying a full load of live missiles. The two crew escaped with bruises and Dutch civilians took them to a pub and they were having their first drink to settle their shaky nerves. Two Dutch customs officials suddenly arrived (this was before the Common Market) and demanded, "Have you any goods to declare?" Blaise says they might at least have asked if the airmen wanted a doctor.

Blaise often had to go out in bad weather to fix floodlights and runway lights. "In one blizzard the two guards didn't want to go out with me, so they said to their German Shepherd, 'Go boy!' and he escorted me instead. I was crouching down trying to get the waterproof cover off, with my torch in my mouth. My British woolen gloves were useless and my fingers were frozen. All the time, this dog was inches from my face snarling at me."

Blaise's tales usually have a wry twist. He says there were always special days at the bases where top NATO brass would drop in and get a parade, aerobatics and fly-past. "At an American base near Frankfurt one time, a big NATO delegation arrived and they had more gold on their sleeves than at Fort Knox. They were put with their women-folk in the viewing stands with top ranks in the best rows. During the aerobatics a Super Sabre crashed and there were bits of it flying everywhere. The top brass trampled over the womenfolk in the panic to get out of the stands."

The Yanks were on a dream wicket in Germany. Kevin says. "Their pay was double ours, they got cheap tickets for Paris nightlife, they could buy cars not just duty-free and discounted but flown over free. Their camps had bowling alleys, movie theatres, dance halls that converted to ice rinks. Back in the States they'd be worse off so lots volunteered to stay in Germany for extra terms."

Blaise: "Brits' conditions were really poor. If you got sent home injured, there'd be raffles and charity drives to look after you. The idea was that you'd been privileged to serve Queen and Country."

Of course, the Brits in turn were far better off than the Soviet forces across the border in East Germany freezing in their trenches, ice and slush, he adds.

After 10 years with the RAF, Kevin eventually ran his own successful business KD Instruments in Perth, and retired in 2001. Blaise came to Australia in 1967 and served 21 more years with the RAAF Reserve

Australia taught them the folly of British class distinctions. Kevin: "RAF officers and men didn't mix, we lived in parallel worlds. At one base, officers in chairs would watch a film while we had to watch it in reverse from the back of the screen."

The officers kept these distinctions up even after they left the RAF. Blaise went back for a Battle of Britain anniversary four years ago, and at the Duxford air museum when they found he'd been a flight sergeant, they took him into a volunteers' lounge room exclusive to former sergeants and warrant officers. "In Oz they never kept up such distinctions," he says.

The British left Geilenkirchen in 1968 and the Germans converted it for Pershing theatre nuclear missiles, again with the US controlling the warheads. Today the base runs early-warning (AWACS) aircraft. The Cold War is long over, but the US still has about 500 nuclear bombs in Western Europe.

Quadrant Monthly, April 2016

The ABC, Communists and ASIO: 50 Shades of Red

Was the Australian national broadcaster ABC asking the Communist Party to organise telegenic protests against the Vietnam War? Documents suggest the security agency suspected as much, but the only thing of which we can today be certain is that the accusation was far from improbable.

◇◇◇

I happened to come across an Australian Security Intelligence Organisation (ASIO) file containing the info below.

SECRET:
Report to Regional Director (WA) OF ASIO, 25/10/68 on
"Communist Influence in the Information Media".

15. "A somewhat unusual incident occurred in this media [ABC TV] *in 1967 when intelligence received from "Q" sources indicated that ABC television operatives had approached the CPA* [Communist Party of Australia] *and asked them to organise a demonstration on Vietnam which the ABC would televise. The demonstration was duly held on 3/11/67 and filmed by an ABC television unit, but no details were obtained as to those persons in the ABC responsible for the approach to the CPA."*

The report says that four persons of security interest (though not directly associated with the CPA) were employed by the ABC in Western Australia in 1968. They were an education assistant, a secretary, and two journalists. The report says, "Potential for CPA influence in television would appear to be limited again to the national [ABC] network. However, apart from the incident mentioned in para 15, there has been no definite evidence of CPA influence."

I sent off the queries below to the ABC's hard-pressed media manager Nick Leys:

> Are the facts in Para 15 correct?
>
> The report says that the alleged facts were only "somewhat" unusual. Have there been other instances of the ABC organising Communist Party demonstrations? If so, I would appreciate details of when, where and why.
>
> Do current ABC reporting guidelines (in general) discourage ABC staff from organising Communist Party demonstrations? If so, which guideline(s) is relevant?

With commendable speed and courtesy, Nick replied:

> Thanks but we won't comment on something that allegedly happened almost five decades ago. However I will point out a central tenet of the ABC Editorial Policies, 1.3, which requires ABC staff to "ensure that editorial decisions are not improperly influenced by political, sectional, commercial or personal interests."

The ABC certainly covered the anti-Vietnam Moratorium in Melbourne in May, 1970, but I make no suggestion that the ABC organised it.

The ABC in Perth in 1967 was a public service monster of 700-800 people in myriad departments housed in a sprawling, 6300-square-metre complex occupying a whole block, from Adelaide Terrace to Terrace Road. Admin/management was concentrated on the Adelaide Terrace frontage, with the radio/TV people semi-isolated down on the river side.

Geoffrey Luck, who was Sydney chief of staff of ABC National News in 1967, says, "I would be absolutely certain this [ABC arranging a CPA demo] would have nothing to do with the News division." News in those days abided by impartiality guidelines, but young staff, radicalised in their university days, were constantly wanting to put their personal views forward. As Luck puts it, "I had to tell a youngster, whose job was to interview celebrities arriving the airport, to take off his anti-Viet-war badge.

"I can't speak for ABC Perth but that demo episode sounds like something our *This Day Tonight* (*TDT*) might have generated. *TDT* was a loose cannon on a bucking ship, hard to control and causing enormous problems for management, like pulling pollies' whiskers just for the fun of seeing how they reacted. Maybe that Perth demo was just something they thought would be fun."

One Perth ABC TV veteran says, "Absolutely nothing would surprise me when it came to the ABC. There was tremendous tension then between the conservative Perth ABC News team and the irreverent and opinionated *Today Tonight* staffers who set out to air provocative stuff."[39]

I trotted over to the State Library of Victoria and checked *The West Australian* (where I worked from 1958-69) for a next-day report of an anti-Vietnam demo on Friday, November 3. Nothing was published. A Communist-led demo may still have happened, but gone unreported. As the ASIO report noted, "*The West Australian* pursues a conservative right-wing policy".

The front-page of *The West*'s November 3, 1967 issue was chock-a-block with controversy over President Johnson's then-current campaign to bomb North Vietnam to the negotiating table, Johnson insisting that it "was the right thing to do." Whitlam was accusing Prime Minister Harold Holt of letting "thousands of Australian, American and Vietnamese soldiers die to prove a political point", and on page three Paul Hasluck was saying there was "no doubt at all that South Vietnam and its allies would win the war." Bad call.[40] I figured that if anything could provoke Perth's Leftists and Communists onto the streets that day, Pages 1-3 of *The West* would suffice, with or without guidance from the ABC's *Today Tonight*.

Now, back to ASIO's secret report. Comprising three typed and single-spaced pages it seems a response to a demand from Canberra HQ for an update on Reds in the Perth media. Putting it together in only nine days for the WA Regional Director J.M. Gilmour was an efficient effort. It covered all print, even including the student paper *Pelican* and the ALP's *Western Sun*, plus all radio and TV stations. I totted up 17 persons named as "of security interest". The print pinks ranged from a staff printer on *The Sunday Times* to a talented and charismatic reporter on *The West* (a certain Anthony Paul THOMAS), along with a hotbed of security risks on *The West*'s afternoon stablemate *Daily News*, where one

---

39 Not to be confused with Channel 7's later Today Tonight.
40 Two months earlier, ABC General Manager Talbot Duckmanton had been personally assured by President Johnson during a White House meeting that the war "was both just and winnable". Ken Inglis, *This is the ABC*.

suspect was the assistant chief of staff.[41]

I would be surprised if the ASIO report's author was sloppy enough to include sheer fantasy about the ABC organising a CPA demo on November 3. From the coding around the summary, it seems the ASIO author had drawn on four internal files about the matter. The ultimate source is described as a "Q source", meaning an agent run by an ASIO staffer. These Q sources were scattered throughout the media at that time – spotters operating much like the IMs in East Germany (but less plentiful of course).[42] For example, in 1966 someone advised ASIO that reporter Anthony Thomas had applied for and been granted two weeks leave from *The West* to go to Darwin. ASIO went into a flurry of checking airline ticketing but concluded, correctly, that he never went.

A Perth ABC source says, "I was told that embedded in the ABC were ASIO spotters; we never found out who they were. They could have been ex-military who were then in ABC administration. The message was to behave yourself, if you don't you will be on report or something. Maybe the ASIO report about the demo was based on scuttlebutt overheard around the ABC coffee pot."

ASIO intense scrutiny of ABC staff and programs at the time makes it even more mysterious that the demo deal was done under ASIO's nose.

For all the ABC's professed independence, ASIO could promote conformity by denying security clearance to individuals. Historian David McKnight says:

> Overall, at least throughout the 1950s and 60s, a security watchdog was peering over the shoulder of the ABC and regularly querying employees' background and program content.

For example, in 1955, ABC Assistant General Manager Arthur Finlay asked ASIO to search ABC Radio's kids' show *The Argonauts* for subversives. Finlay was worried "that dangers lie ahead" (as per *The Argonauts* theme song). Subversives in the Children's Session could disguise their views and gradually exert their influence to put a pink slant on kiddies' fare, Finlay thought. In 1958, the compere of *Kindergarten*

---

41 Several Daily News journalists, including the senior one mentioned, had in earlier years moonlighted from the Daily News at weekends putting together the WA page of the national Communist weekly Tribune. Justina Williams, *Anger & Love*. Fremantle Arts Centre Press, 1993, p157

42 *Inoffizieller Mitarbeiter* – unofficial cooperators.

of the Air, Joyce Hutchison, was a person of interest to ASIO. Finlay also asked ASIO to do a careful check on Children's Session compere Leonard Teale, who went on to to play Senior Detective Mackay in Crawford Productions' long-running *Homicide*.

The programs aired were also monitored by ASIO, alert for any left slant. The mere mention of Prague in an ABC radio travel serial was enough to generate an ASIO report (the show was found not guilty). ABC manager and writer/historian Clement Semmler in the 1960s had this on his ASIO file:

> It is reported that Semmler, described as a strange, highly strung temperamental person, is a close friend of Frank Hardy, a CPA member and author and that Hardy has often called to see Semmler at the ABC.

ASIO applied a doctrine of *lese majeste*, literally. Disrespectful references on or off-air to the Royal Family were followed up and the author's file checked. An artist, Jack Child, wanted a job at the ABC but an informer deposed that Child had been overheard to make "scathing" remarks about the visit of Princess Alexandra. That was the last straw for ASIO, given that Child had a left or Communist past, although one operative suggested that Child was "not a communist" while observing "all artists were 'queer people'".

Perth's Communist Party offices were on the third floor of the southwest corner of the twee-Tudor London Court. Across the wall a fake Big Ben chimed on the quarter hours. Two floors below, Sir Walter Raleigh stood guard in plaster with London Mayor of history and legend Dick Whittington.

The CPA State Secretary in 1967 was Sam Aarons, father of Laurie and Eric, Eastern States party stalwarts (Laurie became National Secretary).

If the ASIO story of the ABC approaching the CPA is true, Sam would have approved the broadcaster's request for a demo. All important party decisions had to come from the top. Hence Sam's personality is germane to my story (plus an opportunity to sex-up my dull narrative).

ASIO described Sam as "of sallow complexion, black curly hair, brown eyes, looks very Jewish". Sam had been a truck driver for the Republicans in Spain – no comfy task as trucks were the prize targets of hostile aircraft.

Fond of purging dissidents and a Stalinist to the end (1971), he also spent a life in fertile pursuit of Communist women, the more beautiful the better. Ironically, he was, pre-war, on the party's three-man Control Commission for moral disciplining of members. He concurrently embarked on a torrid affair with a young party woman Esme Odgers, "one of four beautiful sisters", in the prose of Aarons family chronicler Mark Aarons. ("Esme Odgers" is not a pretty name but we're talking real life here).

Party president, the oafish ex-lift-driver Lance Sharkey, was also vying for Esme's hand and other parts, so Sam lost his moral enforcer job and Esme had to write a Soviet-style grovelling self-criticism, despite which she was back in Sam's arms within a month.[43] Sharkey exiled Aarons to some remote post, but Sam had the second-last laugh when he and Esme went off together to fight for freedom in Spain. There, Esme dumped Sam for a wealthy Spanish husband and disappeared to Venezuela.

Sam arrived in Perth as new WA boss about 1948, once again under a cloud in the party over an affair with a young and married woman, according to poet-playwright Dorothy Hewett.[44] "I find him totally irresistible," she wrote, "A passionate, highly intelligent, charismatic man with a glamorous history." London Court headquarters gained a Marx & Boon quality or maybe 50 Shades of Red quality. Hewett: "He bends me back on the desk in his office, but before we can consummate our affair we are interrupted by the old Party caretaker, locking up for the night…"

Sam tells her, "Sharkey has already told me that if there's any more gossip about me and other women, I'll be on the outer. He's had it in for me ever since I stole his girlfriend in Spain."

They live in a *ménage a trois* with Sam's unwitting wife, until Dorothy finds another lover while Sam is on Eastern States party business. Sam threatens to blacken her name in the party all over Australia. Dorothy reports that, eventually, most of the WA State Committee went east "to

43 Odgers: "My behavior (sic) over the past 12 months has been such that it has been nec-essary for certain organisational measures to be taken against me, and has also necessarily called forth serious criticism of my actions…My renewal of the association with Comrade Aarons is indicative of the fact that I was willing to place my own personal inclinations and desires before the prestige and good name of the party…"
44 Dorothy Hewett, *Wild Card*. McPhee, South Yarra, p. 138.

escape the heavy hand of Sam Aarons."

I'd have to say that Sam was an unlikely collaborator with ABC provocateurs, unless they were beautiful females.

Next question is whether the ambience and culture of ABC Current Affairs, circa 1960s, was compatible with sponsoring a CPA Viet demo? I'd have to say 'yes'. Weirder things happened in that era. For example, Prime Minister Billy McMahon in April, 1971, told Parliament that the government wouldn't permit reporter John Penlington to go to China for *Four Corners* unless he was first positively vetted by Ted Hill, then secretary of the Communist Party of Australia (Marxist-Leninist). Penlington didn't go.[45]

The tone at ABC Current Affairs in the 1960s had been set by Talks supervisor Allan Ashbolt, an ex-AIF commando turned actor and film-maker who led a coterie of aggressive ABC talent. He had been inspired by New York (so-called) intellectuals towards "democratic socialism". In 1963 he took over *Four Corners*, and created a political storm with an unconventional program on the RSL. Though fairly mild, this program included as a talking head one Alec Robertson, editor of the Communist Party newspaper *Tribune*, opining that the RSL was thwarting citizens' desire "to build for themselves a secure and peaceful future". Though qualified for the program through his wartime service as an officer, Robertson looked shifty on the box, "a filling in a front tooth glinting under the lights".[46] Ashbolt was sacked from *Four Corners* but reinstated in 1964.

In 1967 *Four Corners* was joined by a kid brother, *This Day Tonight*, which began in April, 1967, seven months before the alleged ABC/CPA Perth demo in November. Historian Ken Inglis wrote, "The TDT approach was not merely to report events but to create them, especially by having people confront each other...both news and a kind of sport." Shades of the ABC's *Q&A*, circa 2016. Compere Bill Peach wrote, "There was no jealousy more intense than the jealousy between the different program divisions of the ABC." *TDT* sometimes even paid interviewees to appear on *TDT* rather than News.

TDT set out to upset applecarts, and succeeded. An example was

---

45 Ken Inglis, *This is the ABC*. 1932-83, Black Inc. Melbourne, 2006
46 Rob Pullen, *Four Corners, 25 Years*. ABC, 1986.

its second broadcast, which apart from speculating on ABC board appointments, featured author Frank Hardy, live to air, telling yarns. Hardy said overseas tourists loved Australians: "They all said the same thing. Finest people in the world, and the most generous too. They said the Australians would share anything they had, even give you the coat off their own back. The salt of the earth. There was just one thing to watch, they all said."

"What's that?" Bill Peach asked.

"They all said you have to watch out for those white bastards."

The Perth version of *TDT*, *Today Tonight*, at the time of the demo was run by New Zealander Bruce Buchanan, who later went on to become Executive Producer of *TDT* in Sydney. There he became a thorn in the side of ABC top management over what they called "errors of judgement" and what staff called lively TV. Buchanan shook things up in WA with stunts like greeting random people in Albany, "G'day, you old bastard!" to see whether the term still caused offence.

The program's Vietnam War coverage was provocative. Peach wrote that *TDT* was happy to give anti-Viet-war people a platform:

"We thought it was our job to pursue the truth, including the truth that many intelligent and loyal citizens believed that we were on the wrong track in Vietnam. It was TDT's hottest potato, and the source of most accusations against us of bias."

Historian Inglis instances *TDT* devoting an interview segment in 1968 to Communist journalist Malcolm Salmon, fresh from North Vietnam. In that same year, Bill Peach on *TDT* mistakenly claimed that two companies of Regular Army troops were standing by to quell an anti-war demo outside the St Kilda Road consulate of the US embassy. In November, 1971, *TDT* interviewed a draft-resister student on the run from police.

Sadly, despite all my verbiage above, we are not going to resolve whether rogue elements of the Perth ABC organised and filmed a CPA anti-war demo in 1967. The files show ASIO was in no doubt about it. Mad things did happen in those days, but the likelihood that Perth Communist supremo Sam Aarons would kow-tow to ABC journos is low. On the other hand, the gung-ho culture of ABC Current Affairs was amenable to such stunts, but ASIO informers in the ABC were a threat to anyone wanting to liaise with CPA headquarters. We have no newspaper evidence that the November 3 demo happened, but it was a propitious day for such a rally. So is the ASIO story true? I'll give it a definite 'Maybe'.

Quadrant OnLine, 28 August 2015

3

CLIMATE UNFROCKED

Stranded monster lands at Oahu

Now and then giant ocean creatures wash up on beaches in a horrible mess.

At Kalaeloa Airport on Oahu (Hawaii) a similar but aerial creature has washed up in an airport hangar. It's the Solar Impulse 2, a solar-powered plane with a wingspan nearly as long as an Airbus A380's. But it weighs rather less than a Toyota Land Cruiser and has so far cost its sponsors about $US250m.

It was meant to fly around the world – without using a drop of fossil fuel – from March to August this year (2015). Cheering it on were bigwigs Prince Albert 11 of Monaco, ex-UN czar Kofi Annan, Virgin's Richard Branson, the ubiquitous Mikhail Gorbachev and the IPCC's figurehead Christiana Figueres. Among the plane's partners are champagne people MoetHennessy, who supplied refreshments at each stop "to promote their common values" with "beautiful occasions".

Departing Abu Dhabi, Solar Impulse 2 got half-way in 200 days, but it's going nowhere until next April (2016). That's because its solar batteries overheated during a wrong flight pattern and have to be replaced.

The fuel-free plane was meant to show the delicious potential of clean solar energy, "therapy for the planet" and a climate-change stopper, as its founders balloonist Bertrand Piccard and ex-Swiss air force man Andre Borschberg see it. The solar plane's actually demonstrated the superiority of a few drums of avgas.

Its 17,200 solar cells generate 17 horsepower for each of the four props – less than half the grunt of my four-cylinder Camry. It can lift only one person – the pilot. (Freight? Zero, not counting all the "messages" and "positive emotions"). The pilot can last about five days and nights in the air, taking catnaps and using his seat as a potty-chair. Strangely, the Wright Flyer 111 in 1908 carried a passenger.

The solar plane is at the mercy of sun and breezes. It was held up at Nagoya for a month waiting for favorable winds, much like a 17th century galleon.

But there's more. To keep this gossamer confection airborne, an Ilyushin 76 strategic airlifter flies ahead with a blow-up hangar and all the high-tech servicing gear. Aviation buffs call the four-engined airlifter a 'bad-ass', not just because of its ugly nose and droopy jets, but because its takeoffs are real Russian screamers. Once aloft, it burns eight tons of CO_2-spewing avgas per hour.

This behemoth is accompanied by a twin-turboprop ATR72 which can carry a support crew of up to 60, apart from the dozens left at Monaco mission control. The ATR burns a more modest ton of fuel per 90 minutes.

With these two little helpers, the solar plane flies (half) round the world "without using a drop of fuel". Piccard says, "What we have here is the future."

Well maybe. This futuristic plane cruises at about the top speed of a postie's bike, but can sometimes accelerate away to 90km/h.

Charitably assuming the plane does make it round the world in 18 months, that compares with other round-the-worlders such as:

- The Graf Zeppelin in 21 days in 1929.
- Wiley Post in his Winnie Mae, in nine days in 1933
- The Rutan Voyager, non-stop non-refuelled in nine days in 1986
- Bertrand Piccard and Brian Jones by balloon in 20 days in 1999.
- Solo yachter Francis Joyon, in 58 days in 2008, using that other clean fuel, wind.
- Someone could walk the plane's route (somehow) in two years, not much longer than the flight time.

Piccard, who partakes of green delusionism, has summed up the venture: "Protecting the environment should not be perceived as expensive… Fighting climate change is opening-up new industrial markets and offering an opportunity for economic development, job creation and profit."

I can picture a fourth-world peasant looking up from his hoe and saying, "Kids, that's a quarter-billion investment whirring along up there using clean energy. And it's worth it!"

Australian Spectator, 16 January 2016

When Scientists Still Did Science

Gough Whitlam was PM when the notion of climate change began bubbling – not about warming in those days but cooling. The report he commissioned makes sad reading today, not for its conclusions but as a marker of how far and deep the rot has spread.

◇◇

A great embarrassment to the warming-catastrophic community is that 40 years ago the climatology scare was about cooling and onset of an ice age. Warmists today go, "Pooh! That cooling stuff then was just a few hyped-up articles in magazines. Cooling never got any traction in the *real* science community!"

Really? Then explain this away…

Letter from the Australian Federal Minister for Science, W.L. (Bill) Morrison, to the President of the Academy of Science, Professor Badger, January 9, 1975:

> Dear Professor Badger,
>
> I am writing on this occasion to enquire if the Academy could assist the Government by examining, and reporting on, claims recently made in the media, and apparently also by competent scientists that the earth's climate is changing and that a new ice-age could be on the way.
>
> The Prime Minister [Gough Whitlam] is very interested in this subject and is anxious to obtain the best possible advice about it. As an interim measure towards that end, I sought, and obtained, a short report from Dr Gibbs, Director of Meteorology, and Dr Priestley, Chairman of the CSIRO Environmental Physics Research Laboratories…I am now anxious to have the subject examined in more detail and at greater length…Since the enquiry stems primarily from concern about man and the possible effects of climatic changes on him [I think Bill means 'him or her'], it seems to me that it should reflect not only the input of those expert in the physical sciences but also that of those expert in the biological sciences… I would be most grateful to have your views at your earliest convenience.

Hard to get more top-level concern about the possible 'ice age cometh' than this letter – Prime Minister Whitlam badgering the Academy President Badger for an answer. Cyclone Tracy had devastated

Darwin three weeks earlier; Rex Connor was telexing a Pakistani con man who lived on peanuts and potato crisps, asking him to raise $US4 billion; Jim Cairns was nipping at Gough's heels as PM-in-waiting. But Gough wanted to know about the global cooling scare.

The Academy swung into action, mustering eleven of its finest minds and a three-man secretariat for the job. The eventual report[47], delivered a year later, ran to 80 pages.[48]

Good Lord, the stuff you can find in the body text! For example:

> In the 1960s some scientists extrapolated from the warming trend evident between 1895 and 1940 and predicted the melting of the ice caps and the consequent flooding of the world's seaports. There was then thought to be some rational justification for their warnings, namely the warming effect associated with the global increase of CO_2 caused by the burning of fossil fuels (Matthews et al, 1971). However, since 1940 the temperature curve has reversed its direction [despite significant increase in CO_2 emissions – TT]. It is just as precipitate now for scientists to postulate that the present downturn presages an imminent glaciation as it was for their collegues (sic) to forecast the melting of the ice caps 20 years ago [1955]…Nevertheless the historical record…does not preclude a change lasting for some decades or even centuries to a regime colder than what is called by some northern hemisphere climatologists the 'climatic optimum' of the 1940s-50s. (p14)

The terms of reference for the global freezing examination were:

> To consider and report to Council on:
> Reports from overseas to the effect that marked changes in global climate are currently occurring;
> The extent to which man's activities may be causing or contributing to climatic changes;
> Whether the climate of Australia is currently undergoing change, and the predictability of future changes;
> The consequences of postulated climatic changes for agricultural production and rangeland management in Australia;
> …Social and economic implications.

---

47 Report of a Committee on Climatic Change. No 21, AAS
48 There is a copy in the National Library and I found one in the Victorian State Library – in very poor condition with pages falling out.

The Academy team consulted far and wide (including Norwich and Grenoble), grilling experts on everything from paleoclimate to "man made influences" and tree rings – this pre-dating the "tree-ring circus" of Michael Mann in the now-notorious 2001 IPCC report.

The Academy report began:

> During the past few years, there have been reports of a persistent cooling trend in the higher latitudes of the northern hemisphere, crop failures in the USSR, severe droughts in the Sahel region of Africa, and failures in the Indian monsoon rains. Some scientists have interpreted these events as showing that the global climate is changing [i.e. cooling, TT] in such a way as to make conditions of man more difficult and these views have received widespread publicity through the mass media.
>
> Following the concern expressed at the World Food Conference in November 1974 about the possible effects of this predicted climatic change on agricultural production and the world's food supply, the Australian Government requested the Academy to report to it on these assertions. The Government was especially interested in their possible significance for Australia…

The report comes to a ringing conclusion:

> We conclude that there is no evidence that the world is now on the brink of a major climatic change. There is ample evidence that the world's climate has changed widely during the geological past, and while there is every expectation that it will continue to change in the future, **the time scale of these changes is in the range of thousands to hundreds of thousands of years rather than decades or centuries.**
>
> It cannot be too strongly emphasised that year-to-year variability is an inherent feature of global and regional climates and that…large fluctuations leading to severe droughts and floods are bound to occur from time to time. (My emphasis; p9)

The report's summary affirmed that the cooling reports were coming from "some climatologists"[49], as distinct from media beat-ups. It affirmed that cooling from 1940 to 1975 had dropped global temps by 0.3degdC, and together with various droughts, monsoons and other

---

49 The late Dr Stephen Schneider first ramped the "cooling scare" and then the "warming scare" – Rasool S., & Schneider S. Atmospheric Carbon Dioxide and Aerosols – Effects of Large Increases on Global Climate, *Science*, vol.173, 9 July 1971, p.138-141. Schneider was still promoting the coming "ice age" in 1978.

stuff, *"has led some climatologists to suggest that the world's climate is progressing rather rapidly towards another glacial phase, or at least another 'Little Ice Age'."* Any such global rapid-cooling threat to the planet could cause damaging shifts in rainfall patterns and *"the spread of glaciers and ice sheets to the countries of Europe and North America."* (p7)

The report debunks the claims that various weather events, such as the Sahel drought and the 1972 Ukrainian wheat failure were evidence for global cooling: *"Impartial examination has failed to support these hypotheses."* Today's warmists who want to attribute Hurricane Katrina and increased shark attacks to global warming, please note.

Today's finest climatologists like Will Steffen and David Karoly are all about doom and gloom. Yesterday's equivalents in the Academy were not so down in the mouth:

> The dire consequences predicted for the supposed cooling trend in the northern hemisphere would be unlikely to occur in Australia…a slight cooling might produce a climate more, rather than less, suitable for human activities. (p9)

Among prescient statements in the report:

- The influence on climate of the eleven-year sunspot cycle and the 22 year solar magnetic cycle "is indeed plausible, though the physical mechanisms involved remain obscure" and their "utility is not yet established". [These factors, largely dismissed by the IPCC, are now getting serious attention in lieu of problematic CO_2 causation].
- A "major difficulty" with numerical climate models is "inadequate representation of the many feedback processes which occur in the atmosphere". [In the past 25 years the IPCC has been unable to refine its huge uncertainty range about climate sensitivity to CO_2 doubling].
- Models can simulate a 50% increase in CO_2 but "a problem … is that a forecast must be made of the variation of 'external' factors, and this is not always possible." [IPCC modellers still have no handle on cloud cover and feedbacks, nor long-cycle ocean temperature oscillations].
- "We see no prospect of any quick break-through into reliable and

accurate climate forecasting." [97% of IPCC models run too hot and none predicted the 19-year current halt to warming].

In a startling admission – though not seen as an 'admission' at the time – the report says:

> Weather records have been maintained in Australia for over 100 years [i.e. back to 1875]. There does not appear to have been any general rise in temperature in this continent between 1890 and 1940…Temperatures in Australia, New Zealand and the Antarctic coast appear to have risen very slightly since 1940, in contrast to the downward trend in the northern hemisphere…
>
> While there is some evidence for the occurrence of cycles in weather patterns over the years, their recurrence is unreliable. In the present state of knowledge, it is not possible to make useful forecasts of future climatic trends." (p8)

Now, of course, climatologists prove stuff by playing with models on their computers.

The Academy also saw the importance of "the bank of Australian meteorological data" and said it should be "maintained, improved by quality control, and subjected to more detailed systematic analysis… The maintenance and improvement of this data bank is of national importance." Interesting that the Turnbull government last September killed an external audit of the Bureau of Meteorology's highly contentious adjustments and "homogenisations" of the records, which have also been truncated at 1910. The Academy's 1975 report includes graphs of temperature back to 1875.

The report says that despite uncertainties about the climate, judgements based on physical grounds must be relied on to steer the best course between complacency and alarm.

"These grounds must be as objective as possible, and preferably quantified wherever the opportunity exists."

Unlike today, when science and activism have become indistinguishable.

The report said there was no evidence yet that man-made influences had changed the global climate, but if emissions and other human influences kept increasing, they were more likely to create warming than cooling. Fair enough.

The degradation of climate science in the 40 years since that common-sense Academy report is a wonder to behold.

Quadrant OnLine, 4 December 2015

The fine art of scaring children

Ballarat boasts a charming art gallery, but do be careful about taking impressionable children on a visit. Thanks to the climate-change cult, even the most innocuous pictures are now nightmare exhibits of the parched world to come.

<><><><><><><><><><><><><><><><><><><><><><><><><><><><><><><><><><><><><><><><><>

Ballarat has a great art gallery, with its original architecture and gold-boom-financed 19th century acquisitions. I was stooging around there last week after enjoying its show on floral illustrations, dating back to William Dampier. In the main halls it has an "art trail" for children, directing them to half a dozen works. Each has a screed alongside backgrounding the painting and giving the kids some quizzes. So far so good…until I began reading those screeds.

The first involved an aquatic storm scene by ship captain-turned-artist Johan Bennetter (1886), *A Bore on the Hooghli*. Sailing ships and lifeboats thrash about amid surges and spume under a furious sky. (A "bore" is a storm surge after a very low tide).

The screed quickly cuts to the chase:

> Climate change, bringing with it an increase in extreme weather and rising sea levels, means that phenomena like the famous bores on the Hooghli at the Bay of Bengal now threaten the lives and livelihoods of literally hundreds of millions of people. This is one of the places in the world most vulnerable to catastrophe arising out of rapid rises in sea level…
>
> What other changes in natural phenomena do you know of as a result of global warming?
>
> How will predicted climate change affect your life?

Hmmm. The author may be referring to the prediction in 2005 by the UN Environmental Program (UNEP) of 50 million "climate refugees" by 2010.[50] An astute reporter for *Asian Correspondent* realised last year that the prediction had fallen due, but not a single "climate refugee" could be identified. Embarrassed, UNEP and its scientific boosters furtively rubbed out their map of 50 million climate refugees, circa 2010, and shifted the year out to 2020.

Let us move on to the next way-station along the kiddie-art climate trail.

At Kiddie Station 2 we find David Davies (1890), *Under the Burden and Heat of the Day*, which shows a swaggie near-collapsed from heat and being offered a mug of water by his fellow swaggie in the red shirt.

The screed:

> ...Australia is getting hotter and climate change has arrived. There is more on the way, but how much of an increase will depend on us. How do we cope with such heat? Massive air conditioner use threatens peak electrical supply while the electricity used to power them comes mainly from coal. Greenhouse gases are produced to cope with the symptoms of existing greenhouse gases – we are kelpies chasing our tails on a hot day.
>
> Renewable energy, better house design and a reduction in the atmospheric levels of greenhouse gases will all be needed if we are going to beat the heat...
>
> How can we keep cool without making demands on energy supplies? How do we know whether our individual actions make a difference?

It was a fairly hot day outside but cool inside the gallery. Reason: It is air-conditioned.[51]

Kiddie Station 3. A modern work: Tony Cran (2007) – "We've come for what's ours". This shows a kangaroo, a reindeer and a wolf* on the coastline, two of them brandishing a eucalypt swatch.

Our narrator tells the kids:

> In this vision we have poisoned our environment with toxic waste and used up all the natural resources until the earth could no longer support us...In this painting, people are just a memory. The earth has survived and with it some of the plants and animals which lived in

---

50 This was taken up by Oxfam and quite recently Melbourne tramstops were plastered with this horrific scenario, to stimulate donations.

51 Is it just coincidence that "a one-stop shop for people seeking information on sustainable living practices" is only five doors east of the Gallery? This shop is backed by various State departments and businesses seeking to make income from green renovating.

harmony with nature, only taking what they needed and adapting…

We have become reckless with our consumption, buying bigger and better things with more and more packaging [blah blah, insert here more Greens Party boilerplate].

Who should be responsible for the effects of our heavy consumption of resources? How can we reduce the cost of sustaining our natural resources?

To me, this draws the long bow. For a start, although "people are just a memory", a lighthouse in the background is still lit up. Maybe the reindeer is maintaining it. Second, it's nice that the three animals are living in harmony with nature, only taking what they need. Let's hope for the 'roo and reindeer's sake that this particular wolf is a vegetarian.

At Kiddie Station 4, beside *Mardayin Design* by John Mawurndjul, the screed reads:

…Australians are rediscovering how to treat this ancient place after unsuccessful attempts to implement foreign land management practices.

How can we learn about sustainability and solutions to climate change from indigenous art and culture?

Kiddie Station 5 uses Murray Griffin's (1934) *Golden Barriers* to make its, er, educational point. This is a traditional Australian landscape of rolling pastures with scattered eucalypts and old eroded hills in the distance.

"This scene of a rural landscape was painted at a time when the most accessible and fertile areas of the country had been adapted for farming and before many of the problems we are now experiencing were becoming recognised [eg erosion, salinity and poor water quality]."

The blurb goes on to patronise ignorant farmers who had, it said, felled trees for firewood and building materials, and cleared land for crops and grazing. The gallery clearly sees this landscape as an example of what the Germans used to call *entartete Kunst* (degenerate art).

It then asks, "What do you think rural landscapes will look like in the future?"

Our kids' tour is nearing its finale with Walter Withers' (1898) *The Last of Summer*. This shows a row of settlers' cottages still within bushland, paddocks and scrub, with a gathering storm and a solitary female in the middle distance. The dimming light is beautifully handled, a Withers

trademark. Incidentally, there is no human-caused litter in the scene.
Of this we are told:

> Our modern lifestyle encourages us to buy goods with a lot of
> packaging and non-refillable containers, this means we produce a
> huge amount of rubbish, putting pressure on landfill and creating
> enormous environmental problems…Early Europeans who settled
> in Australia produced very little rubbish…They had very little
> packaging…Now we live at a fast pace. Rubbish has become a real
> problem because people buy food at supermarkets, which use more
> packaging and non-refillable containers than small shops. (Blah blah
> from any "sustainability" boilerplate).
>
> Should companies be responsible for disposing of and recycling
> the products and packaging they produce? Should companies be
> regulated for use (sic) specific, earth-friendly materials?

To get with the spirit, I'll do my own screed for an extra kiddie
station, this one inspired by the gallery's *Ajax and Cassandra* by Solomon
J. Solomon (1886).

"This is what climate change looks like. It is too hot to wear many
clothes. A lady tries to hail a taxi but in a desperate attempt to reduce
C02 emissions, her friend carries her home instead. Do you support the
carbon tax designed by the Australian Greens Party, which will prevent
these calamitous climate outcomes?"

(*Editor's note: *A* Quadrant reader believes two members of the eco-avenger
trio in Tony Cran's painting have been misidentified. Rather than a wolf, he believes
the dog-like creature is a Tasmanian tiger, while the antlered one may well be a
sambur deer. That's the thing about socially-aware art; it is a catalyst for debate.)

Tony Thomas doesn't know much about art but knows what he likes.

Quadrant OnLine, 20 November 2012

Shooting Santa to Save the World

If you ever doubted that warmism endorses a preening, totalitarian disdain for the lives and rights of others, take up a copy of "Climate Changed" by graphic novelist Philippe Squarzoni, who imagines how virtuous it would be to go berserk with an assault rifle in a shopping mall. And yes, he's not joking.

~~~~~~

A top scientist of the Intergovernmental Panel on Climate Change, Dr Jean Jouzel, is lauding a comic publication which has the heroine gunning down three Santa Clauses in a supermarket with a military assault rifle. The realistically-drawn massacre in *Climate Changed* by Philippe Squarzoni (Abrams, New York 2014) is meant to symbolise the need to reduce consumerism and CO_2 emissions.

The book was written a year before the Nairobi Westgate shopping mall massacre in September, 2013, in which gunmen killed or wounded 240 people in the name of Islam. But the fictional massacre in the cause of reducing CO_2 emissions is retained in this year's English translation.

The book, 480 pages and 1.2kg, is in the 'graphic novel' genre, now a serious literary form. The book won the Jury Prize at the Lyon Graphic Novel Festival in 2012. (A graphic novel, Maus, by New Yorker cartoonist Art Spigelman, won a Pulitzer in 1992).

In the massacre sequence, Camille, the beautiful partner of the comic's hero, Squarzoni himself, arrives at the "Nuclear Power Christmas Market" with what looks like a Belgian FN assault rifle slung over her shoulder.

The next frame shows her in the supermarket aisle amid shopping trolleys, lifting the gunsights to her face.

The caption reads: "Today, choice about energy issues has been stolen from the people. The decisions are all in the hands of politicians or big multinationals. Economic motivations prevail over environmental needs."

Frame three shows she is sighting on three men in Santa costumes, one holding bottles of Coca-Cola, and another taking a gift-wrapped parcel from a shelf. The caption: "We produce more so we can consume more."

Next frames, she opens fire and the Santas scream in death agonies as bullets rip into their bodies, with blood spattering. She continues firing as they start collapsing to the ground, while a stream of ejected shellcases tumble in the foreground and Cokes and Christmas parcels fly in the air. One Santa lifts his right hand as if to shield himself.

Their suits are riddled with bullets and gore continues to spout. The bland caption for this bloody mayhem reads: "On the demand side, it's up to individuals, households, and local communities to evaluate their own needs themselves, with an eye to conservation."

The final frame shows Camille and author Squarzoni standing over the corpse of one Santa, Camille still training her rifle on him. The caption reads: "Making conservation a positive factor in the future would require a huge change in political direction."

Their massacre by the couple is not followed by any repercussions as the book goes on to lament the Copenhagen summit failure and excoriate "climate deniers", who are drawn as dung beetles pushing a ball of excreta with their hind legs.

The IPCC's Jouzel, who likes the book so much, has been:

- A vice-chair of the IPCC's prestigious Working Group 1 ("The Physical Science Basis") since 2008
- A drafting author, WG1 Summary for Policy-Makers of the 5th IPCC report
- Review editor, sea level chapter, 5th report
- Bureau member, WG1, 4th report, 2007
- A drafting author, Summary for Policy-Makers, WG1 4th report
- Lead author, WG1, 4th report
- Review editor, Paleoclimate chapter, 4th report
- French expert delegate to the IPCC 2nd and 3rd reports

On the book's back cover, Jouzel writes, "What a marvellous way to convey the knowledge accumulated by our scientific community … I am truly admiring of Philippe Squarzoni's great scholarship on all facets of the climate problem… An extremely well-documented work – which is, of course, essential for the perception of the message that it delivers. But its principal merit is, in fact, in the quality of the narrative and the art."

Earlier, the book's Santa figures personify fossil-fuel use and smoke British American Tobacco cigarettes.

Author Squarzoni damns sceptics as "relying on scientists who worked for the tobacco industry in the 1980s to put the science in doubt." This theme is similarly promoted by Naomi Oreskes in her 2010 book *Merchants of Doubt*, now being made into a Hollywood film by Sony as something of a sequel to Al Gore's *Inconvenient Truth*.

I googled for IPCC climate scientists who have taken benefits from Big Tobacco. Who should turn up after five minutes but Squarzoni's guru, Jean Jouzel himself, a recipient of a 1992 climatology prize from the Philip Morris tobacco corporation.

It gets better, or worse. Squarzoni's second-ranked advisory source is Herve Le Treut, a coordinating lead author in the 5th IPCC report. It's taxing my schoolboy French, but under his "Prix et distinctions", one notices, "Prix Philip Morris (1992)". Merde, alors!

Nature complained in April, 2001, that the German arm of Philip Morris had been awarding annual research prizes since 1983 without controversy: "Around 100 researchers in Germany, Austria and Switzerland have received the Philip Morris prize …" it noted. "This year's winners, announced last week, each take home around US$100,000."

Even if not identical, the Philip Morris Prizes that went to Jouzel and Le Treut clearly had a family connection to the US$100,000 Philip Morris Prizes offered in the German context.

Jouzel blurbs about the comic book, "Great scholarship on all facets of the climate problem…a true feast". The book extensively features Jouzel as a talking head and wise dispenser of IPCC platitudes. He is described on the front and back covers and in the source-list as sharing the 2007 Nobel Peace Prize – which is flat-out wrong as the IPCC itself in late 2012 banned members from making such claims: "The prize was awarded to the IPCC as an organisation, and not to any individual associated with the IPCC. Thus it is incorrect to refer to any IPCC official, or scientist who worked on IPCC reports, as a Nobel laureate or Nobel Prize winner." Pulp the book, publisher!

The book's narrative is how author Squarzoni educates himself about climate by interviewing nine experts, who broadly compete to push catastrophism. Three are IPCC sorts. Another three, for some reason, are all eco-economists associated at a high level with a French group called ATTAC (Association for the Taxation of Financial Transactions and Aid to Citizens). To select three economists of that ilk is bizarre. Another of the artist's talking heads is an eco-journalist with *Le Monde*, the author of European best-seller *How the Rich Are Destroying the Earth*. The eighth source is a French nuclear industry scientist (France gets three-quarters of its electricity from nuclear). The ninth source is a corker, Helene Gassin, who ran Greenpeace energy campaigns in France for eight years. In 2001 her activists scaled the Exxon Mobil building in Paris during rush hour, and Gassin announced, "Greenpeace is going to give warnings in the entire world to companies who support this [anti-Kyoto] decision."

The book contains almost 100 pages of talking-head advice from these impartial sources. Unusually for a comic, the book has a comprehensive index so that its, ahem, "science" can be easily looked up, e.g. "ice melting, acceleration of, 113, 200-203".

Under "climate change, denial of, 414-19" we discover that the Melting-Himalaya-Glaciers howler in IPCC 2007 was "the only [error] in the 3000 page report" (the truth: nine errors on that single page alone) and that it came from a mere typo, the year "2035" for the glaciers all to melt, instead of "2350".

IPCC chief Pachauri and UN boss Ban Ki-Moon hardly called in the auditors (the InterAcademy Council or IAC) on the basis of one typo in the IPCC's 3000-page report.

This reality was this: The IPCC took the year 2035 correctly, but unwisely, from a popular Indian science magazine which had done the inverting of 2350 to 2035, and invented and garbled its own material. The IPCC also pretended its source was a WWF report (also garbled) and not the magazine. The IPPC page and its genesis were a mockery of science and scientific rigor.

The porkies in *Climate Changed* follow thick and fast. The IAC, the author claims, "concluded that the work methods were solid and the conclusions of the IPCC were correct." In fact the IAC concluded there were significant shortcomings in every major step of the IPCC process (p13). It also said at the outset that the report "does not examine climate change science or the validity of its representation in the assessment reports."

We also discover in the book that Climategate's famous 'trick' email of Phil Jones was just a method of splicing proxy and real temperature data "to make the results more accurate". In fact, the infamous 'trick's purpose was to conceal that the proxy series was worthless.

Climategate, Squarzoni concludes, was a smear campaign, "just a series of trumped-up scandals, slander and false accusations." He scoffs at what he calls an internet myth that global warming stopped in 1998, and says the hiatus arose by comparing a hot year 1998 with a cool one in 2008. (The IPCC people now acknowledge the 15-year halt and are arguing about what's caused it).

Among the book's 480 pages one finds every example of green zealot mythology. I'll cite just one: the magical 'climate refugees'. The index helpfully takes one to page 239, where we learn that 250 million people could be victims of coastal flooding and 60 million could migrate from arid zones by 2020 (hey, we're nearly there!). The cartoon frame shows a line of climate refugees trudging forward with bundles on their backs.

A boatload of people departs from a tropical island: *"From the Maldives to Kiribati to the Carteret Islands, people are already fleeing the rising sea level"* [no they're not, Maldives is building long-term tourist infrastructure]. "It is estimated that there are already 25 to 50 million eco-refugees fleeing from drought, hurricanes [huh?], floods … and their migration is accelerating," the comic insists. The frame shows an Arab-looking climate refugee sheltering under an umbrella from global warming.

What seems like 150 pages of frames are authorial self-indulgence, showing Squarzoni himself agonising over his personal task to save the planet. He gets offered a trip to Laos for an artist's residency, but this will add to jet-trail pollution. After soul-tearing deliberation across many pages, he rejects the trip. The epiphany of Saint Squarzoni is marred by his incidental jet-setting here and there, including sight-seeing to New York.

Being the product of French intellectuals, perhaps the book's conclusion – that Western democracies must be transformed into a Greens' playground – is no surprise.

The author's cited sources think Al Gore's emission-cutting prescriptions don't go far enough. One of Squarzoni's quoted sages, journalist Herve Kempf, chin resting on right fist, intones, "People like Al Gore are very sincere. Their knowledge and concern are real. But all they promise as a solution is 'green recovery'; new technology, hybrid cars and so on …" Even Obama is a green wimp: he "stays within the ideology of economic growth, and that will not resolve the problem."

Squarzoni concludes lugubriously, "At the end of the day, climate skeptics were able to undermine the [Copenhagen] consensus on global warming."

In technical skill, Squarzoni's illustrations are first-rate, drawing on cinematic and advertising styles while avoiding formulaic Manga-style visual cliches. Publisher Abrams – "The art of books since 1949" – meant well. Its blurb says of the book: "This groundbreaking work provides a realistic, balanced view of the magnitude of the crisis that An Inconvenient Truth only touched on." It adds, "Climate Changed is printed on FSC-certified paper from responsibly-managed, environmentally-sound sources." But Abrams could hardly say no Santas were hurt in production of the book.

UPDATE (it gets worse): *Climate Changed* New York publisher Abrams has issued a "Teacher's Guide to Climate Changed" for 15-18 year olds. It was written in June, 2014, by Peter Gutierrez, curriculum developer and graphic novels expert for the US National Council of Teachers of English.

The guide does not discuss whether the supermarket Santa slaughter offers a role model for armed American teenagers. The guide begins:

> Philippe Squarzoni's rigorous presentation of the relevant science and thoughtful reflection on the implications for policy, both public and personal, allow teachers to integrate economic, political, and individual responses to the realities of climate change that students will experience in their lifetime.
>
> The fact that Climate Changed is also a highly expressive work of graphic nonfiction rich in text features, and thoroughly capable of functioning as a primary and secondary source, make it an optimal text for students at various levels …
>
> For your convenience, this guide is aligned with the Common Core [US] State Standards (CCSS), specifically the 'Literacy in Science & Technical Subjects' strand, and the framework of thematic standards of the National Council for the Social Studies (NCSS).

In the questions for students, the first is, "What convincing evidence exists for anthropogenic climate change?" Students are asked to evaluate "which evidence is most compelling, and why?" On p429, the comic's captions say:

"Over the last two decades, the world has experienced the hottest years since 1880. The summer melting of the Arctic ice packs happened 40% faster than predicted. Greenland's glaciers and the Antarctic are also melting so fast that even specialists in these regions are surprised…

"2008: Hottest October Ever Recorded. We're probably approaching that level of warming, the 3.6 to 5.4 Degrees Fahrenheit (2 to 3 Degrees Centigrade), where the tipping points are. Climate High Alert … that we're better off not approaching."

The final frame shows a cauldron boiling under a fire. Next question – somewhat loaded: "How do the experts represented in the book consider, and refute, evidence for counterarguments?"

Another question: "How might the lack of scientific understanding among the general public contribute to unfounded optimism (e.g., climate change will be far in the future – there will be tech solutions by then), often through the manipulation of data (p. 416)?"

That page refers to 'trumped-up' Climategate scandals, the skeptics' 'smear campaign' creating public doubt, and skeptics deceiving the public about temperatures halting in 1998. The guide finishes with an essay question: "According to the author, how does media coverage of climate change, including its current consequences, hamper the ability of societies to take necessary steps?"

Teachers are then told: "Answers will vary. Examples include the gradualness/ distribution of climate-related deaths (pp. 250 – 51) as well as the "shoddy journalism" shown during the so-called "climategate" incident (pp. 418-19)."

The comic says on page 250: "Global warming causing 300,000 deaths per year" including, curiously, in Vietnam. The captions say, with intended irony, "The victims of climate change die slowly, one after another – no drama, no media coverage – scattered over the whole year over the whole planet. If only they had the good sense all to die on the same day, like the victims of the 2004 tsunami, that would catch our attention."

A few of the questions in the teacher's guide are reasonable, e.g. Consider this statement: "The beginning of the end of the world is beginning (p. 304)". Does it belong in a book about science? Does it make the discussion more authentic and/or state clearly what's at stake in terms of climate change? Does Squarzoni sufficiently prove this point? Why or why not?"

And "Does writing from the perspective of a French citizen enhance or undermine the author's critique of the 'American way of life'? Do you detect any cultural or political biases in the book? Support your opinion with relevant text evidence."

Quadrant OnLine, 19 October 2014

We're Doomed ... Kittens and Puppies Too

If you have a bill of climate goods to peddle, as Naomi Oreskes always does, what better foil than ardent warmist and ABC Science Show compere Robyn Williams? When flogging a book, it is handy to have a radio pal who has never encountered an alleged peril too silly to inspire a raised eyebrow -- not even the mass extinction of household pets.

Global warming is going to "wipe out" every Australian man, woman and child, according to Naomi Oreskes, the much-quoted Professor of the History of Science at Harvard. Revered by catastropharians the world over, she was a guest on a recent edition of Robyn Williams' Science Show on Radio National.

The glum forecast is in her latest book, *The Collapse of Western Civilisation* (co-author Erik Conway). She is so globally famous that her previous book, *Merchants of Doubt*, about the great warming-denialist conspiracy, is now being made into a movie by Sony Pictures Classics. This film-to-be is being touted as the successor to Al Gore's *Inconvenient Truth,* which may be an ironically apt comparison, as Gore still hasn't amended his flick to correct the nine howlers identified in a UK High Court judgement.

Robyn Williams doesn't seem to have read Oreskes book about Western civilisation's collapse, because its forecast of Australians' extinction (at 464/1172 on my Kindle) went unmentioned on his *Science Show.*

What Oreskes predicts is that some people in northern inland regions of Europe, Asia and North America, plus some mountain people in South America, will survive the killer warming. These lucky ones are able to "regroup and rebuild. The human populations of Australia and Africa, of course, were wiped out," she says, writing from a viewpoint some 400 years into the future.

But Oreskes forecasts something much worse than the death by climate for every Australian human. She prophesises the climate deaths of puppies and kittens. One reader, she says, "started crying when the pets die, so I didn't mean to upset people too much … I was just trying to come up with something that I thought people wouldn't forget about, and I thought, well, Americans spend billions of dollars every year taking care of their pets, and I thought if people's dogs started dying, maybe then they would sit up and take notice."

I looked up that bit in the book, and found the Great Kitten & Puppy Extinction occurs in 2023, along with the incidental deaths of 500,000 people and $US500b financial damage. Oreskes writes, "The loss of pet cats and dogs garnered particular attention among wealthy Westerners, but what was anomalous in 2023 soon became the new normal. A shadow of ignorance and denial had fallen over people who considered themselves children of the Enlightenment." To make sure no-one misses the pet die-off, she repeats it in a bold-type breakout.

Radio National's Williams was delighted with Oreskes' pet-panic strategy. He chimed in, "Yes, not only because it's an animal but it's local. You see, one criticism of the scientists is they're always talking about global things … And so if you are looking at your village, your animals, your fields, your park, your kids, and the scientists are talking about a small world that you know, then it makes a greater impact, doesn't it."

Oreskes responded: "Well, exactly. It was about bringing it literally home, literally into your home, your family, your pet, the dog or cat that you love who is your faithful and trusted companion."

As I type this, I look down at my faithful (but not always trusted) spaniel, Natasha, and let my own tears fall.

Oreskes doesn't think she's writing fiction. She told the admiring Williams, a Fellow of the Australian Academy of Science, no less: "Well, it's all based on solid science. Everything in this book is based on the scientific projections from the Intergovernmental Panel on Climate Change. All we did was to add to the social and human aspects to it … and to ask the question; what does this really mean in terms of what its potential impacts would be on people and its potential impacts on our institutions of governance?"

Oreskes starts *The Science Show* by reading from her book. Be afraid:

By 2040, heatwaves and droughts were the norm. Control measures

–such as water and food rationing and Malthusian 'one-child' policies –were widely implemented. In wealthy countries, the most hurricane- and tornado-prone regions were gradually but steadily depopulated…

In poor nations, conditions were predictably worse: rural portions of Africa and Asia began experiencing significant depopulation from out-migration, malnutrition-induced disease and infertility, and starvation…

Then, in the northern hemisphere summer of 2041, unprecedented heatwaves scorched the planet, destroying food crops around the globe. Panic ensued, with food riots in virtually every major city. Mass migration of undernourished and dehydrated individuals, coupled with explosive increases in insect populations, led to widespread outbreaks of typhus, cholera, dengue fever, yellow fever, and viral and retroviral agents never seen before.

Surging insect populations also destroyed huge swaths of forests in Canada, Indonesia and Brazil. As social order began to break down in the 2050s, governments were overthrown, particularly in Africa, but also in many parts of Asia and Europe, further decreasing social capacity to deal with increasingly desperate populations.

As the Great Northern American Desert surged north and east, consuming the High Plains and destroying some of the world's most productive farmland, the US government declared martial law to prevent food riots and looting. A few years later, the United States announced plans with Canada for the two nations to begin negotiations toward the creation of the United States of North America, to develop an orderly plan for resource-sharing and northward population relocation.

The European Union announced similar plans for voluntary northward relocation of eligible citizens from its southernmost regions to Scandinavia and the United Kingdom…

The ever-credulous Williams, instead of asking Oreskes, "Mmm, you're smoking something good?" merely observes that all of the above is "fairly shocking", further wondering why it is only Western civilisation that collapses, leaving the Chinese in charge. Oreskes gave two reasons. One, Chinese civilisation is more durable, and two, authoritarian regimes are better able to deal with climate catastrophes.

It's no surprise that Oreskes is a fan of our very own Professor Clive Hamilton, ethicist and "leading public intellectual". In *Collapse*, she cites approvingly his book *Requiem for a Species*, in which he says that combating climate change will impose moral obligations superior to mere obedience to the law. Hamilton has also welcomed the prospect of emergency measures, such as the suspension of democratic processes. If you're as smart as Hamilton thinks he is, what need to take the views of lesser mortals into account?

Oreskes' other Australian bestie is former Greenpeace International CEO Paul Gilding, of Tasmania, author of *The Great Disruption*. Gilding doesn't quite forecast the extinction of all Australians, but he does say: "I do believe it's going to be catastrophic by today's standards. Potentially, billions will die in famine, there will be conflict between nations, there will be a dramatic change in lifestyle enforced by a war-like effort in response … We should be on a war-footing …"

Oreskes seems to share the same authoritarian yearnings. She said last February that sceptic groups ought to be prosecuted via the Racketeer-Influenced Corrupt Organisations (RICO) statutes that have been widely used in the US to convict leaders of criminal syndicates for helping third parties to commit crimes. In *Merchants of Doubt*, she notes with approval how RICO, conceived to de-rail the Mafia, was later used to prosecute tobacco-industry executives for suppressing knowledge of health impacts.

Oreskes, the frequent object of Williams' gushing admiration, insists 'no one' in the 'scientific community' now thinks global warming can be confined to 2degC.

"Things that only a few years ago scientists thought were unimaginable, almost unspeakable, like a four-degree or a five-degree temperature range, now we realise we have to speak about them because that is where we are heading."

Given there's been a warming halt of between 14 years and 19 years, depending on whose charts you consult, it's hard to see why her climate scientists are suffering such rising panic. The halt even seems to have penetrated Williams' warm brain, since his next (excellent) question was:

> Williams: How much sympathy do you have for the ordinary person who picks up bestselling daily papers and sees that there hasn't been a temperature rise in 15 years, who sees that the IPCC is quoted as predicting that sea level will hardly change at all, that the temperatures won't go up beyond two degrees and they are quoting all this stuff, as if (and you use the word in your book) people like yourself are just alarmists?

Oreskes says:

> Well, I have tremendous sympathy for the ordinary citizen ... We have been victims of two things really; a systematic and organised disinformation campaign ... and then we've also been the victims of a tremendous amount of false equivalence in the media ...
>
> "There are hundreds of millions of people around the globe ... who will say to me, 'Well, I read in the New York Times' or 'I read in The Australian' and then they will spout some nonsense, something that we know is factually incorrect, and yet it has been presented in the media as if it were somehow equivalent to actual scientific data ... The media has done a huge disservice by perpetuating what are really lies – lies, misinformation, disinformation – that ordinary people read and think are true.

Well said, Naomi, except that you're now calling the IPCC crowd liars, since they've acknowledged the 15-year hiatus *(5AR, Policymakers Summary)*.

Williams, or the ABC (the official website isn't specific) introduced the Oreskes episode on the Science Show with a big fib: "The Earth's climate is changing at the highest of predicted rates."

In its draft for its Fifth Report, the IPCC showed actual temperatures running below the lowest bound of the IPCC forecasting. This graphic conveniently disappears from the published report, replaced by this account:

> However, an analysis of the full suite of CMIP5 [modeling] historical simulations ... reveals that 111 out of 114 realisations [forecasts] show a GMST [global mean surface temperature] trend over 1998–2012 that is higher than the entire HadCRUT4 [actual temperature] trend ensemble ... Chapter 9, WG1, Box 9.2.

In other words, actual temperatures are running lower than 97% of the forecast runs, not at "the highest of predicted rates" as claimed by *The Science Show*. Expect a correction from Robyn Williams any day (as I've put in an official complaint).[52]

---

52 Lordy lordy, my complaint to the ABC bore fruit. The Science Show website now includes this Radio National's "Editor's Note", viz., "The original introduction stated that 'Earth's climate is changing at the highest of predicted rates, scientists have given up on the much talked about two degree ceiling ... ' In context these words telegraphed the premise on which Prof Oreskes' work of fiction is based; however, it has been interpreted as a statement of incontrovertible fact and has therefore been removed to prevent any further misunderstanding."

Oreskes finished her interview by claiming, improbably, that some readers of her *Collapse* wanted her book to be longer. She explains, "We didn't want it to be too depressing, we didn't want to go on and on and on, like 300 pages of misery, that really wouldn't be any fun. So we are sort of hoping that the book, despite the fact that it's a depressing topic, it's actually we think kind of a fun read."

Apart from the dead kittens, she means.

Quadrant OnLine, 2 September 2014

The Joy of Yurts and Jam-Jar Glassware

Via Melbourne University's Sustainable Society Institute we visit the enchanted isle of Entropia, the eco-aware settlement where bad poets and oboe players celebrate the death of capitalism with lentil casseroles, home-made port, free love and no small amount of green-haloed self-regard.

〰〰〰〰〰〰〰〰〰〰〰〰〰〰〰〰〰〰〰〰〰〰〰〰〰〰〰〰〰〰〰〰〰

Futurology is a mainstay in the writing about global warming, not just forecasting but the more difficult art of time-travel.

We've had a vice-chair of the Intergovernmental Panel on Climate Change, Professor Jean-Pascal van Ypersele, discovering in 2004 that our own Prince William, Duke of Cambridge, was killed by a warming-caused disease in 2039. Then we had Harvard Professor Naomi Oreskes writing last July that global warming in 2023 would kill our puppies and kittens, our 'faithful and trusted companions". And three months ago, the science-y World Meteorological Organisation lined up real-life TV weather presenters who pretended to be reporting in 2050 about tornados hitting Berlin, a 50-day heat wave in Tokyo and so on.

Closer to home, we have Dr Sam Alexander, research fellow of the Melbourne University's Melbourne Sustainable Society Institute (MSSI) and lecturer with the university's Office for Environmental Programs. Last year he wrote a book: *Entropia: Life Beyond Industrial Civilisation* about someone looking back from a post-apocalyptic year 2099. It is published ($21.99 in paperback) by the Simplicity Institute, of which he is co-founder.

I don't want to give away plot twists, but the narrator describes a low-energy, simple-life community of poet-farmers on an isolated island off NZ after civilisation collapses about 2035. They were "determined above all else to transcend the materialistic values of the Old World."

The book is "an insight into the possibility of a much saner and more satisfying world" according to blurber Ted Trainer, of UNSW, who happens to be a fellow-member of Dr Alexander's Simplicity Movement; a co-author of a paper with Alexander; and subject of a paper by Alexander.

The successfully-simple poet-farmers become a model for contemporary society. As reviewer Paul Gilding, a former Global CEO of Greenpeace, puts it, "This is no escapist fantasy, however, but rather a practical and inspiring reminder of what we humans are capable of – and a wake-up call to action."

Dr Alexander is a doyen of the Melbourne University's Sustainable Society Institute, judging by the five of his papers on its *Publications* website menu. They are "Post-growth economics"; "A critique of techno-optimism"; "Disruptive social innovation for a low-carbon world" – you get the idea. For his Simplicity Institute, he's written lots along the lines of Planned Economic Contraction: The Emerging Case for Degrowth. He co-edited a new book last year, writing in the preface: "As the consumer class expands, we see the face of Gaia vanishing." Consumerism is a "fossil-fuelled perversion that has no future".

Readers may be surprised to learn that promoting Western economic contraction is a respectable academic field. Dr Alexander describes in an MSSI publication how the "Paris Declaration" of 2008 called for "right-sizing" of all countries' economies, meaning contraction in the West and expansion in the third world, but only to consumption levels there "adequate for a decent life". (Wealth transfers from the West are the preferred choice for them). After global right-sizing, world growth should cease.

Alexander further explains: "The primary contribution made by degrowth scholarship is the explicit acknowledgement that sustainability implies … initiating a phase of planned contraction of the 'scale' of developed economies. That is a position entirely absent from mainstream environmental and political discourse, where the ideology of growth still reigns supreme."

His paper's bibliography includes nine self-citations, one of which is *Entropia*, his fantasy tract.

Dr Alexander's 2011 grant and scholarship-supported Ph.D. thesis (Melbourne University Law School), was "Property beyond Growth: Toward a Politics of Voluntary Simplicity". One of its five chapters is written from the future, as follows: "Looking Backward from the year 2029: Ecozoic Reflections. Lennox Kingston, *Possibility* 81(4) (2099)." (Kingston, just so you'll know, is Alexander's future alter ego).

Dipping into the thesis chapter, one reads: "By the end of the 2020s, the Simplicity Movement had become a significant oppositional force, and it would continue to strengthen and expand every year … Furthermore, simple living had become a socially accepted alternative lifestyle, which made stepping out of materialistic lifestyles much less isolating, thus hastening the demise of consumer culture. These changes resulted in discernable social and ecological benefits."

But what are his conclusions? For his post-growth world, he recommends:

> A guaranteed minimum basic income for all
>
> A highly-progressive income tax ensuring a "democratically determined 'maximum wage'"
>
> "Worker cooperatives as the dominant corporate form in the economy"
>
> Tougher environmental laws
>
> "Curtail the laws of inheritance and bequest through high levels of taxation or abolition"
>
> "Redesign labor laws to encourage systematically the exchange of income/consumption for more free time".

Who could guess what you find in Melbourne Uni's Ph.D. theses these days? Alexander explains, "Although I acknowledged that these proposed reforms may well slow an economy's quantitative growth – even to the point of inducing a phase of degrowth – and thereby not maximise a nation's GDP per capita, the underlying argument of this thesis has been that the reforms would at the same time: (1) increase human well-being; (2) promote social justice; and (3) enhance the health and integrity of the planet's ecosystems. This is the potential 'triple dividend' which makes a post-growth property system such an alluring and promising prospect."

He notes: "A profound debt of gratitude is owed to my doctoral supervisor, Professor Lee Godden, who spent countless hours reading and discussing this thesis."

Alexander's thesis bibliography includes Alexander, Samuel (ed), *Voluntary Simplicity: The Poetic Alternative to Consumer Culture;* Alexander, Samuel, 'Looking Backward for the Year 2099: Ecozoic Reflections on the Future'; and Alexander, Samuel, 'Deconstructing the Shed: Where I Live and What I Live For,' *Concord Saunterer* (2011, forthcoming).

In his 2013 future-book *Entropia*, Dr Alexander's narrator just happens to be a part-time lecturer in philosophy and culture at the island's academy, as well as assistant editor at a community newspaper, "The Saunterer", when he's not binding books and picking fruit.

In the 2035 Great Disruption, we are told the island's beautiful Tibetan violin prodigy Nishka, unable to find solace "even in our warm community", sat in the bath with her violin, and with slashed and bloodied wrists, died playing a beautiful, tragic composition. The others remained positive while dining on beans, potatoes and lentils. Although there were a few arguments about how to stay alive, "generally these were measured, mature conflicts. Everyone knew that there was no place for childish egotism … "

For a couple more pages, the narrator describes the non-realisation of Karl Marx's vision, due to the working class becoming distracted by consumerism. Capitalism marched on, "brutally shaping the world according to its cold logic of profit maximisation." But good news! Capitalism collapsed anyway, growing itself to death "like a cancer cell".

On the resource-poor island, the citizens only need 65 litres of water per person per day (from wood and clay storage tanks), and if they use more they get a visit from a social educators "and as such, they are never resented".

Citizens in their densely habited mud-brick and yurt compounds, converted containers and tepees, cut back severely on cleaning themselves and their clothes, since hyper-cleanliness is "fetishistic". They limit showers to 90 seconds, "and often simply wash themselves with a bucket and some soap". In summer they jump into rivers and ponds, a mystical experience "as the sun rises like a warm god over the eastern mount".

Their clothing is made from "functional, easy to grow, low-impact fabrics … derived from such things as agricultural hemp, nettles and wool … a new aesthetic of sufficiency".

Dr Alexander doesn't remark on the aroma of his community of minimally-washed, hemp-clad, yurt-dwelling bean-eaters who drink from old jam jars. Nor does he mention the rigors of low-tech dentistry.

People take on a succession of roles. A person finishing school might become a potter, a carpenter, "a blacksmith, a music teacher, a lecturer, a tailor, a doctor or some mixture of such roles". My women friends are apprehensive about getting a procedure from a blacksmith-turned-medico, but the author assures us that the isle's vegie diet and work-life balance minimise health issues anyway.

The community, run by the "People's Council", involves home-grown food etc, and "artisans also produce specialty goods at the household level, such as musical instruments, paintings or various tools". (Preferred painting styles are chocolate-box scenery and "a revolving series of mostly colourful abstract works").

Women delight in use of long-lasting treadle sewing machines, pausing to welcome friends over to share a nutritious bean meal and play the musical instruments.

The booze on tap is suggested by one lady's diary. During a stroll she met an 83-year-old "full of poetry and wisdom", who played the ukulele to her. Arriving home she bottled pears, "worked a little on my novel", mended a hole in her sweater and then joined some friends in the garden "where we sipped on home-made port and threw ideas around about organising a series of dawn plays in the summer". The home-made-port-sipping continued till midnight so the play scripts probably got a bit ragged.

However, the narrator is convinced that the community "is awash with the most thrilling novels, plays, poems, music, sculpture, paintings, tapestries and all other forms of art, beyond historical precedent and beyond historical imagination".

Dr Alexander's narrator provides a sample of the thrillingly-beyond-imagination poetry, which I think would do credit to William Topaz McGonagill. Here we go:

Witness O mysterious other, Who wanders in from beyond, Like mist emerging from the woods, To settle on the pond, With etiquette poetic, Charm refined without pretence, You seem a gentlemanly brother With many dollars, but fewer sense.

It goes on for four pages and ends with the audience entranced and 'eager to hear more'. But instead they get an oboist. "Thus in our simplicity, we are happy", the chapter concludes.

The narrator says, "While strict equality is not enforced on the isle, we recognise that significant disparities of wealth are socially corrosive and politically dangerous". The narrator seems to have studied not only Marx but Marx's famous interpreter J.V. Stalin, who knew exactly what to do with socially-corrosive elements, such as millions of slightly-wealthier peasants (kulaks) and their families.

I took a prurient interest in the sex lives of this community. For starters, marriage has been dumped because of all its 'baggage' marginalising gay relationships. Relationships are open or closed, according to what anyone wants. "Expanded relationships that sometimes form on the Isle raise no eyebrows and certainly draw no moral censure."

I visualise an Entropian dinner party: *"I'd like you to meet my three partners Trent, Noah and Roslyn, and Daisy my cocker spaniel. Do let me pour you a jam jar of port."*

The narrator/Alexander is a bit weak on the essential task of controlling the island's population. To have more than one baby poet-farmer, you need a permit, but what if a couple has an accident (quite likely in the absence of latex factories and pill laboratories), or the couple tells the People's Council to get stuffed? The narrator says lamely that social disapproval of multi-birth families tends to bring the fecund poet-farmers into line. (If dad heads off to join someone else, the new couple gets an extra-baby permit).

The book ends unusually, "Would you be interested in helping to fund and participate in the creation of an Entropia Ecovillage outside of Melbourne, Australia, based on the ideas in this book? If so, please register your interest at www.bookofentropia.com/ecovillage."

I therefore emailed Dr Alexander:

Hi Sam, I have just finished reading your book Entropia and was bowled over by the ambition of your vision. I think the idea of an eco-village near Melbourne including yurts, tepees and shipping container housing could be the answer to affordable housing.

I own (with my wife) a house near Coburg that is really more of a burden because of all the unnecessary appliances, like washing machines and dishwashers, that are always breaking down, and if my wife agrees, we could sell the house and sink the proceeds into sustainable housing in your village project, without wasteful appliances, especially as I for one, like you, see industrial civilisation soon to collapse under the burden of ever-more-expensive oil. All the best with your project, Tony.

Forty minutes later, Dr Alexander responded enthusiastically to my conditional offer, "I'm heartened to hear that my book spoke to you."

In fact, the ecovillage is not only well underway but, in the past 18 months, the founders have built "a small Earthship, a mud house, an earthbag abode, and a 'tiny house' from reclaimed timber and iron." They have a yurt in transit from WA and have started an orchard, chicken coop etc.

What's more, a documentary film-maker (sounds like the ABC, but I may be wrong) is onto their case, and up to 10 people will stay at the property to film a 'simpler way' documentary based on the ideas in his *Entropia* island book. The film would present a deep green alternative to mainstream life and illustrate 'one planet' living.

I was invited to sink the proceeds from my (conditional) house sale into buying neighboring blocks for $215,000 or $485,000. A nearby $900,000 block was mentioned, but probably out of my price range. "Having someone like-minded buy the neighbouring properties would be absolutely amazing," Dr Alexander wrote.

Soon after, he did a bit of googling and was disappointed to find that I am a *Quadrant* writer and as such, unlikely to be a genuine sympathiser with earth-bagged earthships, tiny houses and home-made contraception.

Quadrant OnLine, 15 January 2015

The Fishy 'Science' of Ocean Acidification

With an obstinate atmosphere failing to warm as predicted, another peril was needed to sustain the junk-science industry and keep lazy reporters supplied with bogus scoops. No problem! Conscript a Disney character, garnish with misrepresentations and there you have it: "ocean acidification".

How scary is "ocean acidification"? Very scary. The previously scary "global warming" stopped 19 years ago, but do stay scared because all that CO_2 since 1997 has instead been "acidifying" the oceans. Please imagine baby oysters dissolving in the equivalent of battery acid, and hermit crabs raising a nervous feeler to discover that their protective shells have disappeared. Curse you, horrible human-caused CO_2 emissions!

In one celebrated episode involving Climate Science™, a lone oyster farmer in Maine put his oysters into a bucket and then found that the bivalves at the bottom were crunched because their shells were weakened. Can any reasonable person ask for better scientific proof of ocean "acidification"?

"Ocean Acidification", the evil twin of global warming, is scary because the chemistry is so simple. For example, the Australian Academy of Science in its curriculum for secondary schools, organises an experiment for 16-year-olds where crushed ocean shells go into a test tube of sea water. You add acid or vinegar or something, and then watch the shells fizz and dissolve!

Two years ago, I noticed in Melbourne's Fed Square a $50,000 competition for schoolkids for the best drawing about ocean "acidification", sponsored by the green Ocean Ark Group. The theme was "Imagine losing all this color and life". Guidance text included, "There are approximately 10,000 Coral Reefs and we are destroying one every other day … Left unchecked Ocean Acidification could trigger a Great Mass Extinction Event …"

Now that union corruption has been exposed, maybe our next Royal Commission should be into Abuse of Children's Intelligence, and the Academy and Ocean Ark could justify their teachings under cross-examination.[53]

Meanwhile, a trans-Atlantic team of top "ocean acidification scientists" has published a scary op-ed in the *New York Times*. Congrats to skeptic blogger Steve Milloy at Junkscience.com for successfully obtaining under FOI the emails among them collaborating over the op-ed draft. This material runs to 440 admittedly repetitious pages.[54] The named op-ed authors were Richard W. Spinrad, chief scientist of the U.S. National Oceanic and Atmospheric Administration (NOAA), and Ian Boyd, chief scientific adviser to UK's Department of Environment.

The trove of FOI emails include some beauties. Here's what NOAA's Dr Shallin Busch had to say, privately, to her NOAA colleague Madelyn Applebaum on September 30 about the draft. They had been asked by the *New York Times* to sex it up with some specific hurts allegedly being caused by all this acidification. The editor asked:

> It's very interesting, but in order to work for us it needs to be geared more toward the general reader. Can the authors give us more specific, descriptive images about how acidification has already affected the oceans? Is the situation akin to the acid rain phenomenon that hit North America? What can be done to counteract the problem?

Dr Busch, who works for NOAA's Ocean Acidification Program and Northwest Fisheries Science Center at Seattle, responded to Ms Applebaum:

> Unfortunately, I can't provide this information to you because it doesn't exist. As I said in my last email, currently there are NO areas of the world that are severely degraded because of OA or even areas that we know are definitely affected by OA right now. If you want to use this type of language, you could write about the CO2 vent sites in Italy or Polynesia as examples of things to come. Sorry that I can't be more helpful on this!

Dr Busch had the integrity to admit that science can cite "NO" significant ocean "acidification" impacts. But she was nonetheless happy

---

53 "…Some of the octopuses in the ocean can't breathe from gas pollution … I started off my poster design of drawing the octopus first and wanted to make it look as if he was dying. Then I drew dead coral coming and surrounding him like there's no escape from the acid ocean…" – one child's entry in the Victorian schools contest for "ocean acidification" art.
54 Strangely, NOAA has been fighting tooth and nail to thwart Republican congressmen's requests for its emails about a NOAA study by Karl et al purporting to show there has been no 15-year pause in warming. It is now conceding defeat and starting to hand over documents.

for the article to include, as agitprop, the effects of natural CO_2 venting through the ocean floor, as though this somehow corroborated the "acidification" story.

Dr Busch, in the course of vetting many drafts, also wrote to Applebaum:

> Thanks for letting me chime in on this piece. My two general impressions are the following:
>
> 1) This article is mostly gloom and doom, which research has shown that people don't respond to well. In fact, people just stop reading gloom and doom environmental stories. It could be good to highlight ways we can and are dealing with OA [Ocean Acidification] now and that we have an opportunity to prevent the major predicted impacts of OA by stopping carbon emissions before larger chemistry changes happen ...
>
> 2) I think it is really important to resist the NYT editor's impulse to say that OA is wreaking all sorts of havoc RIGHT NOW, because for ecological systems, we don't yet have the evidence to say that. OA is a problem today because it is changing ocean chemistry so quickly. The vast majority of the biological impacts of OA will only occur under projected future chemistry conditions. Also, the study of the biological impacts of OA is so young that we don't have any data sets that show a direct effect of OA on population health or trajectory. Best, Shallin.[55]

And here's Dr Busch on the Great Barrier Reef. (The "Chris" she refers to is Chris Sabine, director of the NOAA Pacific Marine Environmental Laboratory).

> I'm not sure that I agree with Chris's statement about the impact of OA on the Great Barrier Reef, [namely] 'but underlying all of those factors is the fact that the corals are so stressed from ocean acidification that they can't recover from those other impacts the way they used to be able to recover.' Given my knowledge of the literature, OA is more of

---

55 The 2014 5th IPCC report Summary for Policymakers, written by politico-bureaucrats, waxes fearful about ocean acidification. But the scientists themselves in their non-sexed-up findings in body text, WG11 Chapter 6, say, for example,

• "Few field observations conducted in the last decade demonstrate biotic responses attributable to anthropogenic ocean acidification" pg 4

• "Both acclimatization and adaptation will shift sensitivity thresholds but the capacity and limits of species to acclimatize or adapt remain largely unknown" pg 23

• "To date, very few ecosystem-level changes in the field have been attributed to anthropogenic or local ocean acidification." pg 39.

a future problem than a problem right now for the Great Barrier Reef. I think it is important to resist the NYT editor's impulse to say that OA is wreaking all sorts of havoc RIGHT NOW, because for ecological systems, we don't yet have the evidence to say that.

If you'll permit a digression, Dr Sabine's CV notes that not only was he a NOAA Employee of the Month in 2007 but his awards include: *Nobel Peace Prize (co-shared with Al Gore and other members of IPCC) - 2007*.

As an aside, I keep reminding these people of an IPCC ruling banning them from claiming Nobel Peace Prize status. Sometimes people like Deakin University's Vice-Chancellor Jane den Hollander even referred to the (subsequently) abruptly-resigned ex-IPCC head, accused sex criminal and all-around dirty old man Rajendra Pachauri as a "Nobel Prize" winner.[56] Our own CSIRO is full of bogus Nobel Peace Prize winners. The best solution would be for the IPCC to issue them all with lab coats recognising their special status, e.g. with a purple satin sash, gold buckles and ostrich plumes.

Digression over, in the *NYT*'s other wordage and pics, we learn from the top scientists that sea butterflies, a food for salmon and herring, undergo shell weaknesses, *"showing why ocean acidification is often called* [by whom?] *'osteoporosis of the sea'"*. The *NYT* editor had been badgering the authors for pics to go with the article in order to spruik all this damage from "acidification". The authors, via the indefatigable Madelyn Applebaum, were desperate to find such before-and-afters — a dauntingly hard quest, given there isn't any damage.

So what did Applebaum come up with to make the *NYT* happy? Why, twin pics from NOAA of sea butterflies (*Pteropods*). The first had lived in a laboratory tub with "normal waters" (whatever "normal" means) for six days, and was in the pink of health. The other specimen inhabited a tub with "acidified water" for the six days. (Did the animal anti-cruelty people sign off on sea-butterfly torture?). Would you believe, the poor little acid-dunked *Pteropod* showed a tracery of white lines where the acid had etched its shell surface. What more pictorial proof of the harm of ocean "acidification" could a *NYT* editor (or climate scientist, or

---

56 "As well as helping fulfil Deakin's prophecy, teaming up with TERI is a major coup for Deakin University. The organisation's Director-General is Dr Rajendra K. Pachauri, the No-bel Prize winner".

Academician) possibly require?[57]

All such articles have to point to harm to people too. We read emails that "Human health, too, is a major concern." This is because the NOAA labs show toxic growths when water in the tubs is artificially acidified. So assuming (heroically) the same thing happens in the wild, the authors warn that people could get sick from eating acidy shellfish. Eating this nasty sea-stuff could "sicken, even kill, fish and marine mammals such as sea lions." I imagine that right now, hundreds of NOAA IT people are modeling ocean-life die-offs based on that algae in a NOAA lab tub.

To climate scientists, the most important sea creatures in the entire planetary eco-system are not whales[58] or other coelacanths but Walt Disney's celebrated clownfish. That's because little Nemo is a sure-fire tear-jerker in any climate-catastrophe scenario.

In the long piece about the global oceans by the top dogs of US/UK climate science, we learn:

> We cannot yet predict exactly how ocean acidification will affect connections among the world's many different marine organisms, but we do know the consequences will be profound. [i.e. we don't know but we do know. Send more grant funding immediately.] Research already points to the unnatural behavior of coral clownfish in an acidified environment. These fish wander farther from their natural protection, making them more vulnerable to predators.

This published reference to clownfish was the fruit of much angst involving the UK department's determination to shoe-horn Nemo into the PR exercise.

Jane Phenton, Senior Flack for UK Environment Dept, 30/9/15: "The [UK] team have added some examples (Nemo the clown fish a particularly good one I think!) and a few thoughts.

Comments on a draft: "Hearing loss/impairment in Nemo, the coral clownfish, is just one of many potential impacts that have been identified in laboratory studies …"

Oh no! Nemo, too, has been subjected to laboratory acid torture, but in a good cause. The boffins found "he" began wandering further from his protective home, inviting danger. But couldn't Nemo, if still right

---

57 Or the Australian Academy of Science, which has recycled the Pteropod before-and-after pics for schoolkids.

58 Some say whales aren't fish, but I say they look more like fish than coelecanths.

side up in the tub, now be fitted with a sea-going Cochlear implant? [Editor: shouldn't that be a <u>conch</u>lear implant?].

However, things got more complex, because, says a NOAA scientist, "Apparently one study called Nemo 'deaf' – problem was attributed to brain damage that affected capability to hear. I'll word carefully."

Someone else chips in, "He [Nemo] can't smell his predators when they are near, and engages in risky behavior, making him more vulnerable to predators."

Someone else bells the cat, or fish, by pointing out that Nemo's lab tub isn't literally acidic, just less alkaline. And, anyway, Nemo might work out how to adapt [assuming Nemo's brain damage isn't terminal].

Then on September 30 the NOAA heavy Dr Chris Sabine, Director, Pacific Marine Environmental Laboratory, weighs in to Madelyn:

> I have asked everyone I can reach and nobody is aware of a study that suggests that Nemo's hearing would be impaired by ocean acidification. I did find one article on the web that suggested the opposite. I am aware of studies indicating that Nemo would lose sense of smell or ability to detect predators and therefore would be more likely to be eaten. Perhaps you can ask the UK people to check on that sentence.

Be aware that these collaborators obsessing about Nemo are taxpayer-funded scientists and PR flacks, all hard at work on a journalism piece to puff their organisations. The article continues, "In the past three decades, the number of living corals covering the Great Barrier Reef has been cut in half, reducing critical habitat for fish and the resilience of the entire reef system."

I looked up the 2014 Great Barrier Reef Marine Park Authority's Outlook Report which re-quoted a 2009 study, "There is little detailed information about the status and trends of many habitat types within the Great Barrier Reef … However, there is some evidence of a small decline in coral reef habitat over recent decades."

A "small decline"? So what's this halving that NOAA is talking about? It seems to come from a 2012 paper by De-ath *et al* from the Australian Institute of Marine Science.

By analyzing 27 years of data, the authors found that the Barrier

Reef's coral cover was down from 28% to 13.8% by area, in other words, half the initial coral cover had been lost. But why? The losses were due to cyclones (48%), crown-of-thorns starfish (42%) and coral bleaching (10%) – none of this involves the "acidification" peril. And the pristine northern Reef area showed no decline. If it wasn't for the cyclones, starfish and bleaching, the coral overall would have grown by nearly 3% a year. Even with cyclones and bleaching, the coral would grow by nearly 1% a year if the starfish were neutralised. To stay politically correct, the authors added that climate change had to be (somehow) stabilised, otherwise there would be more bleaching and cyclones, they think.

The *NYT International* piece was published under the ludicrous headline: Our Deadened, Carbon-Soaked Seas. A graphic showed a big fish whose head above water was intact but whose body underwater was reduced to an acid-etched skeleton.

The scientists' preferred headline had merely been *"In a high CO2 world, dangerous waters ahead"* and the authors had nothing to do with the lurid graphic. But the *NYT* likes to greenwash its readers with terrifying climate capers. The broadsheet gives several pages of boilerplate specs for contributors on fact-checking, and has an army of its own fact-checkers to ensure against embarrassing corrections. But this "professionalism" is trumped by a headline-writer's whim and an artist's ignorant sensationalism. As with our own demented and dying Fairfax papers, sensationalism is given the tick of shock-horror approval all the way up the editorial chain.

The top-tier science authors commiserated among themselves about the "quite inflammatory" re-write of their headline, but made not one word of complaint to the *NYT*. After all, the luridness was in the right direction – mega-scariness – and the authors were keen to get more *NYT* coverage in future. Principles be damned.

The *NYT* article made a lot of mileage out of US west-coast oyster industry problems ostensibly caused by ocean currents pushing "acidified" water towards the oyster beds, causing "baby oysters" to expire. The infant oysters had in fact been killed by a faecal organism *Vibrio tubiashii* from sewage.

And in any event, that pesky Dr Busch throws in an email saying: "In fact, production in the Washington oyster industry is higher now than at the start of the [supposed acidification] crisis … Just as an FYI, we can't yet attribute any large patterns in shellfish yield to OA" [ocean acidification].

Dr Busch also wrote, re specific fish communities, "It might be good to mention that some species will be harmed by OA, some will benefit, and some won't respond at all!" This is complete heresy, as global warming must always be presented as a bad thing. But Dr Busch knew what the NOAA playbook demanded and constructed a new draft paragraph dotted with the conditional — words like "may affect some fish populations" and "may" re-order ecosystems. In this way any references to positive impacts on marine life are made to disappear.

The Australian Academy of Science in its educational materials is likewise unable to actually admit that lower pH can have positive impacts on sea life. Instead, it glooms, "not all calcifying animals react in the same way to lower pH conditions. But although some animals and plants may not fare so badly as others, the impacts upon marine biodiversity have the potential to be severe."

The *NYT* piece revels in ridiculous analogies and apparently-massive numbers isolated from any planetary context, eg:

> "Over the past 200 years, the world's seas have absorbed more than 150 billion metric tons of carbon from human activities. Currently, that's a worldwide average of 15 pounds per person a week, enough to fill a coal train long enough to encircle the equator 13 times every year. Hence ocean and coastal waters around the world *are beginning to tell* a disturbing story". (My emphasis. Note how the italicized words fudge that there is actually no story so far).

Innocent readers might imagine NOAA embarked on this op-ed project to educate the public about a serious scientific matter. No, the project's prime and explicit function was to puff NOAA as a funding-worthy institution, and to add ammunition to the COP21 climate talks in Paris in December, 2015. As Dr Libby Jewett, director of NOAA's Ocean Acidification Program, briefed: "The article would fit well with NOAA's resilience and observational priorities and could go an important distance in recognising NOAA's leadership in growing an international ocean observing system…We want visibility for NOAA's pioneering global leadership to be prominent, too!"

The final 250 words — 20% of the 1250-word *NYT* piece — are all about the need to send money to the scientists for their planet-saving endeavours:

> Smart investments in monitoring and observing are critical to building resilience and hedging risks that can directly affect economies at all levels. There is urgency to such investments. The U.S. National Oceanic and Atmospheric Administration conducts round-the-clock monitoring of global CO2. The rate of increase has never been higher than during the past three years, accelerating the ocean acidification process … We ignore the risks of ocean acidification at our own peril, and that of future generations.

Tim Flannery, head of Australia's Climate Council, is of the view that CO2 falling into the ocean produces "carbolic acid" or phenol, that useful disinfectant which can still be bought on eBay in the form of soap bars. Flannery is, as always, correct in terms of the prevailing hysteria, if not real-world facts. His prophecy is affirmed by Ocean Acidification International Coordination Centre (OAICA) and the International Atomic Energy Agency (IAEA), which agree that "Too much carbon is flooding the ocean with carbolic acid, with devestating (sic) effects on life in the sea." This is devestating (sic) news for chemistry textbooks.[59]

Here's a contrary view to all that. The Centre for the Study of Carbon Dioxide and Global Change, run by sceptic scientists, agrees with the orthodox group that, since pre-industrial times, the oceans have become less alkaline by about 0.1 pH unit. But it views as far-fetched any results from modeling that posit a further pH reduction of between 0.3 units to 0.7 units by 2300. The Centre marshaled about 1100 peer-reviewed studies on impacts of lower pH on ocean life and, after excluding those with wildly unrealistic assumptions, checked the rest in terms of five factors: calcification, metabolism, growth, fertility and survival. It plotted the experimental results involving pH falls from 0.0 to 0.3, the latter number being what the IPCC predicts for 2100, and found that the fall in pH led to "an overall beneficial response of the totality of the five major life characteristics of marine sea life to ocean acidification" which

---

59 The OAICC and IAEA warn that climate is putting the world "in a dangerous position, just as the US was when it was bombed at Pearl Harbor… This segment reports on "global warming's evil twin", ocean acifidication, which results from too much carbon in the water." The audio segments begin with air-raid sirens and crashing bombs.

result is vastly different from the negative results routinely predicted by the world's climate alarmists.

It said the results would be even more positive if studies had also allowed for the ability of generations of sea life to adapt to changed conditions. The studies testing lower pH on life forms typically involved a mere four days duration and some trials lasted a mere few hours, preventing any favorable evolutions, it said.

Footnote: My studies in high-school chemistry ceased at age 16, but here's my take on ocean acidification technicalities.

The oceans' alkalinity (pH) varies from place to place, in a range 7.9 to 8.3 on a logarithmic scale where 14 is most alkaline (or basic), 7.0 is neutral and below 7 to zero is acidic. The log scale means each change of one unit is ten times the value of the adjacent unit.[60]

The scare term "ocean acidification"[61] first popped up in *Nature* in 2003, followed by the Royal Society in 2005. Climate scientists now "calculate" that the average ocean alkalinity has declined from 8.2 to 8.1 on the scale since pre-industrial times, except that the measurement error margin is several times the alleged reduction (and each of the five oceans has its own pH characteristics). pH levels at given points can also swing markedly even within the 24-hour cycle.

In past geological ages CO2 levels in the atmosphere were ten or more times what they are now (400ppm) and ocean life thrived. Indeed our current fossil fuels are the residue of vast oceanic life that thrived and died in such super-high CO2 environments.

In the parts of the oceans where alkalinity is low (i.e. tending towards neutral), fish, corals, and sea flora have managed and adapted perfectly well. Freshwater lakes and rivers are slightly acidic (pH of 6 to 8), as is rainwater, pH 5.6, and drinking water, 6.5 to 7.5. Life has adapted and thrives in fresh water notwithstanding the, ahem, "acidification".

Quadrant OnLine, 1 January 2016

---

60 Vinegar, for example, at 2.5, is almost a million times more acidic than seawater.
61 Compare it with its twin verbal Orwellism, "carbon pollution".

4

HOW FEMINISTS EMASCULATE THE MILITARY

Attack of the Gender Warriors

The sisterhood is grimly determined to see women in every unit of the armed forces, objections on grounds of physical capability, logistics, group psychology and lowered standards being dismissed as mere phallocratic prattle. Let us hope that peace prevails while commonsense does not.

◇◇◇

"For the strength of the pack is the wolf, and the strength of the wolf is the pack."
– Rudyard Kipling

Western feminists are getting a good scorecard on feminising the Western military, starting with the all-powerful US forces. The sisterhood's pack, apart from the likes of our own Lt-General (Retd) David Morrison and politicians, include the human rights bureaucracies, the Left, and "diversity" advocates. The plan, branded as "equality", is to have women accelerated to one-star rank (roughly Colonel/Brigadier-General) and beyond. Those so elevated can then drive the feminising from atop the system.

There is a problem, though. Currently, women without prior combat experience struggle to secure the loftiest promotions, so the campaign is on to lower combat fitness standards. "Equality" to the Left -- and the current crop of top brass – means "discrimination" if women don't represent suitably proportionate numbers in elite units. To conservatives, "equality" means equal opportunity to pass a necessary military test. If women don't get through, too bad.

So, do women do well at war? From 2001 to 2013, 154 US servicewomen were killed on duty in Iraq and Afghanistan, many by IEDs which, admittedly, do not discriminate. Nineteen mothers returned to their toddlers and children, but in body bags.[62] All studies suggest that women's casualty rates become disproportionate the closer women get to combat – and close to half US women troops reported hostile action in those two war zones.

But to the Sisterhood, these are trivial issues compared with the need for equality, "fairness" and "civilising" the rude military. If the push leaves the West less able to deal with, say, ISIS and/or Iran, North Korea, Islamic "caliphates" and thousands of lone-wolfers, well, that's just tough for the West. Feminists, so reluctant to denounce Islamic misogyny, perhaps hope that they and their sisters will be the last consigned to sexual slavery and life in a burka'd sack.

Last December, US Defense Secretary Ash Carter announced lifting of all gender-based restrictions on combat and infantry roles, most in infantry and armor units and including the elite Rangers and SEALS. [63] [64] The Marines had wanted the toughest jobs, such as machine-gunner and field reconnaissance, to stay male-only. They lost partly because the US, conveniently for politicians, has faced no serious opposition in the field since Vietnam. There has been no extreme combat to test the fragility of mixed-sex combat units.[65]

Secretary Carter's professed rationale – prompted by females' lawsuits and pressure from the Obama White House — was to increase the pool of potential recruits for 220,000 new unrestricted roles. Low ability of women to pass existing physical tests (developed from generations of combat experience) may shrink the pool to just a birdbath, hence the

---

62 Robert L. Maginnis, *Deadly Consequences*. Regnery Publishing, Washington DC. Kindle 3016.
63 Among the fall-out from the decision is that US women aged 18-26, along with US men 18-26, should now be registered and subject to possible call-up. Women had been previously exempted because of battlefield restrictions. Standards must now be similarly enforced against countless flabby, overweight male NCOs.
64 The Navy integrated its fighter pilot career fields in the 1990s
65 In the past decade, 300,000 US women were deployed to Iraq and Afghanistan. More than 9,000 earned Combat Action Badges. About 800 were wounded and 160 died from combat- and noncombat-related incidents.

push to drop standards.

Prior groundwork has included such comical stuff as rolling out courses for US non-commissioned officers and combat veterans, starting on Japanese Marine bases. The instructors donned fake 12kg bellies and boobs and, thus clad, went through the PT regime in order to feel greater empathy with pregnant soldiers. These courses were mandated whether or not a team actually had any pregnant soldiers.

The Services' *Stars And Stripes* newspaper reported that at Camp Zama, Japan, 14 non-commissioned officers took turns wearing the "pregnancy simulators" over three days' training. There were nine authentic baby-bellies among the troops.[66] The newspaper said Army-enlisted leaders "all over the world" were being ordered to take the Pregnancy Postpartum Physical Training Exercise Leaders Course, or PPPT. Sgt. Michael Braden, a veteran helicopter chief (78th Aviation Battalion), with no pregnant soldiers to teach, had misgivings but "strapped on the empathy belly and spent Tuesday morning learning low-impact aerobics moves like the 'grapevine' and the 'V-step'." One maverick blogged, "They ought to make female paratroopers wear a fake penis and scrotum when they put on a parachute harness."

US combat jobs began opening broadly to women in 2013. The standards-dropping for females is discussed overtly in high circles. General (retd) Martin Dempsey, ex-chair of the Joint Chiefs of Staff and earlier Commanding General, Training Command: "Importantly, though, if we do decide that a particular standard is so high that a woman couldn't make it, the burden is now on the service to come back and explain to the Secretary, why is it that high?" It's not hard for underlings to crack a superior's verbal code and grasp its meaning.

In Canada, the Human Rights Tribunal opened all Air Force jobs to women as of 1987. Military experts began studies on best employment of women in Army/Navy combat without compromising unit performance. But the Human Rights Tribunal immediately mandated full integration of women without limit into combat roles.

Training standards had to be lowered to bring in women. Barely

66 Wiki says Camp Zama is home to the U.S. Army Japan (USARJ)/I Corps (Forward), the U.S. Army Japan Aviation Detachment Japan "Ninjas", the 441st Military Intelligence Brigade, the Japan Engineer District (U.S. Army Corps of Engineers), the 78th Signal Battalion and the Central Readiness Force and 4th Engineer Group of the Japan Ground Self-Defense Force.

100 women in the first year showed interest in infantry and a 100% training failure rate prevailed through to 1990. As of 1995, only three women had finished armored corps training, only one was employed (tank gunner) and she was asking for a transfer because she had no other women to talk to.

In both Canada and Holland there are quotas or 'pink seats' for promotions of female officers who lack combat experience – quotas resented by capable women. In Britain, more of the same, brass hats falling in love with their Royal Navy poster girl, Lt-Commander Mandy McBain, who had been nominated as a top-100 gay/lesbian influencer in the 2010 Pink List and became "widely publicised by the Royal Navy as a role model for all personnel."[67]

The Sisterhood is indifferent to studies showing that women's health can't stand combat qualifying (let alone combat itself). Marines Captain Kate Petronio, a combat engineer in Iraq and Afghanistan and, earlier, a star college athlete, has written that armed forces in the US and elsewhere have not come close to understanding the special and long-term toll on female bodies. Few or no women could endure the military milieu for long enough to reach late-career flag rank, she said.

During her ten-month Iraq deployment, Petronio began breaking down after maximum-effort, 16-hour days. For example, a march with combat kit of 60kg could easily compress a woman's weaker spine.[68]

> By the fifth month into the deployment, I had muscle atrophy in my thighs that was causing me to constantly trip and my legs to buckle with the slightest grade change. My agility during firefights and mobility on and off vehicles and perimeter walls was seriously hindering my response time and overall capability.
>
> It was evident that stress and muscular deterioration was affecting everyone regardless of gender; however, the rate of my deterioration was noticeably faster than that of male Marines and further compounded by gender-specific medical conditions.
>
> At the end of the 7-month deployment, and the construction of 18 [patrol bases] later, I had lost 17 pounds and was diagnosed with polycystic ovarian syndrome (which personally resulted in infertility, but is not a genetic trend in my family), which was brought on by the

---

67 Contrary to most people's impressions, male-on-male sexual assaults in the US forces rose sharply after Obama relaxed the "don't ask, don't tell" policy re gay troops.

68 *Marine Corps Gazette*, July 2012.

chemical and physical changes endured during deployment.

Regardless of my deteriorating physical stature, I was extremely successful during both of my combat tours, serving beside my infantry brethren and gaining the respect of every unit I supported.

Regardless, I can say with 100 percent assurance that despite my accomplishments, there is no way I could endure the physical demands of the infantrymen whom I worked beside as their combat load and constant deployment cycle would leave me facing medical separation long before the option of retirement.

I understand that everyone is affected differently; however, I am confident that should the Marine Corps attempt to fully integrate women into the infantry, we as an institution are going to experience a colossal increase in crippling and career-ending medical conditions for females.

There's a famous account by a Marine squad leader Ryan Smith of cramming with 24 other 'jarheads' in an assault vehicle for 2003's dash down the highway to Baghdad. The squad saw no combat, just that blitzkrieg trip. Read the extract and then imagine the Sisterhood having succeeded in getting the desired small (perhaps three?) band of female combat Marines into the squad. To repeat, the trip involved no fighting.[59]

We rode into war crammed in the back of amphibious assault vehicles. They are designed to hold roughly 15 Marines snugly; due to maintenance issues, by the end of the invasion we had as many as 25 men stuffed into the back. Marines were forced to sit, in full gear, on each other's laps and in contorted positions for hours on end. That was the least of our problems.

The column would not stop for even a company commander to go to the restroom. Sometimes we spent over 48 hours on the move without exiting. We were forced to urinate in empty water bottles inches from our comrades.

Many Marines developed dysentery from the complete lack of sanitary conditions. When an uncontrollable urge hit a Marine, he would be forced to stand, as best he could, hold a (Meals) bag up to his rear, and defecate inches from his seated comrade's face.

During the invasion, we wore chemical protective suits because of the fear of chemical attack. They are equivalent to a ski jumpsuit and hold in the heat. We also had to wear black rubber boots over our desert boots...

69 *Wall Street Journal,* 23 Jan 2013

Due to the heat and sweat, layers of our skin would peel off our feet. However we rarely had time to remove our suits or perform even the most basic hygiene. We quickly developed sores on our bodies.

When we did reach Baghdad, we were in shambles. We had not showered in well over a month and our protective suits were covered in a mixture of filth and dried blood. We were told to strip and place our suits in pits to be buried immediately. My unit stood there in a walled-in compound, naked, sores dotted all over our bodies, feet peeling, watching our suits burn. Later they lined us up naked and washed us off with pressure hoses...

In Israel, women troops are far more restricted against engaging in combat than under the new US and Australian guidelines. When shooting starts, IDF policy generally is to get its females out of harm's way. Retired Maj. Gen. Yiftach Ron-Tal was top commander of IDF land forces in 2006. He at first supported deploying women in direct land-combat situations, but reversed that view in 2011: "Stress fractures suffered by soldiers is dozens of percentage points higher among women than among men. As a result, the female soldiers are not required to carry as much weight.

"I cannot even imagine a female soldier serving inside a tank or in elite infantry units, mostly because of operational considerations. The army must not allow this thing to interfere with its operational ability... Expanding female service will be a grave mistake that will damage the prowess of the army."[70]

US studies in the 1990s showed that women failed most, or close to all, combat tests. In body strength, youthful female combat recruits averaged at the grade of average 50-year-old men. Women had 20% less aerobic power, 40% less muscle strength, and nearly 50% less lifting strength. They route marched 26% slower. Injuries knocked them out at twice the male rate. Their bones broke more easily. Their non-deployable rate was three times higher. Even given lower entry standards for combat readiness, most women still flunked – in one case, 63% of the female group, compared with 1% of men. More recent studies by the Marine Corps found that male-only infantry units shoot more accurately, carry greater burdens and move more quickly through some tactical maneuvers.

70 Arutz Sheva, 23 July 2011

Modern equipment can be operated with fingertip pressures, but there is never a guarantee that a woman operator won't be called upon to unexpected heavy tasks. If the loader of an M1 tank is injured, for example, a woman stand-in's capacity, as judged in the light of the Marine standards cited above, to lift and swing 20kg shells into the breach at a rate of four shells a minute must be considered dubious, the ability to change 40kg road wheels even more so.

Further, an infantryman – perhaps that should be infantryperson – is expected to close with the enemy while carrying weapon and more than 40kg of gear. Women have evolved without such power and endurance. In a unit, the women's weakness is inappropriate to the training intensity and forces a reshuffling of heavy labor roles, lowering morale and team performance, the Marines study concluded.

Nor can women necessarily be kept in the rear. A notorious example was when Iraqis in 2003 ambushed wayward trucks and captured supply clerk Private Jessica Lynch.[71]

Army traditionalists focus on the need for group cohesion and morale. A wag might wonder if the Australian Defence Forces' decision to underwrite the cost of sex-change surgeries for serving members might be a neat trick to gain the advantages of the male physique while officially lifting the number of "women", at least as recognised by military policy.[72]

Retired US Army Lt-Col Robert Maginnis's excoriates top brass for their "cowardice of silence" in kowtowing to politicians and political correctness, rather than protesting by resignation at lowering of performance standards. Such 'craven behaviour' was particularly life-threatening to the same young women the generals were agreeing to place in harm's way, Maginnis said.

As it happens, I have a friend who is a Marine in Utah and agreed to give his views.

> Opening all combat roles to women would be a logistics and expense nightmare. Women will bond with us OK on combat duty, maybe

---

71 The Pentagon then morphed this pretty and honest woman into a poster-girl for women recruitment, ignoring the black and Hispanic women who suffered equally in the incident.
72 Australian taxpayers spent $648,000 in 2012-14 for 13 sex changes and 15 breast enhancement procedures for serving members of the Australian Defence Force (ADF).

differently and with more effort perhaps. It can work great.

But why add them in anyway?. We're not short of male combat trainees. I don't like change. The machine's not broke, why try to fix it?

Marines take care of their own; people say that excessive risk would be taken to rescue a wounded woman Marine. We would take excessive risks for any comrade, white, black, male, female.

A woman in combat should be strong enough to endure the same hardships and loads. I've worked with some who could carry a 180kg comrade and kit off the field. But even the regular Marine Corps includes weaker, less bright guys who become the unit's weak links – they simply can't carry their kit up the mountain . Weak-linkers multiply with women who haven't passed the physicals; we have to take up the slack.

I've had few dealings with women Marines, mainly in admin and nursing, and they're all great professionals. But suppose at an Okinawa base there's a few who are pretty and available. I've sat one night in a bar and saw four jealousy fights over one girl – maybe she had been switching her favors. She can take her pick of 500 guys.

Practical issues swarm in. "In the field we all get filthy together and it's not such an issue," he said. "Back at base, they need their own rooms, showers and toilets with doors, two structures down through all the units."

To conform to the Obama mindset, top generals have developed a deranged focus on non-war-fighting issues.[73] Apart from elevating climate change (which stopped nearly 19 years ago) to a primary security threat to the US, generals have fast-tracked Muslims up the ranks. That turned out badly in 2009, when Major Nidal Hasan at Fort Hood in Texas, shot 13 comrades and wounded 31 others. Now awaiting execution, he had been pre-posted to Afghanistan. Earlier he was an email pal of a notorious jihadist and had even delivered an in-house presentation that included the admonition that, "Muslim Soldiers should not serve in any capacity that renders them at risk to hurting/killing believers unjustly." The Department of Defense chose not to charge him with terrorism – although it was the worst terrorist attack in the US since 9/11. The

---

73 A blogger's comment: I am a retired US Army Officer and continue to work for the Federal Govt as a DoD civilian and cannot believe the level of testicular atrophy that has occurred among the senior leadership of the US Armed services.

official description of the massacre was "workplace violence."[74]

Army Chief of Staff George Casey then announced that he was fearful of a backlash against US Muslim soldiers. He said, "Our diversity, not only in our Army, but in our country, is a strength. And as horrific as this tragedy was, if our diversity becomes a casualty, I think that's worse."[75]

That is, potential loss of "diversity" disturbed him more than his own troops being massacred by a traitorous Islamic renegade. In a sane world, Casey would have been met with horrified laughter. As it is, having dismissed out of hand all questions of Muslim loyalty, the military's social engineers and their agents in the Pentagon took up the feminist cause of reducing readiness, performance and unit capability. #

Quadrant OnLine, 16 February 2016

Neutering the Army's 'Warrior Culture'

De-gendering society inspires shrieking enthusiasm in womyn's studies classrooms, where academic notions of equality make minimal contact with the real world. In a foxhole things are different, which explains why the feminist push to "reform" the armed forces is so very worrying.

In an epochal change in late 2011, Labor's Defence Minister Stephen Smith announced that virtually all remaining military restrictions on women in combat would be lifted before 2016. Women in the Australian Defence Force (ADF) are now available to kill or be killed at the bleeding edge.

This followed the Australian Defence Force's own announcement in April, 2011, to the same effect. Those signing off on it were General David Hurley, Chief of the Defence Force; Navy chief Vice-Admiral Ray Griggs; Army chief Lt-Gen David Morrison (current Australian of the Year); Air Force chief Air Marshall Geoff Brown; and Major-General Gerard Fogarty, Head, People Capability. Hurley began the statement: "After thirty-five years in the Infantry, I know the rigours of life as an

---

74 A day after a radicalised Muslim couple shot down 14 co-workers at a health centre in San Bernardino, Calif., on December 2, President Obama said, "It is possible that this is terror-ist-related, but we don't know; it is also possible this was workplace-related."
75 Tabassum Zakaria, Reuters US, 8 November 2009.

infantryman. My decision to support the opening of combat positions in the Australian Defence Force to women comes from experience and knowledge … A robust and agile ADF relies on every member having the opportunity to contribute fully and equally to Defence operations and capability. We all share the responsibility to work towards a fair, just and inclusive ADF. After all, gender equality is the whole community's responsibility."

The statement was emphatic that standards would not be lowered for women's entry. It was accompanied by a "Risk Management Plan" of high formality but little substance (maybe the nitty-gritty details are for military-eyes only). Meanwhile, Defence got a new employee, a "permanent full-time cultural change manager to assist with implementing cultural change within Army."

Concurrently, the government tapped the Australian Human Rights Commission's Sex Discrimination Commissioner Elizabeth Broderick, a lawyer, to do annual reports on discrimination against females in Defence. As might be expected from someone of her legal background, she endorsed the brass's combat deal in a sentence of two, then swung back to hundreds of pages of public service trivia about gender pay gaps, leave and flexiwork.[76]

Broderick's thoughts on military life began with the complaint that the 86% of males in the Defence Force were evidencing excessive "masculine norms", thus neglecting their "feminine side". In an exercise that mixed reverse-sexism with pitiful sarcasm, she wrote: "Men should always 'be a winner'. Men should be 'tough' both physically and emotionally. Men should never be seen to be in any way feminine or acknowledge their 'feminine side'. They should be 'a man's man' – one of the boys."

Such male bastions weren't "the types of environments in which healthy, respectful attitudes towards women are likely to thrive" and, thus, correctives should come from the top and middle. Thus challenged by a warrior feminist, Hurley folded like a cheap card table, and rushed

---

76 To the extent that skilled members who quit cost the forces well over $600,000, she has a point that work conditions should be positive.

to begin his forces' feminisation.[77]

Broderick seems unaware that the appropriate environment for warfare training involves encouraging troops to put their lives in danger while grasping that it is their duty to kill those on the other side. This is a horrible job and not everyone is capable of doing it. To instead put soldiers – men or women – in this role to meet a political objective, or to gratify feminists, seems extremely dangerous.[78]

The Gillard era announcement caused barely a ripple at the time, and to this day the change is treated as just another nod to female equality. The politically correct class, including the Anglicans who've draped a huge "Let's welcome all refugees" sign from the spire of Melbourne's St Paul's Cathedral, seem less interested in what happens to women soldiers' minds and bodies on the literal front line. Major General Gerard Fogarty, managing the process, boasted 18 months after the announcement, "We've had very little criticism from any segment of the community."

Once, men went to war while women kept the home fires burning. What was good enough for Odysseus and Penelope is now passé, and the casualty lists are reading differently. US servicewomen who came home to their toddlers in body bags include Lori Ann Piestwa 23, mother of two pre-schoolers, Melissa J. Hobart 22, mother of a 3-year-old; Jessica L. Cawvey 22, single mother of a 6yo; Pamela Osborne 38, mother of three; and Katrina Bell-Johnson 32, mother of a one-year-old.

Part of the community silence in Australia must surely be because the physical entry standards are so high very few women have managed to pass them. Indeed, the standards were tightened, rather than loosened, concurrent with the announcement, and embodied in the new Physical

---

77 As changes drive down from the top, the lower Defence bureaucracy has become a seething mass of clerical political correctness e.g. "The Review has also been advised that the Values, Behaviour and Resolution Branch (formerly Fairness and Resolution Branch) informally considers every new piece of policy from a gender and general diversity perspective, as part of the new formal process by which all Defence Instructions are developed and periodically reviewed."

Another comment from a Broderick appendix reads that these clerks had formulated an Action Plan for diversity, including social networking and a "Young Female Leaders Network". It continued, hilariously, "Although in April 2011 progress against these tasks was reported as 'good', in November 2011, the position was that none of these tasks have been completed."

78 A search on the word "combat" in one 72-page Broderick opus turns up virtually nothing except a few anodyne sentences — brain-snaps urging women into combat.

Employment Standards (PES).[79]About 30% of women Army recruits were flunking the easier test, ten times the male flunk rate. The PES are supposed to be a health-and-safety initiative to "ensure that we don't hurt anyone", as Lieutenant-Colonel Peter Conroy put it; pity our potential enemies don't concur.

The policy for equal combat for women evolved python-like from an Australia-ratified UN Convention on the Elimination of All Forms of Discrimination Against Women (CEDAW) in 1983. Originally, we put in get-out clauses exempting women from combat, but those have been progressively abandoned. The UN General Assembly is dominated by corrupt Third World blocs whose style is actually more inclined to burka-enforcing and female genital mutilation than combating discrimination against women.[80]

The Gillard announcement came on September 27, 2011, but the nuts and bolts weren't endorsed by Cabinet until June, 2012. The doors opened to women across the board on January 1, 2013, and those changes are to be fully phased in (technically) from next year, as of June 30.

In the Army, the new categories for women include infantry, tanks, artillery, bomb disposal and combat engineers. In the Navy, women divers are welcome to tackle mines, while Air Force women serve in cockpits, control centres and as airfield guards.

Defence watchdog Australia Defence Association says any weakening of traditional infantry-type standards, and introduction of gender targets and weaponry to suit women, would be deadly, irresponsible and immoral.

But if standards were maintained pre and post-transfer, there would be no issue with psychological/emotional/social relating to women in

---

79 The old tests involved a 2.4km run plus push-ups etc, adjusted according to age and gender. The new tests have no age or gender allowances, for example soldiers must march 5km in full kit in 55 minutes, then carry two 22kg jerry cans of water for 150m as proxy for a stretchered casualty. They also have to do fire-and-movement in 12 sets of 6m rushes, and lift 25kg up 1.5m as if loading sandbags or a truck. Infantry tests are tougher still – and special forces tests, extreme.
80 The 2013 UN President John Ashe (Antigua) is currently indicted on $US1.3m bribe-related charges.

the tough squads and deployments, it said.[81] This contrasts with my reading of numerous US studies emphatically stating the opposite. For example, corrosive jealousies among males in previously well-bonded units can arise whether or not a female comrade is sexually active.

The ADA continues that women should be allowed to opt in or out of fiercely hazardous combat tasks, but confuses itself while simultaneously baffling observers by stating that males *can't* opt out. So where's the gender equality? How can field commanders plan for combat if some soldiers have a choice about whether to become involved? Imagine the resentment among male soldiers if the dirty work always falls to them.

Elizabeth Broderick speaks of modern warfare involving new technological skills "rather than simply manual or physical strength", as if any front-liner – an artillery trooper, for instance – can be quarantined from huge exertions. She wants the women-friendly squads to be hand-picked to ensure women are treated well, and there should be "no less than two women in each work section of ten or less, with the grouping of women within a category to achieve as close to a critical mass as possible."[82] More than that, she also wants to lift more women up the chain of command and achieve this goal by means of quota, not equal treatment (so far, about 5% senior officers are women and 8% of NCOs). Quotas are a common technique of the Left to get their favorites into powerful positions when they cannot get there by ability.

Broderick disparages the front-line "warrior culture" and "war-fighting mission" as barriers to accepting that women can make good combat troops. By her reckoning, less warrior culture in the Army

---

81 "Arguments commonly mounted to oppose female participation on psychological or emotion grounds are invariably incorrect factually or conceptually. Similarly, most social and cultural arguments posed against broadening female participation in combat roles have been disproven by ADF and allied experience gained in existing mixed-gender units."

82 After all her fuss about sex harassment in the forces, Broderick had to quote a survey by a female officer demonstrating that the 25%-of-women rate was the same in the forces as in the general community. As her "urgent priority" she secured installation of a top-level anti-harassment bureaucracy, "reporting directly to the Chief of the Defence Force"

would be a good thing![83] Further, the promotion of women should not require combat experience as "leadership" and "ability" are enough: "Strong ADF leaders should come from a range of ADF occupations not just the combat corps... Though indisputably important, a lack of combat experience is just one of a range of obstacles to women's career progression..."

She concedes combat experience lets 'real' (male) soldiers gain the respect and regard of their peers, in turn cementing their authority as leaders. But she countered that line of reasoning by insisting that more than 40% of Australian women veterans reported past exposure to "hostile action". That could mean anything. To get around combat-bias among promotion board members, she urges "diversity" on promotions boards (women? Indigenes? Muslims?) and even seeks to install non-military members, tasked with helping the original and befuddled board members reach her idea of correct targets for high-ranking women. Says one military critic in correspondence with the author: "I'm buggered if I'd jump out of the trench on the say-so of someone who has spent their life shuffling paper. Orders from a Patton or a Montgomery — they're different."

As to Broderick's specific suggestions, she wants the Army, Navy and Air Force to start with a model squad involving not less than two women in a unit of ten people "with clustering of women within a category to achieve as close to a critical mass as possible." In a bizarre example, she laments the lack of women mine-clearance divers, asserting that frogwomen would inspire many other women to join them. Similarly, they should be appointed to "key roles", such as army combat officers in infantry and armour. Alarmingly, she seems to labour under the misconception that "non-combat" officers include those attached to

---

83 A Canadian official report she quotes says more cautiously: "Hyper-masculinity appears to be deeply embedded in combat unit culture and plays an important if unmeasured role. Constructive change in combat units will involve more than 'tweaking' current training to strip proscribed 'masculine' manifestations and reproducing the mixed culture of support units which is unproven in sustaining close battle. Battles and wars are won by cohesion. The fact that cohesion in mixed support units has proven sufficient for supporting roles is not proof that the same culture will be adequate for those whose job is to kill and maim at close quarters. If manifestations of hyper-masculinity are simply treated as misogyny and dogmatically prohibited without persuasive explanation and this is allowed to be understood by male soldiers as emasculation of their established combat identity, the consequence may be at odds with intent: resentment, demoralisation and clandestine ostracism of women."

the artillery and engineers.[84] For someone with such sweeping plans to "reform" the military it seems passing strange that she is unaware of Coral Fire Support Base near Saigon in 1968 being partly over-run by North Vietnamese regulars. One soldier who cracked under pressure had to be handcuffed to a stake behind the gun line to keep him out of the way.[85]

The new, gender-liberated combat roles would never attract more than 4% of female recruits, Broderick theorises. She continues, "But we are doing this because, to sustain the workforce into the future, we want to access our fair share of the talent in the Australian labour market, which is increasingly female." So women are to fight and die to help the ADF improve its recruiting, and those recruits may well be slotted into roles they can't handle, endangering themselves and their comrades, male and female alike.

She has little to say about sexual shenanigans with women among testosterone-fuelled men, but quotes some conservative male officers on the topic. They told her they feared to discipline women because female underlings might retaliate with sexual harassment claims. (This is a serous issue in civilian employment as well). One officer said that when he told a woman she was no good at her job, she went up the line with complaints and left him "shit scared". "Since then," he lamented, "I won't speak to a female one-on-one." Another suggested why bonding in combat units is necessarily weak in mixed-gender units: males sleep in their own tents separate from women; men are also reluctant to relax with them in case something said is misinterpreted.

In middle ranks, as the US experience has demonstrated, the ban on sexual relations within a unit are often (if not usually) viewed as a challenge to be circumvented. In any year, 10% of US servicewomen have an accidental pregnancy, twice the national average. In the Gulf War, despite an official and total ban on sexual fraternisation, 5% of deployed servicewomen got pregnant. In Australia, policy-makers simply don't know how much sex goes on during training and operations and what disruptions to unit cohesiveness result.

Anne Summers in a piece on women soldiers in *The Monthly*

---

84 "In Army – Combat Officer roles including Infantry Officers and Armoured Officers; non-combat officers including Field Artillery Officers and Engineer Officers."
85 Personal communication with ex-Vietnam Major, 13 February 2016.

inadvertently made the case against mixed-gender military squads by noting that women are not always acculturated to tough locales, such as misogynist Arab backwaters. She cites Matina Jewell, who a decade ago was a uniformed Australian officer with UN peacekeepers in Lebanon. Summers writes, "A [Lebanese] civilian leeringly masturbated in front of her … She is critical of the lack of support she received from her superiors." Her Australian commander "confirmed to (her) that he did not believe that the incidents was significant enough to report". (A fortnight earlier she had been grabbed in daylight by two would-be rapists but kicked them off). Jewell in her book, *Caught in the Crossfire,* says the flasher was identified as a local nutter and pervert. Jewell went into distinguished retirement as a major in 2009 after war injuries and, make no mistake, is a credit to our country. Pardon me if I feel a little sympathy for her then-commander, who is still getting stick some ten years later for not having rated her complaint about the pervert as high official priority. Would a male soldier have demanded official follow-up, one wonders, if he had been propositioned by a gay harasser?

A retired military-sector chief says: 'Will full integration give us the capability to kill more enemy soldiers?' Malcolm Turnbull, Lt-General Morrison, and the Human Rights crowd would find that question offensive and disgusting. But what else are infantry for?"

Summing up, Australia's new policy of killer female soldiers has been launched but is so far having no positive effect, with significant potential for distracting the Defence Force from its primary mission of defending Australia.

The Sisterhood and its Defence acolytes and enablers will, in my view, shortly be campaigning to drop entry standards to elite jobs to make the policy work their way. You read it here first.

Quadrant OnLine, 19 February 2016

5

THE HORROR OF ABORIGINAL VIOLENCE

'Yabbered' to death" – The PR and the Reality

"Community safety in remote Aboriginal communities in the Northern Territory has improved in recent years."
— Closing the Gap: Prime Minister's Report 2013.
(No supporting data was provided, other than comments about unspecified community surveys).

Australian governments' policies towards "closing the gap" of Aboriginal disadvantage generate heaps of flowery prose. The policies' impacts on domestic violence, child abuse/neglect, and crime, are at best negligible. The violence and abuse have worsened dramatically in the past decade, after also rising significantly in the prior 20 years.

The absurdities of official policies are suggested by South Australian government spending of $360,000 on 30 motorbikes for youths in the remote South Australian desert (the bikes stayed unused in storage). At $12,000 apiece, each bike was only a tad less expensive than a Harley-Davidson XL883L SuperLow, at $14,000. SA bureaucrats also bought for the remote locals five heavy-duty microwaves and six washing machines ($10,000 each); and four baby-change tables imported from the US at $2400 apiece.[86]

These are the same Ngaanyatjarra Pitjantjajara Yankunytjatjara (APY) lands where Australian Crime Commission figures show women are 67 times more likely than Australian norms to be the victim of domestic homicide, largely from bashings. In a population of 6000, 14 women

---

were killed by partners from 2000-08, including six in 2006-08.[87]

Meanwhile, deep discussions about Reconciliations, constitutional recognitions, treaties, social justice, disadvantage and 'negative social indicators' continue, a type of national conversation that Peter Sutton dismisses as "yabber". Professor Sutton is a linguist and anthropologist with a lifetime's work for Aboriginal progress. He writes, "Such [bureaucratic] language…moves in a territory somewhere between euphemism, banality and propaganda. A murdered mother is not 'disadvantaged' – she has lost her life."[88]

Reconciliation, he says, has now "attracted the hideous Orwellian language of management-speak. In glossy-brochure land, in a galaxy far, far away, we were to read about governance, capacity building, partnerships, whole of government, benchmarks, stakeholders, leadership, targets, measureable outcomes, role models – and so it goes…It is the language of managerialist welfarism. But if you believe the media releases, it's the *Breakfast of Champions*. And where is our Kurt Vonnegut when we need him?"

To pad out these official narratives, bureaucrats now insert colorful "Case Studies", each involving an individual Aborigine who has become a success story thanks to Program XYZ. Of course, there is never a case study involving failures. Suggested case studies of failure:

- In Alice Springs, there is quite a gap to be closed, with Aboriginal women there 80 times more likely to be hospitalised after assault than women living anywhere else.[89]
- There is so much persistent ear disease in the communities that 40% (urban) and 70% (remote) Aborigines have hearing loss and difficulties.[90]
- More than a third of the Indigenous children under 14 are in over-crowded housing. In remote communities, more than half the children live over-crowded.[91] About a third of the housing is also deficient in washing, sanitation and food storage and cooking facilities. Even where new building and repair programs were active in the NT,

87 Stephanie Jarrett, *Liberating Aboriginal People from Violence*. Connor Court, Ballarat, 2013, p. 9.
88 Peter Sutton, *The Politics of Suffering*. Melbourne University Publishing, 2011 p. 76.
89 *Sydney Morning Herald*, 20 November 2012
90 http://nrha.ruralhealth.org.au/conferences/docs/papers/6_E_3_1.pdf
91 *Doing Time – Time for Doing: Indigenous youth in the criminal justice system*. House of Representatives Standing Committee on Aboriginal and Torres Strait Islander Affairs, June 2011 p. 18.

housing occupancy would fall on average only from "the high to the early-teens" – presumably from about 18 to 13 people per house.[92]

- The rate of abuse and neglect confirmations nationally for Indigenous children under 17 years has risen from 2.2% of the Indigenous child population in 2002-03 to 4.2% in 2011-12. Protection orders similarly have risen from 2.3% to 5.5%.

- In the NT in the decade to 2010, child removals grew from 175 to 555, a 215% increase, including a 40% increase in 2008-10.[93] Worse, removals are forecast to escalate while availability of Aboriginal carers diminishes.[94]

The normally level-headed Productivity Commission cites one bizarre finding that, despite appalling living conditions in remote communities, the settlements "also possessed protective factors that can safeguard children and families from psychological distress, such as spirituality and connection to land, family and culture."[95]

Bureaucrats and politicians are prone to one-day flying visits to remote settlements. Peter Sutton describes how Aborigines smirk at these people 'tippin' elbow' (checking their watches) "as the afternoon of their brief transit in the tropics wears on."

Sutton says the worst forms of violence are often ignored as too awful to tackle, and staff themselves may be threatened and assaulted, or just suffer burn-out. He concluded, "In the 2000s the statistics are now proving one vital point above all others: approaches to dealing with community violence in the recent past have been a hopeless failure."

Sutton quotes anthropologist and author Inga Clendinnen, in a rather odd comment, complaining, "From the 1970s on, a relative silence promoted and policed by the Left and by a number of Indigenous activists created a vacuum in public discussion on these (violence) issues that in the 1990s began to be filled by those pursuing ideologically conservative agendas".

Examples of 'burying' the violence problem are common. In the mid-1990s, when half of Indigenous children were said to be victims of family violence or abuse, the Aboriginal & Torres Strait Island

92 *Promoting the Safety and Wellbeing of the Northern Territory's Children.* Report of the Board of Inquiry into the Child Protection System in the Northern Territory 2010. p. 113.
93 Ibid., p. 38
94 Ibid., p. 40
95 http://www.pc.gov.au/__data/assets/pdf_file/0018/111609/key-indicators-2011-report.pdf 8.4

Commission (ATSIC) was spending only $1.3m out of its billion-dollar budget on programs to curb domestic violence – and even that small amount had to be clawed out of its multi-million-dollar travel and information budgets.[96]

The 1997 Bringing Them Home report of Ronald Wilson is 700 pages. Of those pages, only one page discusses family violence as a cause of child removals. (Incidentally, the NT Families & Children division has been arbitrarily putting Aboriginal children in and out of care, "with very little notice or appreciation of the devastating impacts of such decisions on both the children, the carers, and the natural children of carers."[97] So much for Kevin Rudd's apology of 2008: "The injustices of the past must never, never happen again".

Only two years after Bringing Them Home, the 1999 Queensland Aboriginal & Torres Strait Islander Women's Task Force on Violence Report, headed by Professor Boni Robertson, was writing:

"Violence is now overt: murders, bashings and rapes, including sexual violence against children, have reached epidemic proportions with both Indigenous and non-Indigenous being perpetrators." The atmosphere in Aboriginal communities was described as one of "continuing fear from which there is no escape…Sexual abuse is an inadequate term for the incidence of horrific sexual offences committed against young girls and boys in a number of Community locations in Queensland over the last few years.[98]

Failure of passive welfarism was predicted by the distinguished anthropologist Professor William Stanner as early as 1968: "Possibly the most dangerous theory, though it is scarcely that, is that things are now going well, that all we need to do is more of what we are already doing, that is, deepen and widen the welfare programs, and the rest will come at a natural pace in its own good time."[99]

Two decades later anthropologist Colin Tatz was writing of "an abysmal absence of historical perspective in Aboriginal affairs, resulting

---

96 Louis Nowra, *Bad Dreaming*. Pluto Press, North Melbourne, p70
97 *Promoting the Safety*. Op. cit., p42
98 Hannah McGlade, *Our Greatest Challenge: Aboriginal children and human rights*. Aboriginal Studies Press, Canberra, 2012. p125-6
99 Peter Sutton, op. cit., p42

in a policy and administration myopia that is staggering in its implications and results. No one learns from the past, no one listens, no one learns, and hardly anyone stays around long enough to osmose anything. Everyone re-discovers the wheel."

Anthropologist Professor Paul Memmott examined 130 remedial violence programs in communities in the 1990s. Only six had ever been formally evaluated. "There was, in fact, a total absence of discussion of program failure in the literature on the programs…"

Remarkably, the same criticisms were made again in June 2011, this time by the House of Representatives standing committee inquiry into Aboriginal over-representation in the justice system.[100]

The committee quoted a Menzies School of Health Research report that interventions continue to be short-term, sporadic, un-rigorous, lacking in corporate memory and hence unable to learn from past successes and failures. Each new failure feeds into the downward spiral of powerlessness and cynicism among providers and clients, the School said.

The committee said continuing government inability to identify what works and why, leads to wasted public money and bad relations between government and non-government providers, as well as with Aborigines. "The Committee insists that Australians cannot wait another twenty years to address this national crisis and urges that the Committee's recommendations are responded to within six months from the tabling of this report," it said.

Fat chance. Nearly 24 months have elapsed with no serious response from the Gillard team. The intergenerational effects of the unsafe, violent communities may well be generating new crises in 2033. As just one example, numbers of Aboriginal children in out-of-home care through abuse and neglect at home, are skyrocketing. And there is a very high correlation between out of home care and later entry into the criminal justice system.

A further factor suggesting the problems are going to spiral, is the high annual population growth of around 2% in remote communities. By 2050, Arnhem Land could have more than 34,000 people and now-

---

100 *Doing Time – Time for Doing. Indigenous youth in the criminal justice system.* House of Representatives Standing Committee on Aboriginal and Torres Strait Islander Affairs.

small communities like Yarrabah, Qld, 6000.[101] This natural increase will be augmented nationally by the compounding increase in Aboriginal self-identifiers. (Between 2006-11, 90,000 more people identified as Aboriginal).

There are testable targets in Closing the Gap for half a dozen indicators – some important, like early-childhood mortality, and others flakey, such as enrolment in pre-school facilities (whether attended or not – NT Aboriginal children in 2010 comprised 43.3% of the child population, but represented only 10% of children attending early child care services).

But despite all the recommendations, there are no Closing the Gap targets for reduction of the horrific violence against women, or the vast over-representation of Aboriginals in the criminal justice system. Rates of young Aborigines' incarcerations are now worse than during the 1991 "Deaths in Custody" hearings, despite huge increases in miscellaneous program funding and bureaucratic resources.

 From 2000-10, the rate of Indigenes in prison rose 51% to nearly one in 50 (1891 per 100,000), while rates for non-Indigenes remained steady. In WA the per capita rate rocketed to about one in 25 in custody, about 24 times the rate for non-Indigenes.

From 2000-10, Indigenous males in custody rose 55% and females, 47%. They now comprise a quarter of Australian prisoners.

In 2008, over 40% of all Indigenous men in Australia reported having been charged formally with an offence by police before they reached the age of 25.

Young Aborigines are about 60% of all youths in detention, and their rate of detention is 28 times higher than for non-Indigenous juveniles. About 22% of the young Aboriginals in detention are 14 or under.

A hidden but crucial issue in "Closing the Gap" is the rate of foetal alcohol spectrum disorder (FASD) among young Aborigines. It is caused by excessive drinking by pregnant women. (Some women get to blood-alcohol readings of 0.4%). The children often suffer life-long brain damage and frequently get into conflicts with police.

Recent findings from Fitzroy Valley community in WA (pop. 4500, 80% Indigenous) involved a sample of 127 children. Half have FASD.

---

101 Peter Sutton, op. cit., p.75

The Fitzroy data is a wake-up call, given Indigenous FASD has normally been estimated at a mere 3-5 babies per 1000 births, or 0.05%.[102]

Dr Sharman Stone (Murray, Liberal Party), chairwoman of Parliamentarians for the Prevention of FASD, suspects Australian Indigenous communities have the world's highest rates of FASD. For comparison, in Western Cape province in South Africa, FASD rates are 68-89 children per 1000, i.e. under 10%. Those rates have been viewed as high-end.

June Oscar, Chief Executive Officer, Marninwarntikura Women's Resource Centre, who is helping the Fitzroy study, says: "This is the biggest issue facing the nation and I cannot understand why Australia has been so slow to recognise it as a major public health issue as it is in Canada and the United States."

The needs of the FASD children alone are sufficient to swamp available health services. Follow-up treatments needed at Fitzroy Valley include occupational therapy, 53 % of children; speech pathology, 53%; psychology, 50%; physiotherapy, 31%; optometry, 10 %; and dietician, 4%.

Sharman Stone says, "[The disorder] is filling jails with young kids who break the law. It is a drain on the health system and to police, and is linked to high incidence of youth suicide and chronic unemployment." FASD is even promoting 'cultural genocide' as youngsters become incapable of learning their traditions, she says.

The federal government is providing about $7m for FASD work. This compares with $10m gifted towards a campaign by Reconciliation Australia to promote constitutional recognitions, and $63m over four years for the new Indigenous TV channel.

One scourge in remote communities is simply parental neglect. In the NT, the bulk of child removal cases involve parental failure to provide food, shelter, clothing, supervision, hygiene or medical attention. Drugs and gambling distract parents from supervising children, and introduce many strangers into homes. Environments where there is substance abuse and where gambling is prevalent will also impact on parental vigilance and the supervision of children, and can involve entry of strangers in the home, propagating vice to children.

As a much lesser health issue, a third of Aboriginal adults are obese,

102 http://pubs.niaaa.nih.gov/publications/arh341/121-132.pdf

compared with a sixth among non-Aboriginals. Aborigines are also smokers at two and a half times the rate of non-Aborigines.

How "Closing the Gap" can succeed in the face of such data, is a problem. It's difficult even to get Health departments to cooperate with Justice departments on offenders with FASD.

Many children are growing up without their family. From 2007 to 2012, Aboriginals in out-of-home care increased from 36.3 to 55.1 per 100,000 Aboriginal children, whereas non-Aboriginal care cases rose only slightly.

One study found children in care were 68 times more like to face a court than other children. Nearly half the Indigenous adults in NSW prisons in 2009 had been in care. Moreover, high numbers of inmates said a parent had been in care.

In New South Wales, 9.1% of sexual assault victims under the age of 18 years were Indigenous, and 12.6% of under-18 victims of domestic violence were Indigenous.

Victims of child abuse and adult violence also tend to move on to prisons. About 70% of Indigenous women in NSW gaols said they had suffered sexual abuse as children, 44% had been sexually assaulted as adults, and nearly 80% had been violence victims as adults. Virtually all those sexually assaulted as children now had a drug problem.[103]

The Representatives' committee concluded by noting that each young Aboriginal now winding up in the justice system, is likely to re-offend and create fractured families with absent kin. (A little-recognised fact is that, for the past five years, Aboriginal deaths in custody have run at only half the rate of non-Aboriginal deaths).[104]

So what is being done about these community-safety and prison issues?

There was a Council of Australian Governments (COAG) round table on community safety in 2009. Ministers agreed that unless communities could be made safe, the other big Closing the Gap targets in health, education and housing would be unattainable. Understandable, given that Aboriginal women are about 35 times more likely to be hospitalised for domestic assault than non-Aboriginal women.

---

103 *Doing Time. Op. cit.,* p. 46
104 Productivity 8a.16. Op. cit.

Through 2011-12, Aboriginal groups were lobbying COAG for targets on safe communities. As the National Congress of First Peoples complained:

> As at June 2012, discussions between the Commonwealth, State and Territory Governments were at a preliminary stage. It is not clear what the timeframe will be for finalisation of the [community safety] Strategy, whether Aboriginal and Torres Strait Islander organisations will be consulted, or what might be included in the Strategy. There now appears to be no commitment from the Commonwealth Government to a National Partnership Agreement...

But at the December 7, 2012 COAG meeting, such targets didn't even make the agenda for discussion. Fast-forward to the latest COAG meeting on April 19, 2013. It found time to consult and issue communiqués on purchasing locally-made cars and sorting out the States on the Royal Succession, but Safe Communities for Aboriginal Women and Children again failed to get a mention.

Hence there is still no agreed national funding strategy for the community safety issue, despite previous pledges by the Gillard government to negotiate such a strategy. There is only the 2012 Federal "Stronger Futures" deal with the NT involving $620m over ten years. But there are plenty of National Partnership Agreements (with funding commitments) on other topics, including health, housing, early childhood development, and even "Remote Indigenous Public Internet Access".

Here's a glimpse of how things subside in the bureaucracy:

Several years ago, the Federal Attorney-General's Department, according to First Assistant Secretary Katherine Jones, was supposedly working with state counterparts on closing-the-gap justice targets, for approval in mid-2010. As the House of Representatives committee put it in June 2011:

> At the time of tabling this report, the Attorney-General's Department informed the Committee that no further developments have been made on Indigenous justice targets.

This committee then urged that the Commonwealth develop a National Partnership Agreement for Safe Communities and present it to the Council of Australian Governments by December 2011. It is now mid-2013. Action: nil.

Katherine Jones hinted at one aspect of the inertia: not only do the Commonwealth and the States pass the buck rather than cooperate, but within the States there is buckpassing and territorialism among agencies for corrections, police and justice.

Individual workers on Aboriginal programs may be champions, but as a WA Magistrate complained, "Then very soon they are shifted to some other location and all of their good work is lost."

Katherine Jones at the time was running the AG's Social Inclusion Division. Her portfolio ranged from human rights (whatever they are) to wild rivers and distinctions between traditional owners and native title holders. She has since moved sideways to work on combating international crime. A certain Kym Duggan now runs the "Social Inclusion Division" with its forlorn heritage on national cooperation for safe Aboriginal communities.

In February, 2013, Prime Minister Gillard reported that her government is working towards 'an overarching policy framework' on community safety, 'with a view to developing advice to COAG…later in 2013'. Naturally, 'significant progress continues to be made'. I'm sure Peter Sutton would put all that in his 'yabber' category.

Par for the course in government agencies is duplications, gaps, role confusions, and funding by multiple agencies for the same thing in the same place, rather than complementary activity. Planning goes uncoordinated and with unrealistic time frames, such as rushed building of inappropriate housing. Agencies refuse to share their data, putting alleged privacy considerations ahead of client welfare. Huge staff turnovers and inadequate training arise from impossible case-loads, leaving agencies with chronically unfilled positions and poor supervision and morale. Talented staff are ruthlessly headhunted from existing jobs.

One example of gaps in service is the Larrakia Nation Aboriginal Corporation Night Patrol in Darwin, described in the 2011 report. The people manning it were volunteers with no legal power, but they operated seven nights a week and picked up about 150 people per night, mainly drunks and unsupervised children. The patrol was funded by the NT Department of Justice. But there was only one 32-bed sobering up shelter in Darwin, and only two re-hab clinics, each with long waiting lists. The service needed also to operate in daytime, but has great difficulty winning funding tenders from governments. It has limped along but last year the NT mini-budget cut its funding and it was facing closure this June. In April it was rescued with some federal funding.

There are many similar small Aboriginal groups in youth justice work, which are unable to negotiate the government funding labyrinth, against competition from professional white groups.

Peter Sutton's blueprint for improvement is for governments to scrap the plethora of racial-identity-based programs and simply focus resources on where needs exist: "Aboriginality itself, of course, would not be removed, any more than Jewishness or Greek ethnicity are negated by their absence from the state apparatus."

He says many, if not most, of the Indigenous elite live in middle-class suburbs, marry non-Indigenes, and enjoy a professional lifestyle. Their common factor is not race or culture but descent from an Aboriginal ancestor, no matter how remotely.

Given the high out-marriage rate with non-Indigenous people (71.4% in 2006), "it will not be too many more generations before most Australians share some Indigenous ancestry. That might defuse the issue if it is still with us. Or will the racial wall be downed by then?"

His priority areas would be early childhood socialisation, health and education; communities safe from endemic violence; primary and preventative health care; encouraging job and social mobility between settlements and mainstream Australia; ending of heavy funding of non-viable communities; and seeking reconciliation as a personal matter rather than a collective and bureaucratic one.

Quadrant OnLine, 6 May 2013

The long history of Aboriginal violence

It is not polite to say that pre-contact Aboriginal society was abusive to women and generally violent. This would undercut the long-standing official view that current violence in Aboriginal communities reflects colonial dispossession and on-going victimhood.

For example, a 2010 fact sheet from the federal government's Closing the Gap Clearing House says that, as is typical for Indigenous populations elsewhere, Aboriginal disadvantage "is a consequence of the historical and *continuing* impact of colonialism and dispossession, which has left many (Aboriginals) impoverished, marginalised, discriminated against, in a state of poor physical and mental health, and with inequitable access to necessary public and private services."

Aboriginal lawyer Dr Hannah McGlade in "Our Greatest Challenge" similarly blames colonialism: "The linking of Aboriginal culture to family violence and child sexual assault diminishes the grave harm inflicted on Aboriginal people through colonialism…the way in which colonisation systematically deprived Aboriginal people of basic human rights."[105]

But feminist author Stephanie Jarrett, in her introduction to "Liberating Aboriginal People from Violence, says, "It is important to acknowledge [the] link between today's Aboriginal violence and violent, pre-contact tradition, because until policymakers are honest in their assessment of the causes, Aboriginal people can never be liberated from violence…Deep cultural change is necessary, away from traditional norms and practices of violence."[106]

Bess Nungarrayi Price, in her foreword to Jarrett's book, says, "My own body is scarred by domestic violence…We Aboriginal people have to acknowledge the truth. We can't blame all of our problems on the white man…This is our problem that we can fix ourselves …

"The Racial Discrimination Act was there to protect us from white racism and we needed that protection. But it has not protected our people from ourselves. We need an act, we need laws that recognise that the problem now is blackfellas killing blackfellas and killing themselves."

Jarrett says that misogynist violence and child abuse in Aboriginal communities are at "catastrophic" levels. At the same time, Aboriginal culture must not be criticised, as though the violence sits outside the culture. Liberal democracies should welcome diversity, but not customs that violate human rights, she says.

Dave Price, non-Aboriginal husband of Bess Price, was shocked by elders' open comments in 2009 that their women could and should be executed for sacrileges. The comments came after a policewoman drove onto men's ceremonial grounds while young men were being initiated at

---

105 Hannah McGlade, *Our Greatest Challenge: Aboriginal children and Human Rights*. Aboriginal Studies Press, Canberra, 2012. p56

106 Stephanie Jarrett, *Liberating Aboriginal People from Violence*. Connor Court, Ballarat, 2013, p.1.

Lajamanu in the remote NT. Lindsay Bookie, chairman of the Central Land Council, told ABC TV news:

"It's against our law for people like that breaking the law, they shouldn't be there. Aboriginal ladies, they're not allowed to go anywhere near that. If they had been caught, a woman, aboriginal lady got caught she [would] be killed. Simple as that."

Dave Price said Bookie had, for once, openly expressed what all involved with the traditions know but keep silent about. "Both men and women are threatened with execution and grievous bodily harm for offences against the Law. Rape was added to possible punishments in the case of women…This is a fact of life. Lindsay didn't invent this Law, it is unchanging, it comes from the Jukurrpa, the Dreaming.

"It wasn't Lindsay's statement that disturbed me so much. It was the deafening silence of the human rights activists, the opponents of capital punishment, of the feminists and domestic violence activists, of that army of righteous whitefellas inflamed by any public expression of what they deem to be racism or sexism that happens to pop up in the public domain … So I can only assume that threatening to execute women is OK in Australia as long as it is done by someone who is male and indigenous, it is done for cultural reasons, and the women threatened are also indigenous. It's OK. It's their culture. They know the rules. They have to cop it sweet."[107]

Some male Aboriginal groups have acknowledged their culpability. In 2008 there was an apology from nearly 400 men from the Central Australian Aboriginal Congress (CAAC):

"We acknowledge and say sorry for the hurt, pain and suffering caused by Aboriginal males to our wives, to our children, to our mothers, to our grandmothers, to our granddaughters, to our aunties, to our nieces and to our sisters."

However, Jarrett says there is also willful blindness to traditional causes of violence, focusing instead on blaming whites. Such a rationale allows men to retain core privileges of law, gender hierarchy and kinship obligations.

Jarrett spends more than 30 pages critiquing the 2002 National Aboriginal & Torres Strait Island Social Survey (NATSISS) of 9,359

---

107 Ibid., p292

Indigenes. This survey was the basis of influential work by Lucy Snowball and Don Weatherburn, purportedly showing that current violence is not an outcome of traditional culture but rather reflects poor living conditions and substance abuse. The researchers concluded:

"Our findings provide strong support for lifestyle/routine activity theory, moderate support for social deprivation and social disorganisation theories, but little or no support for cultural theories of violence."

Their multivariate analysis did not find violence strongly correlated with traditional homelands, Aboriginal-language speakers, and remote communities.

These findings have involved on-going academic debate, both over the original survey validity and the researchers' methodology. Jarrett for example, notes that the most violent households are too dangerous for survey-takers to approach. In many other vengeful households, only a foolhardy woman would admit to having suffered violence. Jarrett says household violence is catastrophically worse in the remote communities, compared with Aborigines in mainstream locations, and this fact destroys the rationale for encouraging "traditional lifestyle in self-determined communities". The political problem, she says, "is blunting critical scrutiny of Aboriginal violence statistics even at the highest echelons of data analysis and report-writing. This is a national travesty."

Author Louis Nowra complains that sometimes a whole community will protect a vicious abuser. In November, 2006, Judge Michael Finnane, in sentencing the Aboriginal rapist Phillip Boney to 23 years jail, criticised the Moree Aboriginal community, which refused to help police find the rapist after his first attacks. By protecting him, the community allowed Boney to rape again. Within the space of one month, he kidnapped the woman on three occasions, assaulted her and raped her five times.[108]

Indigenous communities, Nowra says, have to recognise they are part of Australian society and grasp the idea of personal and individual responsibility for their actions. Romanticising remote life is dangerous. There have been instances of white women or urban Aborigines moving into relationships in remote communities. After getting their first or subsequent "proper good hiding" they are lucky to escape.

Violence levels are evidenced for thousands of years into pre-history.

108 Louis Nowra, *Bad Dreaming*. Pluto Press, North Melbourne, p72

Paleopathologist Stephen Webb in 1995 published his analysis of 4500 individuals' bones from mainland Australia going back 50,000 years. (Priceless bone collections at the time were being officially handed over to Aboriginal communities for re-burial, which stopped follow-up studies).[109] Webb found highly disproportionate rates of injuries and fractures to women's skulls, with the injuries suggesting deliberate attack and often attacks from behind, perhaps in domestic squabbles. In the tropics, for example, female head-injury frequency was about 20-33%, versus 6.5-26% for males.

The most extreme results were on the south coast, from Swanport and Adelaide, with female cranial trauma rates as high as 40-44% — two to four times the rate of male cranial trauma. In desert and south coast areas, 5-6% of female skulls had three separate head injuries, and 11-12% had two injuries.

Webb could not rule out women-on-women attacks but thought them less probable. The high rate of injuries to female heads was the reverse of results from studies of other peoples. His findings, according to anthropologist Peter Sutton, confirm that serious armed assaults were common in Australia over thousands of years prior to conquest.

From 1788, British and French arrivals were shocked at local misogyny. First Fleeter Watkin Tench noticed a young woman's head "covered by contusions, and mangled by scars". She also had a spear wound above the left knee caused by a man who dragged her from her home to rape her. Tench wrote, "They are in all respects treated with savage barbarity; condemned not only to carry the children, but all other burthens, they meet in return for submission only with blows, kicks and every other mark of brutality."[110]

He also wrote, "When an Indian [sic] is provoked by a woman, he either spears her, or knocks her down on the spot; on this occasion he always strikes on the head, using indiscriminately a hatchet, a club, or any other weapon, which may chance to be in his hand."

Marine Lt. William Collins wrote, "We have seen some of these unfortunate beings with more scars upon their shorn heads, cut in every

---

109 Stephen Webb, *Palaeopathology of Aboriginal Australians.* Cambridge University Press, Cambridge, 1995. p2
110 Nowra, op. cit., p10

direction, than could be well distinguished or counted."

Governor Phillip's confidant, Bennelong, in 1790 had taken a woman to Port Jackson to kill her because her relatives were his enemies. He gave her two severe wounds on the head and one on the shoulder, saying this was his rightful vengeance.

Phillip was appalled that an Eora woman within a few days of delivery had fresh wounds on her head, where her husband had beaten her with wood.

In 1802 an explorer in the Blue Mountains wrote how, for a trivial reason, an Aboriginal called Gogy "took his club and struck his wife's head such a blow that she fell to the ground unconscious. After dinner... he got infuriated and again struck his wife on the head with his club, and left her on the ground nearly dying."

In 1825 French explorer Louis-Antoine de Bougainville wrote "that young girls are brutally kidnapped from their families, violently dragged to isolated spots and are ravished after being subjected to a good deal of cruelty."[111] George Robinson in Tasmania said in the 1830s that men courted their women by stabbing them with sharp sticks and cutting them with knives prior to rape. The men bartered their women to brutal sealers for dogs and food; in one case such a woman voluntarily went back to the sealers rather than face further tribal violence.[112]

Also in the 1830s ex-convict Lingard wrote: "I scarcely ever saw a married woman, but she had got six or seven cuts in her head, given by her husband with a tomahawk, several inches in length and very deep."[113] Explorer Edward John Eyre, who was very sympathetic towards Aborigines, nevertheless recorded:

> Women are often sadly ill-treated by their husbands and friends... they are frequently beaten about the head, with waddies, in the most dreadful manner, or speared in the limbs for the most trivial offences...
>
> Few women will be found, upon examination, to be free from frightful scars upon the head, or the marks of spear wounds about the body. I have seen a young woman, who, from the number of these

---

111 Joan Kimm, *A Fatal Conjunction: Two Laws Two Cultures.* Sydney, Federation Press, 2004. p76,
112 Op. cit., Nowra p12
113 Op. cit., Kimm p46

marks, appeared to have been almost riddled with spear wounds.[114]

Tribal warfare and paybacks were endemic. In "Journey to Horseshoe Bend", anthropologist T.G.H. Strehlow described a black-on-black massacre in 1875 in the Finke River area of Central Australia, triggered by a perceived sacrilege:

"The warriors turned their murderous attention to the women and older children and either clubbed or speared them to death. Finally, according to the grim custom of warriors and avengers they broke the limbs of the infants, leaving them to die 'natural deaths'. The final number of the dead could well have reached the high figure of 80 to 100 men, women and children."[115]

Revenge killings by the victims' clan involved more than 60 people, with the two exchanges accounting for about 20% of members of the two clans. (When Pauline Hanson, then member for Oxley, quoted this account in 1996, an Aboriginal woman elder replied, "Mrs Hanson should receive a traditional Urgarapul punishment: having her hands and feet crippled.")

Escaped convict William Buckley, who lived for three decades with tribes around Port Phillip, recounted constant raids, ambushes, and small battles, typically involving one to three fatalities. He noted the Watouronga of Geelong in night raids 'destroyed without mercy men, women and children.'[116]

Historian Geoff Blainey concluded that annual death rates from North-East Arnhem Land and Port Philip, were comparable with countries involved in the two world wars, although Blainey's estimate could be somewhat on the high side.[117]

Other black-on-black massacres include accounts from anthropologist Bill Stanner of an entire camp massacre, an Aurukun massacre in the early 20th century, Strehlow's account of the wiping out of the Plenty River local group of Udebatara in Central Australia, and the killing of a large group of men, women and children near Mt Eba, also in Central Australia.

114 Op. cit., Jarrett p123
115 http://tghstrehlow.wordpress.com/1922/10/11/wednesday-the-eleventh-day-of-october-1922/
116 John Morgan, *The Life and Adventures of William Buckley*. Canberra: Australian National University Press, 1980 (1852), p. 189.
117 Op. cit., Sutton p91-92

Strehlow's wife Kathleen Strehlow wrote:

> It would be no exaggeration to say that the system worked as one of
> sheer terror in the days before the white man came. This terror was
> instilled from earliest childhood and continued unabated through life
> until the extremity of old age seemed to guarantee some immunity
> from the attentions of blood avenger or sorcerer alike for wrongs real
> or imaginary…children were not exempted from capital punishment
> for persistent offences against the old tribal code.

The Murngin (now Yolngu) in NE Arnhem Land during 1920s
practiced a deadly warfare that placed it among the world's most lethal
societies. The then rate for homicides of 330 per 100,000 (which Jarrett
suggests could be grossly under-estimated) was 15 times the 2006-
07 "very remote national Indigenous rate" of 22, and 300 times the
2006-07 national non-Indigenous rate. That Murngin rate was worse
than in Mexico's present Ciudad Juarez drug capital (300 homicides
per 100,000), and more than three times worse than the worst national
current rate (Honduras).

Jarrett says that surely no aspect of Murngin culture, such as
polygamy, was worth the lives of the many young men sacrificed in war
to maintain it.

Yolngu punishments are deemed valid for wives if they leave scars
but do not kill. In one 2008 case, a husband stabbed his wife multiple
times with a steak knife, which was within traditional bounds. The
husband got a short sentence and this minor punishment was quashed
by Southwood J.

Jarrett wrote: "Even if Australian governments on grounds of harm
minimisation allow traditional physical punishment, there are some
settings – wrong or disputed accusations, a person's refusal to submit
to traditional punishment, and traditional punishment for non-crimes –
where such appeasement is either unworkable or particularly immoral."

Mass violence today can involve large numbers of Yolngu, with a
300-person riot in 2008 and another of 400 people on Elcho Island. At
Galiwinku Council Offices in late 2010, 500 people were involved.

Quadrant OnLine, 7 May 2013

A blacked-out past: the lot of Indigenous females

One hears much of Aboriginal suffering from those who would pin the blame on "invaders". Politically expedient as those excuses may be, they omit a richly documented record of appalling sexual violence and mutilation.

Warfare was only one aspect of death-dealing traditions in pre-contact Aboriginal society. Death could result, for example, from accidentally witnessing ceremonies, or performing them incorrectly. According to T.G.H. Strehlow, "it was this readiness to kill persons who had committed sacrilege either knowingly or unwittingly that caused a great revulsion against Aboriginal religion in Central Australia after the arrival of the white population."[118]

Violence against girls and women is reflected in many accounts in the past century. Noted anthropologist Bronislaw Malinowski surveyed the literature for his 1913 book on the family in Aboriginal society: The husband "had a nearly unlimited authority, and in some cases, when he had special reasons (and undoubtedly deemed himself to be within his rights), he might use his authority for a very brutal and severe chastisement."[119]

Solicitor/historian Joan Kimm wrote: "The sexual use of young girls by older men, indeed often much older men, was an intrinsic part of Aboriginal culture, a heritage that cannot easily be denied."[120]

Playwright and author Louis Nowra concurs: "Despite local variations, there is a consistent pattern of Aboriginal men's treatment of women that was harsh, sexually aggressive (gang-rape for instance) and, in our term, misogynist. Given its pervasive nature across the whole of Australia, we can say that it was ancient and long-lasting."[121]

Nowra quotes Walter Roth (1861-1933) a doctor, anthropologist and Chief Protector of Aborigines in Queensland. Roth described at the turn of the 20th century how, when a Pitta-Pitta girl first showed signs of puberty, "several men would drag her into the bush and forcibly

118 Stephanie Jarrett, *Liberating Aboriginal People from Violence*. Connor Court, Ballarat, 2013, p. 107.
119 Peter Sutton, *The Politics of Suffering*. Melbourne University Publishing, Carlton 2011, p99
120 Joan Kimm, *A Fatal Conjunction*. Federation Press, Leichardt, 2004, p. 64.
121 Louis Nowra, *Bad Dreaming*. Pluto Press, N Melbourne, 2007, p. 24.

enlarge the vaginal orifice by tearing it downwards with the first three fingers wound round and round with opossum string. Other men come forward from all directions, and the struggling victim has to submit in rotation to promiscuous coition with all the 'bucks' present."

Even worse was his description of practices around Glenormiston:

"A group of men, with cooperation from old women, ambush a young woman, and pin her so an old man can slit up the shrieking girl's perineum with a stone knife, followed by sweeping three fingers round the inside of the virginal orifice. She is next compelled to undergo copulation with all the bucks present; again the same night, and a third time, on the following morning."

In Birdsville, a hardwood stick two feet long with a crude life-sized penis carving at the top, was used to tear the hymen and posterior vaginal wall.

"In the Tully area, a very young man would give his betrothed to an old man to sleep with her and train her for him. The idea was that the elder would 'make the little child's genitalia develop all the more speedily'. There was no restriction on age or social status at which the bride would be delivered up. As Roth observed, 'It is of no uncommon occurrence to see an individual carrying on his shoulder his little child-wife who is perhaps too tired to toddle any further."

Accounts from the missionary era are daunting.

In 1905 the local telegraph operator at Fitzroy River reported that a five-year-old half-caste girl, Polly "was out with the old woman, Mary Ann, when a bush black took her away for two nights during which time the blacks here said he made use of her. Such actions as that of Polly and the men are very common among the natives."[122]

Anglican lay missionary Mary Bennett in 1934 testified, "The practice to which I refer is that of intercision of the girls at the age of puberty. The vagina is cut with glass by the old men, and that involves a great deal of suffering…I remember my old Aboriginal nurse speak with horror of the suffering which she had been made to undergo."

A practice as bad as female genital mutilation is still inflicted on hundreds of boys annually – involuntary sub-incision, the slitting open

---

122 Keith Windschuttle, *The Fabrication of Aboriginal History: The Stolen Generations.* Macleay Press, Sydney, 2009, p. 443.

of the male urethra.

The controversy continues into the current period.

In the 1970s John Coldrey, later a judge of the Victorian Supreme Court, appeared for a Central Australian Aboriginal Legal Aid Service client in Alice Springs. The traditional man, drunk, had inflicted 201 separate injuries on his wife who then bled to death. She had been passively crouching, and there were no defensive wounds. The man was punishing her for having been with other men that day. He had not wanted to kill or seriously injure her, he said. J. Coldrey belatedly discovered that the wounds were on traditional punishment areas of the body, and the conviction was then of manslaughter, not murder.

Peter Sutton finds it distressing that in north and central Australia, relatives of small children "cruel" them by inflicting pain to make the child angry and violent, even from six months old. He believes this is a tradition dating from earliest times when aggression needed to be instilled in children.

Nowra wrote his book "Bad Dreaming" after a spell in Alice Springs hospital in 2005, when he saw numerous Aboriginal women and young girls with severe injuries from domestic violence. He visited outback communities and found them astonishingly brutal:

"Some of the women's faces ended up looking as though an incompetent butcher had conducted plastic surgery with a hammer and saw. The fear in the women's eyes reminded me of dogs whipped into cringing submission."

In contemporary Australia, polygamy and traditions of promised-brides continue in Arnhem Land and other remote areas. Until recently, the judiciary was lenient in such cases involving forced under-age sex. Jarrett writes,

"There are Aboriginal men who still claim these modern young girls as their promised possession, and have cars, guns, outstations and kin to help them secure and punish these resistant girls, well away from public purview ... A man's traditional sense of entitlement, and use of violence to enforce it, can still triumph over the emancipation of a young Aboriginal woman's mind."

In 2004 at Yarralin near Katherine, a 55-year-old married man physically and sexually assaulted his 14-year-old promised bride for two days while she pleaded she was too young for sex. In August, 2005, in an under-the-tree session, Justice Brian Martin noted the cultural context, and gave the man a one-month sentence suspended. On appeal the sentence was increased to three years and a defence appeal to the High Court was lost. Justice Martin later admitted he had been too lenient.

In 2002 at Maningrida, Jackie Pascoe Jamilmira, a 50-year-old wife killer, had forced sex on a 15-year-old promised bride, for whom he had given presents to the 'bride's' parents. He then fired a shotgun into the air to warn off the girls' family members. Justice John Gallop of the NT Supreme Court sentenced him to 24 hours gaol for unlawful sex, saying the matter should never have come to court. Pascoe, he said, was exercising his conjugal rights in traditional society and the girl 'knew what was expected of her. It's surprising to me [that the defendant] was charged at all'.[123]

The North Australian Aboriginal Legal Aid Service relied on expert anthropological evidence to argue that promised marriages were common and morally correct under Aboriginal law, and supported his application to the High Court.

Nowra also cites the case of a middle-aged Aboriginal man who anally raped a 14-year-old promised bride, and who was sentenced merely to detention for the duration of the NT court session.

Lawyer Joan Kimm recounts the tragic case of 37-year-old Jennifer Cook on Bathurst Island, who killed her husband David Mungatopi. She had been promised to a very old man, who had bequeathed her to his grandson. Mungatopi. That man flogged her daily for 18 years. In May, 2000, after a remorseless beating, she stabbed him. Justice Riley said that 'after years of [her] black eyes, and coughing blood, he did not think that she ought to serve an actual sentence'.

However, she then became a pariah on Bathurst. Mungatopi's relatives took her six children and Mungatopi's memory is so honored that the local Snake Beach was closed for two years in tribute.

The Gordon inquiry in WA in 2002 had referred the issue of whether violence to women and abuse of children were 'traditionally sanctioned', to the WA University Centre for Anthropological Research.

The Centre found that family violence or abuse "are invariably within

---

123 Hannah McGlade, *Our Greatest Challenge*. Aboriginal Studies Press, Canberra, 2012, p.149.

the sphere of traditional practice, ritual or the operation of customary law. We have found little material that suggests that violence or abuse per se are condoned, or took place with impunity, outside traditionally regulated contexts."

Gordon concluded that "that family violence which occurs in traditional societies appears to be no different to any other societies in the world." However, the comment ignored the sanctioned violence.

In fact, says Kimm, the Gordon report had established that young girls were the property of their community, the arrangement for the promise was made without their consent, they were 'handed over' and they were the reward for 'male accomplishment'. It is a matter of little grace that actual marital sexual relations did not start until after puberty when this could occur at ten years ...

Lawyer Hannah McGlade, however, quotes her mother, Mingli Wanjurri McGlade, a Noongar elder, who talked to an East Kimberley elder, who told her "We have to look after our women. They look after us, they cook for us, they mind us when we're sick, they give us our children. They are very precious."

Mingli also mentioned that Catholic male elders of Turkey Creek commented about 'their promise' (bride) – "it was very clear that there had been no consummation or intent to consummate those traditional marriages with young girls. Minglie's experience on law grounds in Broome and Kununurra was that women talk about respect for men's law, and men talk about respect for women's law."

"In Noongar culture women were always very strong, and sexual violence against children unimaginable." She quotes Pat Baines, an anthropologist who says that traditional Noongar culture featured strong women. Baines quotes a 1988 film by Indigenous filmmaker Tracey Moffatt, conceived by some Perth based aboriginal women, including McGlade, promoting strong Noongar women, "not because we are 'cultural revisionists' but because it is what we know to be true from our own knowledge of our history and culture ...

"Noongar people will also say that we have no words to describe the sexual violence and abuse of children that is occurring today – it is not part of our culture, but something that has happened as a result of colonisation and the breakdown of our Noongar ways."

Kimm argues, however, that male Aboriginal leaders have focused not on women's rights to security but on political rights such as land rights, treaties, sovereignty, self-determination and the need for customary law. "The continued public denial that violence is part of traditional culture remains a large part of the 'root of the problem'."

Kimm's specific examples of abusive traditions are disquieting.

"[An Aboriginal] Ngabidj related a Kimberley practice, the prelude to which, in his account, was of a child bride being taken crying from her parents, who then go far away. The child then had to bear sexual relations by many men before being taken over by her husband."

In Warrabri in the 1960s "…old men looked upon their young wives 'as their pension ticket'; it was also a matter of prestige to have a young wife. The wives'; parents also benefited. In the 1970s when a young girl from Yirrkala was badly beaten for refusing to marry, a journalist observed that with the conversion to money economy, bride prices to be paid to the parents were from $500 to $1000."

In a 1997 case, a man, his wife and her brother were drinking around their campfire. The husband said something out of place to his wife, and the brother, instead of punishing the husband, hit his sister on the head with a heavy stick, massively fracturing her skull. An elder of the Ngukurr gave evidence that this was a hangover from customary law: "That's her punishment – you know. She got to take that…In olden days, you know if one breaks down, one little thing, he's dead. You know, speared – just like that!"

One man at Ernabella in 1978 still felt guilty because, when he was very small 35 years earlier, he had crept out to watch a corroboree. The next morning the group killed his mother over it and he was deposited by the group into the care of Ernabella Mission.

Men could inflict "sacred rape" on a woman or group of women as punishment, to prepare a girl for marriage and penetrate girls upon puberty.

"Women were offered in conciliation to raiding warriors. If their sexual services were accepted it signified there would be no fighting. In the Kimberley a woman might be sent over to a whole group of men visitors.

If a Kimberley woman was thought to be 'running around', a group of men would take her into the bush, and so cut her genitals that she would be incapable of ever again having sexual intercourse."

Other Kimberley accounts tell of girls of nine being impregnated and suffering long and severe labour, only to die at the end. Mother and the baby, whether dead or alive, were buried together.[124]

Boys have been subjected to sometimes equivalent violence. Boy-wives as young as five were assigned to young unmarried men as lovers. In 1992 Fred Hollows was filmed talking about the practice of Aboriginal elders in some remote communities sodomising boys during initiations, and he complained about the HIV infections. The footage was aired only recently (mid-2000s). Nowra says, "It is highly probable his comments were considered too inflammatory and regarded as culturally insensitive."[125]

Lyla Coorey in a 2005 report to the Senate, said some elders were abusing boys in fake initiations. Gary Lee, an indigenous researcher, said boys as young as eight are being used for sex, with almost cultural sanction.

In 2004 in a remote NT community, three brothers under 10 were tied to a tree, stripped naked and sexually assaulted repeatedly by a gang of men. The distraught mother had been abused since 13 and fled with the boys to the bush for weeks living off plants until picked up by the police.

In 2005 a four-year-old boy from a Northern Kimberley community was raped by a man until the boy lost control of his bodily functions, had surgery in Perth, was sent back to his community and then brutally raped again, this time by a 12-year-old.

Between April and August 2006, five men and five youths aged 12-39, were charged with sexually assaulting an 11-year-old boy 37 times, initially when he was stoned on marijuana. He was raped by all nine, then later by another three. Later when swimming, he was threatened and assaulted by five men, one of them raping him with a 20cm stick. On the way home he was raped again by the five. The case was unconcluded when Nowra wrote the book, but the five men had been granted bail.

Sutton relates that "at Watha-Nhiin in the 1970s (a girl named Ursula

---

124 Op. cit., Jarrett, p132
125 Op. cit., Nowra, p50

Yunkaporta) had been one of a number of lively, sassy, school-age kids. In the 1990s she presented at Aurukun Hospital scores of times over a two-year period of heavy drinking, repeatedly bashed by her boyfriend and others with whom she also fought. She was treated after being savaged by dogs at night, and was twice examined after giving details of how she was pack-raped by local boys. In the end she took her own life by hanging, at twenty-seven…"[126]

Sutton concluded his book, "If men refuse to do anything then they are responsible for the slow death of the many wonderful aspects of their culture, traditions and customs, and their communities will continue to be on a nightmarish treadmill to cultural oblivion."

Quadrant OnLine, 8 May 2013

Indigenous Violence: When the horrific is mundane

Sexually mutilated infants, toddlers raped, children sodomised, women so badly beaten they come to envy dogs. Stripped of cant and buck-passing, beyond a patronising and indulgent judiciary, remote Indigenous communities are being eaten alive by the cancers of grog, misogyny and endemic violence.

> *There are so many appalling stories within the indigenous community in Australia and it is hard to know where to start to do something about it… We must stop this appalling violence being inflicted one upon the other by members of the Indigenous community.*– Victorian Supreme Court judge Betty King, April 26, 2013.

The brutally fatal rape of a 23-year-old Indian woman, known as Braveheart, in a New Delhi bus last December shocked people worldwide, including in Australia. So did the two-day series of rapes and torture in the same city, of a five-year-old girl in April. Few Australians comprehend the equally horrific violence that can be inflicted on Aboriginal women by Aboriginal men. This is not to disparage Aboriginal traditional culture *per se*, which I find captivating in its knowledge of the environment, complex social life and droll 'take' on life's ups and downs.

Violent misogyny in some Aboriginal communities, however, is

---

126 Op. cit., Sutton, p.2-3.

endemic. Even to read these instances is daunting. Although Prime Minister Gillard abhors violence against women, she is yet to recognise the dimension of the problem in Aboriginal communities. As she told high school students on the ABC's *Q&A* this week [May 6], *"I mean, we've still got problems and challenges,* but if we look at our near neighbours, you know, PNG, many of the islands of the Pacific, many of the countries in which we do aid and development work, the violence against women there is truly staggering" (*My emphasis*).

Solicitor/historian Joan Kimm wrote in 2004: "The intensity of this violence needs to be understood by non-Indigenous Australians. When working as a solicitor with non-Indigenous clients, I encountered infanticide, homicide, suicide, betrayals, violence, incest and other child abuse. These were tragic cases but in none was the violence equivalent to the horrific circumstances of Aboriginal violence…Aboriginal women are disadvantaged in that Aboriginal culture has become an inviolate space in our society where abuse of women often occurs with impunity because of distorted views of the respect which must be paid to Indigenous rights."[127]

The local instances below start several decades ago but current data show the violence remains appalling and in the past few years has soared.

In 1980, an Aboriginal man, Ivan Imityja Panka, was angry with his wife because she refused to cook meat for him. Both were drunk. He decided to punish her for being 'cheeky'. After thrashing her within an inch of her life, Panka forced a piece of rippled reinforcing steel up her vagina, killing her. [New Delhi's "Braveheart" died from a similar assault by thugs who used a jack handle]. Panka's defence relied on a husband's traditional rights of chastisement if provoked.[128]

In Numbulwar, NT, a man severed a limb off his sister while he was drunk. He went at her with an axe as well as a spear."[129]

Veronica Hudson 42, on April 26, 2013 was gaoled for six years for manslaughter for stabbing her partner Woody Heron in the chest in Bendigo on December 26, 2011. Three days earlier, he had slit her throat from ear to ear, though not deeply, and cut her arm and hand. She was

127 Joan Kimm, *A Fatal Conjunction.* Federation Press, Sydney 2004, Preface, p3
128 Louis Nowra, *Bad Dreaming.* Pluto Press, North Melbourne, 2007, p30
129 Op. cit., Kimm, p. 11

then released from a psychiatric hospital into Heron's custody the day before she killed him. Heron had been gaoled for five years for assaulting her by kicking, biting and stomping on her head, breaking her jaw. He had also pulled her teeth out with pliers. On sentencing, Hudson sobbed to Justice Betty King: "I just want to say I'm sorry. I didn't mean it."[130]

Recent child-abuse cases, from Central Australia and Queensland, included a seven-month baby taken out of her home and raped, and who needed surgery under general anaesthetic. A two-year-old girl left unattended while her mother drank, was sexually assaulted by a man and also needed surgery. A three-year-old was sexually assaulted by three men, and ten days later another man raped her twice, once using a mangrove stick

A six-year-old girl was followed to a waterhole and while playing there was anally raped while being drowned. A 10-year-old girl was tied to a tree and repeatedly raped. One health worker examined a 14-year-old girl 'so raw from being raped – she had been abused since the age of three – that she screamed throughout her examination.'[131] [132]

Morgan Jabanardi Riley, 27, sexually assaulted a two-year-old at Tennant Creek in 2004, digitally penetrating her vagina and anus as she screamed in pain. He got 4.5 years non-parole, later increased to 6.5 years.

Gerhardt Max Inkamala, 21, in 2003 digitally penetrated a 7-month-old girl's vagina, causing serious injury, at Hermannsburg. His sentence was increased after appeal from only five years to nine years, with non-parole of seven years.

These cases are in the minority which get to court, author Louis Nowra wrote. The Robertson report in 1999 estimated near 90% of rapes in the Indigenous communities went unreported.

The Aboriginal Child Sexual Assault Taskforce (ACSAT) 2006, visited 29 NSW Aboriginal communities and child sexual assault was described as a 'huge issue' in every one of those communities. Aboriginal witnesses told the inquiry that the assaults on girls and boys were massive, epidemic, and a way of life. They were perpetrated by grandfathers,

---

130 Press reports, various, April 26-27, 2013
131 Op. cit., Kimm p5
132 Op. cit., Nowra p45

fathers, stepfathers, uncles, cousins and brothers, often important men, and including some non-Aboriginals.

Writing in *Quadrant* last November, Bubbles Segall, a worker for 36 years in Northern Territory community health, instanced these cases of violence:

> A woman is repeatedly evacuated from a remote community health centre to hospital with multiple fractures to the bones in her hands and burns to her vagina. On each of these occasions, her husband, in fits of jealous rage, has put burning sticks into her vagina and broken the bones in her fingers…
>
> A nurse is called out at midnight to attend to a woman who has been brutally bashed by her husband. She is six months pregnant with her first child. In a jealous, drunken rage, her husband accused her of talking to another man earlier in the evening. She is bleeding profusely from a head wound caused by a partial avulsion of her scalp. She has also sustained a partial tear to an earlobe. She is bleeding copiously from her vagina. Her husband has kicked her repeatedly in the abdomen. Her wounds are treated, she sustains a miscarriage and is evacuated by air ambulance to the nearest hospital that night.

Segall finishes: "These situations are not unique or far and few. They are everyday occurrences in many communities, and there are thousands of similar examples which to health workers gradually become overwhelming and disheartening."

These instances could be called anecdotal. For those preferring data, see the NT crime statistics for 2007-12, released late last year by the new CLP government.[133] They show that nearly 11% of Indigenous NT women in 2011-12 were assault victims, more than 12 times the non-Indigenous rate. The number of victims was up 61% from 2006-07.

When examined by age group, the victim rate in 2011-12 for 15-17-year-old Indigenous girls was 11%; and in the group 20-39 years, an extraordinary one-in-five Indigenous women that year were assault victims. The contrasting rate for NT non-Indigenous women overall was under 1%. In the six years from 2006-07, the Indigenous woman who was most assaulted suffered 20 assaults. Keep in mind that these figures only involve assaults that come to official attention.

In the most remote areas of the NT, assault rates were up 66%,

---

133 www.nt.gov.au/justice/…/nt_annual_crime_statistics_2012.doc

compared with 2006-07, including a 19% rise in the latest year. There were a third more alcohol-related assaults than in 2006-07, but 175% more non-alcohol related assaults.

Louis Nowra published his 90-page essay "Bad Dreaming" in 2007. He wrote then that the brutality was increasing, with spears, rocks, knives, bottles and bricks used [in other words, violence has been accelerating both pre and post-2007]. Rape and especially gang-rape had become more common, Nowra said, with violence more ferocious and sometimes beggaring belief.

"Victims are viciously gang-banged, during which they are smashed with iron bars, rocks, pieces of concrete or lumps of wood that cause massive physical injuries and permanent facial deformities. A particularly nasty strain of this violence that is showing an alarming rise, is the number of women being set on fire."

The Age's Russell Skelton in 2006 reported a case where a young man doused petrol on his 18-year-old girlfriend's stomach and genitals and set her clothes on fire when she refused to have sex.

Nowra quotes Dr Kate Napthall of Darwin who on one Friday night from 5pm to 8am at Tennant Creek Hospital saw 28 cases of domestic assault – and those were just the ones that presented. The worst case she recalled was a woman of about 28 who had a saucepan of boiling water poured over her face, scalding her eyes beyond recognition. "When I looked in her files, she had between 40 and 50 similar presentations of assault against her by her husband," Napthall said. (Tennant Creek Indigenous assault victims have risen 19% since 2006-07. The assault rate there is now well over three times the NT average – which itself is high).

Some women became sleepwalking targets-for-violence, rather than human beings. One woman was so inured to injuries she no longer felt them. Her husband put a barbed spear right through her arm and another man pulled it out. No-one reported the incident because she was attacked so routinely with knives, stones and sticks. Women would be on the ground being kicked in the belly but no-one would help her: "You just didn't do that. You could watch, but weren't allowed to butt into people's fights," one woman told a 1999 inquiry.

These reports include a case where wife of an elder was repeatedly bashed and stabbed over the years at Alice Springs, refusing police protection out of fear. Eventually she was beaten to death, tied up and left on an ant's nest for a week.

In May 2005 at Araru outstation on the Coburg Peninsular, NT, Trenton Cunningham 27, beat to death Jodi Palipuaminni, his pregnant wife and mother-of-four, because she didn't bring him a cup of water while he was burying his dog. Her screams for help the night before she died were ignored, and she was dead by morning. The husband was on parole for assaulting his wife with a steel bar and pouring boiling water over her, resulting in skin grafts to 20% of her body. She had become his promised wife soon after her birth. She had complained 29 times to health workers about him. He had whipped her with wire, kicked her in the stomach while pregnant, stabbed her with scissors and scalded her. Cunningham was sentenced to a non-parole period of 6.5 years after his charge was reduced from murder to manslaughter.[134]

- At Maningrida it was common for men, drunk or sober, to bash their wives when the women returned from a holiday or trip, just in case they had done anything wrong while away.
- Merrillee Mulligan in Derby, described as "a respected worker for her people", in 2000 threatened to expose her brother in law Jeffrey Qualla for molesting a seven year old girl. That night while she was asleep he bashed her head and dragged her into a vacant block and attacked her with a file. She died. He was charged with willful murder but the prosecutor Robert Cock QC accepted a please of manslaughter. Qualla was to serve less than two years in prison. Cock commented that the juries view alcohol-fuelled violence in Aboriginal communities as so everyday that it was difficult to prove intent to kill.

The SA Government's Commission of Inquiry into child sexual abuse on Anangu Pitjantjatjara Yankunytjatjara (APY) lands found in 2008 that sexual abuse there was normalised, with adult men holding an attitude of 'she's big enough' towards young girls, and the view that 'if you've got the body you do the thing'. Aboriginal girls came to accept that they would be sexually assaulted and abused, as the inquiry noted: "It is expected of them. They simply believe their resistance is futile."

The sufferings of many young girls will go forever unrecorded – particularly if they face the 'double-silencing' of cultural fear plus

---

134 Paul Toohey, "Last Drinks". Quarterly Essay, 30/2008, e-book Loc 710

English language inabilities. For example, one concerned teacher on APY lands noted a young Aboriginal girl who had otherwise been a bright, happy child. One day the girl came to school and 'just laid her head on my lap and sobbed. Like, heartbreaking, wrenching sobs. There was snot and tears dripping down my legs and she sobbed probably for about 20 minutes.' The girl's siblings' behavior soon changed for the worse as well, but the teacher left the school not knowing whether her report to the department had achieved anything.[135]

These are instances of violence from the past six months.

- In November, a Darwin court was told that riots at Wadeye – a particularly violent community – over a gang leader's death were the worst in 50 years.

- After a 13-year-old boy from a remote community was found dead [presumably suicide] at a Darwin boarding school last March, a former staff member and whistleblower told the press that "violence is the norm where they come from".

- A Daly River school had to be shut until further notice in February after two female staff were punched in the face. One of them, 56, lost a tooth and another, 66, was hit on the side of her face. The principal and eight unhurt staff were rushed from the community because of fears for their safety. The alleged assailant was an Indigenous woman.

- At the Milingimbi NT school in March, a student threatened teachers with a tomahawk and had to be restrained by six staff and given three doses of sedatives.

- In May, Angurugu School on Groote Eylandt was closed after a teacher was hit on the neck from behind with a baseball bat, following smashing of the principal's window with an axe, and a teacher suffering a broken hand after a student threw a chair and table at her. Another teacher was left bleeding after a bite, and a staff member was stabbed in the leg with sharpened pencils. Earlier a woman teacher at the school had to be flown out after a student threatened to rape her. Another student there tried to choke a 66 year old male teacher. The teachers' union says violent assaults happen daily and weekly in remote NT schools The union claims the Education Department is covering up the violence because they wanted to maximise attendance statistics.

- An emergency safety summit called in February to discuss violence,

---

135 Stephanie Jarrett, *Liberating Aboriginal People from Violence*. Connor Court, Ballarat, 2013, p.158.

feuding and alcohol abuse in the 18 housing associations in Alice Springs, collapsed after walkouts by NT Indigenous Advancement Minister Alison Anderson and NT Police Commissioner John McRoberts. The summit followed two murders in the previous ten days. One involved a group bashing a man to death over a prolonged period. Pre-summit, the Tangentyere Council chief executive Walter Shaw said people were under siege and living in fear from alcohol related violence. Federal Indigenous Affairs Minister Jenny Macklin was in Alice Springs but did not attend the summit. The town camps have been the recent recipient of $150m in federal money, but many of the 240 homes involved have been trashed or degraded. (One estimate of the life of a house in such places is seven years). About concurrently with the aid funding, the break-in rate against Alice Springs housing has more than doubled, commercial break-ins are up 30%, and the Indigenous female victims of assault are up nearly 80%.

- In NSW, the town of Bourke (pop 3000) is more dangerous per capita for assaults and crime than any country in the world, despite having 40 police in the town. Moree Plains and Cobar are not far behind. Dr Don Weatherburn, of the NSW Bureau of Crime Statistics, said that 25 years ago, "bashing someone for their wallet was something you just did not do in country towns". Bourke police said they had difficulty returning youths to their homes at night and during school holidays, because the homes themselves were unsafe for the youths.

NT politician Bess Price told the Parliament that gaol was safer for young people because there was no alcohol, three meals a day, the company of family members and language groups, and a healthier environment. The same point was made by a Bourke, NSW magistrate, Roger Clisdell, who set some Aboriginal children were deliberately seeking gaol to escape "constant and brutal domestic violence." He said endemic violence against women and children, often unreported, drove children out on the streets late at night.

The following incidents all occurred with a few days in northern Queensland in March. A Cape York Mayor was charged after allegedly using a spear to incite a brawl and assaulting police. At Doomadgee, a riot squad was flown in after a local allegedly hit a female police officer in the face with a torch and broke her nose. When a 52-year-old was arrested, a large crowd stormed the police station and smashed doors.

At Yuendumu, 300km northwest of Alice, about 50 women threatened a group of 15 families inside a store last July. A bus used in an inter-clan attack was burnt out. Police went to one camp and were met by 80 people armed with axes, nulla nullas, steel pipes, spears, star pickets, wheel braces, axles and rocks. Police were strengthened to 13, in a town of 800.

At Mutitjulu, (pop 300), police answered a distress call last December and found 30 to 40 people fighting. That group threw rocks, bottles, and sticks at the police vehicle, and police reinforcements were also targeted. A female nurse who was treating an assaulted woman, was allegedly punched to the head and threatened with an iron bar. Both nurse and victim were taken to the clinic for treatment.

At Aurukun, the town went into lockdown as police hunted a gunman who fired a volley of shotgun shots during a 200-strong street fight. The hospital, school and shops were barricaded as armed men roamed the streets making death threats against rival clans.

Professor Peter Sutton wrote in 2010, "In the early 1970s Aurukun, when I first went there, there were occasional large-scale battles, and many minor squabbles, but mostly there was relative peace. Alcohol still found its illicit way in, but only every now and then, and was drunk in secret. Homicide, a common feature of the region from earliest records to the 1950s, had been eradicated. Suicide was unknown. People who survived the rigors of infancy and early childhood had a good chance of living to their seventies. Child abuse, if it occurred, found the records only on the rarest of occasions. Local men mustered cattle and ran the local butcher shop, logged and sawed the timber for house-building, built the housing and other constructions, welded and fixed vehicles in the workshop, and worked in the vegetable gardens, under a minimal set of mission supervisors. Women not wholly engaged in child-rearing worked in the general store, clothing store, school, hospital and post office. It wasn't heaven, but it certainly wasn't hell. That was to come later."[136]

Sutton mentions sardonically that after Aurukun got a regular grog supply in 1985, people from nearby Coen, which itself was a disaster zone, began referring to Aurukun as "Beirut".

None of the above fits the federal Labor government narrative of buoyant progress, as outlined by Prime Minister Gillard in her annual

---

136 Peter Sutton, *The Politics of Suffering*. Melbourne University Press, 2010. p40

"Closing the Gap" reports. As she put it last year:

> The transformation of Alice Springs, the advances in community safety and food security in the wider Northern Territory, the new or refurbished housing on the ground in remote Australia, the Australian Government's Education Revolution, the acceleration of private-sector support for Indigenous employment and the roll out of the Indigenous Chronic Disease Package are all building towards achievement of the ambitious Closing the Gap targets. ...Above all, Indigenous people are rising to the challenge and taking responsibility for making these changes with governments.
>
> *Quadrant OnLine,* 9 May 2013

6

A MISCELLANY OF ITEMS

Peter Ryan, Crimebuster

Quadrant readers know Peter Ryan, author and man of letters, who died last week at 92, for his columns, mellifluous prose and erudite wit. Many light-fingered former Melbourne University students and staff harbour less cheerful memories.

◇◇

Peter Ryan, a hero of WW11, of publishing and of authorship, ran Melbourne University Press (MUP) from 1962 until 1988. He died at 92 on 13 December 2015, having delighted *Quadrant* readers for years with his back-page essay and sterling sentiments, always in the prose of a master story-teller. I met him only a couple of times, and on both occasions was amused by how often this frail old gent's stories involved desires or threats to punch hypocrites and equivocators on the nose.

He was not just physically fearless. He also delivered powerfully written punches. Best known is his demolition of the MUP's own pet author, historian Manning Clark. Less known is his exposure of the culture of thieving by students (and occasional academics) at Melbourne University during his MUP days. This involved the virtual tolerance of larceny by the university's Grand Pooh-Bahs and student union.

When he arrived at MUP as Director, book thieving from the MUP's on-campus bookstore was out of control. His fight against the thieves was thwarted at every turn by his soft-spined overlords. Between the thieving and the university's bureaucratic incompetence, he estimated that the financial performance of MUP during his tenure was degraded by some $20 million. In the Sixties, when dollars were worth something, Ryan estimated his bookshop was losing $250,000 a year to thieves.

Moreover, the thieves' victims were not the university *per se* but the honest students who had to pay book prices inflated to cover "shrinkage".

Here I'll confess to some thieving of my own: I'm drawing all my material from his book *Final Proof: Memoirs of a Publisher* (Quadrant Books, 2010).[137] So sue me, Keith Windschuttle!

The index to *Final Proof* has only names, so the accounts of the thievery are to be found scattered among the 200 pages. Apart from campus thieves, Ryan also had to deal with authorised and forcible extraction of the public's money via papermakers' cartels and monopolies. Those cartels were rife through every section of Australian business until the Lionel Murphy anti-cartel legislation of 1974, striking down literally thousands of trade-association's price-fixing agreements.[138]

Yet another legal variety of enforced money-extraction was the frequent refusal of the big publishers and book retailers to pay their MUP bills, not merely when due but sometimes only at the point of a summons. After one successful court action, Ryan had to visit the offending publisher/customer and wait outside the CEO's door until the cheque was grudgingly produced. He then hurried to the bank to ensure its validity.

So let's begin. On first arriving at MUP, Ryan learnt of the uncontrolled shoplifting at MUP's Bookroom. This was no small bookshop. It had 25 staff and, at one stage, ranked as the biggest single-store retail book outlet in Australia. Ryan at once persuaded the MUP board – despite some timidity there – to hire private detective Ernie to assess the situation.

A good operator, Ernie turned up in a tweed sports jacket with authentic leather elbow patches, puffing a pipe and browsing the shelves with a learned tome tucked under an arm. On other days he wore or carried a white lab coat. No customer paid him any mind. Ernie also loitered in the student union café, overhearing details and names. He was able in short order to provide Ryan with a report on how MUP was being robbed blind.

---

137 Peter in his facing-page inscription to me wrote, "Peter Ryan, 3/12/2101". Would that he had written essays for so long.

138 When Ryan wrote a Financial Review piece accusing paper-maker APPM among others of holding the entire printing and publishing industry to ransom, APPM issued a libel writ but did not follow up on it

The two-dozen staff were unfazed by thievery. The Bookroom was so badly designed and operated that customers were almost invited to by-pass the till. Customers were even allowed to carry in their bags and attaché cases, the better to carry away plunder en masse. Many of the staff took the view that they were "professional book people, not policemen". Ryan read them the Riot Act, and half-a-dozen departed with severance pay the same afternoon.

The thieves were largely male enrolled students, but other students imbued with ill intent from other establishments of higher learning also were frequent visitors. "Several members of Melbourne's [University] teaching staff were also apprehended, and some later convicted in the Carlton Magistrate's Court", Ryan writes (p112).

Student thieves included casuals, but the real damage was inflicted by students stealing textbooks to order for other students and commercial customers, usually at 50% of list price. The student union's "book exchange" facility became at times little better than a whitewashed fencing operation. "There was a regular and substantial trade in stolen books which went into second-hand bookshops off campus," he says. Students even staged two night-time break-and-enters, carting away multiple copies of valuable textbooks by truck, "later to appear as stock on the shelves of commercial bookshops," Ryan wrote with some bitterness.

Ryan knew MUP could even be bankrupted by the thieving and sought exemplary punishments for those caught. In that pre-scanning era, he tightened supervision and put up notices saying thieves would be referred to the police.

To the police? This caused outrage, even with his own MUP board. Un-spined professors lamented that it would be a sad day whenever police came on campus to monster students and blight their careers with convictions for theft. Fortunately, the MUP chair William Macmahon Ball told them politely to shut it. Staff were directed to refer all cases to Carlton police. A few students were convicted. Ryan: "The news spread like a bushfire; shoplifting sharply diminished."

Problem solved? No way! Melbourne University's governing council stepped in and forbade MUP to refer any more enrolled students to the police. Instead, these wayward lambs in the university's flock would be handled by the university's own Disciplinary Committee (non-students could still face court).

A stream of malefactors was subjected to the internal processes. All were either acquitted or fined a paltry $5. In 20 years, the largest fines were a $50 penalty and a $25. Again, word spread. Tough and realistic student thieves swung back into action, confident that the worst case would involve a small-change "licence fee" while their cash upside was unlimited. Morale of the bookshop staff plummeted.

In vain the MUP board argued its case for severity to the university council, the counter-argument being that students were a sacred species. "Over the two decades a limp-wristed university allowed millions of dollars of public money to filter through its feeble fingers to thieves. If Council had made 'sending down' [expulsion] from the University the standard penalty for stealing, shoplifting would at once have become a rarity" p. 114.

Next, Ryan was asked from on high to "discuss" the problem with the Student Representative Council. The SRC President was a "slim and gingery young man" who argued against any blighting of thieves' future career prospects. Moreover, said the student president, in the cause of student autonomy, prosecutions should not even go to the University committee but to the SRC's own disciplinary committee. That aggrieved young man was Gareth Evans, currently ANU Chancellor. His plea to Ryan was that, "Students would appreciate being judged by their peers" (pp. 114-15). Ryan asked what sort of conviction rate the student committee might exact, but the young Gareth, now AC and QC, hadn't thought that far ahead. The two men left with a polite agreement to differ.

So for 20 more years the theft industry boomed. Each student caught involved MUP in preparing a legal case for University Council, involving a typical cost of $100 (in what was then real money).

One non-student was caught and a police car drove on campus to take him away. Students rioted to free the oppressed prisoner, who was too traumatised to actually make his escape from the car.

One Arts student was caught stealing exactly 90 minutes after he enrolled for studies. An overseas law student racked up 35 book-theft charges in his first term of study.

Twenty irate students invaded the Bookroom, occupied the manager's office and stole some of his own books.

A Monash student visitor was convicted by the Carlton court and given a 12 months bond. One day after the good-behaviour bond expired, he was arrested again for book theft – but from Monash University's bookroom.

A showcase of MUP's latest books was displayed in Wilson Hall for the public's benefit. Within months the glass was smashed and the specimen books were stolen, presumably by students, Ryan says, though no-one was caught.

Ryan happily conceded that most students were honest and hardworking, but chided them for supine attitude towards dishonest peers and for voting for ineffective representatives.

"I feel sad that 26 years service in the University of Melbourne inspired me with no very exalted view of undergraduate idealism or aspiration," he wrote. "This judgment may be unfair, and perhaps unduly influenced by daily exposure to costly and degrading student dishonesty in the Bookroom."

Ryan waxed at length at the University's money-wasting through absurd bureaucratic processes, but that's another story I won't steal today.

Quadrant OnLine, 24 December 2015

The Naughty Nation of Nauru

In the film *The Mouse that Roared* (1959), the fictitious Duchy of Grand Fenwick, in the Alps, declares war on the United States. The Duchy wants to lose and then enjoy American postwar largesse. I don't want to spoil the plot, but the Duchy stuffs up by winning.

Turn now to the nation of Nauru (population 9400), at 21 square kilometres the area of Perth's Rottnest Island. Nauru has in real life defeated Australia (population 23 million). President Sprent Dabwido continues to dictate the surrender terms to Prime Minister Julia Gillard. When I last checked, Nauru was demanding a visa fee of $1000 per asylum seeker per month. That will cost us $90 million or so to 2017, a windfall of about $9500 per Nauruan.

Australia has propped up Nauru for a decade, thanks to asylum-seeker politics. One would expect Ms Gillard to offset the new visa fees against our $32 million annual aid. But because her surrender to Nauru was unconditional, the visa fees will be extras.

One word sums up Nauruan affairs: *bizarre*. It is the world's equal-second-smallest state by population (Vatican City, population 800, is smallest, and Nauru's fellow UN member Tuvalu is comparable). Nauru has the same clout in the UN General Assembly as China or India, hence has a valuable vote on offer.

In 1998, during the plundering of Russia's assets, the St Petersburg mafia washed US$70 billion (plus kickbacks) through banks in Nauru. There were *450 banks*, including the Panacea Bank, domiciled in the same two-room shack, staffed by a woman with a broom. From 2000 to 2003 the USA classified Nauru as a rogue state for money laundering and indiscriminate sale of passports – Nauru had sold about a thousand for a reported $1500 each, including at least a couple to Al Qaeda operatives.

Nauru today receives aid at one of the highest rates per capita ($3500 plus) in the world. GDP per capita, surprisingly, is more than $7000 per capita (equal to the Ukraine), although this seems to include the aid. Nauruans pay neither business nor personal tax, which is nice for any politicians who put aside some lazy millions somewhere during the good old days. The Australian economist Helen Hughes estimated in 2004 that Nauru from 1968 to 2002 could and should have invested $1.8 billion (in 2000 dollars) from phosphate surpluses. Instead, most Nauruans now live in near-destitution: a quarter of the children are stunted from malnutrition and half those under five are anaemic. Half the men, and more than half the women, smoke. Life expectancy is only fifty-six for men and sixty-five for women. Alcohol-fuelled violence against women is rife.

Getting priorities right, Australian bureaucrats in 2008-09 busied themselves with what they called a "successful" pilot rollout of then Prime Minister Kevin Rudd's one laptop per child program. Schooling in Nauru was then not even compulsory. It became so in 2010, when daily school time was also raised by two hours to whatever is normal in the Pacific. Heaven knows how few hours were worked by teachers previously, in structures officially described as health hazards and with children, if they turned up, too hungry to study.

Another Australian priority for Nauru is global warming, on which two local public servants work full-time "implementing measures to address climate change" (local salary item: $15,360) with a third climate-change-fighter planned. The evidence for the climate threat: "The people of Nauru have noticed changes in their climate. Elders sense that these changes are not normal."

By 2004, the island was not merely broke but enormously in debt. Today, according to the New Zealand government, Nauru's public debt is around A$869 million, though lots of debt remains undocumented or disputed.

The Australian government emits streams of debt figures for Nauru that seldom make sense. In the 2008-09 Nauruan budget, external debt was put at more than $500 million. Last October (2012) AusAid said that Nauru's external debt had reduced from $370 million to $70 million between 2007 and 2010, but added that internal debt had risen from $265 million to $480 million, thanks to belated recognition of debts to depositors owed by the Bank of Nauru, which failed in 1998 soon after the local elite had whipped their money out. Today Nauru has no bank and no insurance company: people use cash or bank online with Australia. (Nauru's official currency is the Australian dollar.)

Squandering of aid seems to continue. In 2011 the nation of 9400 had more than 1200 public servants, which is an improvement on the days when it had (whether notionally or in reality) more than 3000. Other estimates of public service numbers put the peak lower, at 1600. The serious government work is done by what are politely called "in-line" officials, that is, aid-paid Australian expatriates. These include Nauru's secretary for finance (who gets more than $190,000 tax-free in supplementary aid pay) and two deputy secretaries in the Finance Ministry. They have certainly improved the national book-keeping.

Nauruans have led a sedentary lifestyle for two generations, while snacking on trashy imported food. The result is that 82 per cent of them are overweight, possibly the world record. Nearly a quarter of adults have diabetes (among Nauruan women over fifty-five: 53 per cent). While it is possible to grow fruit and vegetables on the coastal strip, Nauruans are disinclined to do so.

How Nauru became one of the world's least-functional societies is a moral fable. The Nauruans were originally part of the canoe-based dispersion of Polynesians through the Pacific, but their single island is particularly remote. The dozen clans of Nauruans managed by fishing, farming and coconut gathering in the forested uplands. Their main problem became lethal inter-clan warfare. Nauru was never a tropical paradise, no matter what hundreds of journalists have written.

In 1886 Germans took over the island, supposedly appalled by the warfare there but also attracted by copra prospects. Ten years later, a Henry Denson took what he thought was a rock of petrified wood back to his job in Sydney with a phosphate business. For the next three years the lump served as a laboratory doorstop. In 1900 a chemist named Albert Ellis arrived and decided to test it. The rock graded at a record-high phosphate content.

Nauru's interior uplands were found to be marine phosphate, with bird droppings as the icing on the cake. Australia administered Nauru from 1920 as part of a "sacred trust" handed down by the League of Nations. The "sacred trust" in practice involved creating a British Phosphate Commission (BPC) to sell phosphate to Australia, Britain and New Zealand at a third of the world price, with royalties to Nauruans at a halfpenny a ton.

The mining work was actually done by imported labour, particularly Chinese. Fearing a communist takeover, the Nauru on-site administrator from 1949 to 1951 received 600 units of what he quaintly called "lachrymose generators" (tear gas grenades). Canberra also despatched twenty .303 rifles and bayonets to Nauru, labelled as "merchandise". Eventually someone found an interpreter and the Chinese turned out to be supporters of Chiang Kai-Shek on Formosa. When the administrator in 1954 tested the grenades, they were found to include six of the lethal fragmentation variety.

Around that time Australia realised the phosphate would eventually run out and the Nauruans should be settled elsewhere, in the same way that the 700 Banabans of Ocean Island (Nauru's distant phosphate-endowed neighbour) had been resettled, painfully, on the then-British-owned Fijian island of Rabi in 1946.

First, the Nauruans refused to be disappeared into the Australian community as integrated citizens. Next up for their new home was Fraser

Island off Queensland, but Queensland timber harvesters scotched the plan. (How interesting if the plan had succeeded!) Third choice was Curtis Island near Gladstone, but negotiations stumbled because the Nauruans wanted the island as their new sovereign state, a version of Cuba hanging off the USA. They also wanted continued sovereignty over Nauru's phosphate – the last thing the Phosphate Commission had in mind.

Nauruan delegations were invited to Queensland for a look-see but ran into overt racism, including insults to their wives. The exact words went mercifully unrecorded but an allied example was a Curtis Islander who talked of "punching on the nose the first n****r who comes ashore".

Ensconced on Nauru, the Nauruans agitated instead for a better share of the phosphate earnings. The tri-nation trustees argued that their sacred trust involved giving the Nauruans what they "needed" rather than what Nauruans might expect commercially. In 1962 the Nauruans astutely recruited the Australian Council of Trade Unions and Helen Hughes to push their case, and got the phosphate price trebled to world level. Because the Phosphate Commission refused to open its books, the Nauruans' goal switched to statehood. This was despite Nauru's minuscule population, which even today is less than a tenth of my local municipality.

In 1968 the flags of Britain, Australia and New Zealand came down and the Nauruan flag went up. It's a nice one symbolising the equator, the Pacific and a twelve-pointed star for the twelve clans, savouring a phosphate fortune. This revenue by 2002 totalled $3.6 billion (in 2000 dollars). The peak year was 1975 when phosphate earned $363 million, giving Nauruans a per capita GDP of $50,000, second only to Saudi Arabia.

Hughes in 2004 wrote that if the cost of production was 30 per cent and another 20 per cent was spent on private and public consumption, this left $1.8 billion (in 2000 dollars) for investment. Invested conservatively at 7 per cent a year, the capital would have grown to more than $8 billion or (assuming five persons per family) nearly $4 million per family. Instead, Nauru's communal net assets appeared to be, at best, worth $30 million, she wrote, adding: "Some Nauruans, however, have accumulated considerable private fortunes."

Things had started well, with investment advice from parties such as Australian consultants Philip Shrapnel & Co. However, the island became a magnet for carpetbaggers, offering get-richer-quick schemes that contrasted with the pathetic returns recommended by former colonialists.

The most famous scheme involved only petty cash, about $4 million. The Nauruans financed a musical in London's West End, *Leonardo [da Vinci], a Portrait of Love*. The whole Nauruan cabinet flew up to enjoy it but it bombed in a month.

Hughes says that Nauru was advised to invest $60 million in dubious bank instruments through the law firm of Allen, Allen and Helmsley. One of Allen's partners skipped with $6 million. The total losses were never established.

A police chief bought himself a yellow Lamborghini, although Nauru has only a few kilometres of road. When it arrived, he was too fat to get into it. The road became littered with wrecks of four-wheel-drives and Honda Goldwing bikes piled up by drunks and unskilled riders. Nauruans took to game fishing, and forgot the art of building canoes. Golf? The Bahamas beckoned.

Phosphate revenue became insufficient in the late 1990s to bankroll the Nauruan lifestyle. The politicians maintained their high life by borrowing against the trust assets. General Electric Capital Division consolidated the debt by lending $236 million against the property portfolio, and foreclosed on it in 2004. When the receivers inspected Nauru House's penthouse in Melbourne, used as a home-away-from-home and occasional football field by Nauruan big-wigs, they found twelve crates of unopened Grange Hermitage dating from the 1970s.

Most bizarre of all was the 2003 invitation or ultimatum from the CIA to President Dowiyogo: if he wanted aid funds, could he please cease rogue state activities and help open a Nauruan embassy in Beijing? The CIA needed an embassy as a way-station for defecting North Korean generals and scientists. A Nauruan-flagged embassy car would assist the logistics. The operation's code-name was Weasel. Dowiyogo tried to comply but Beijing smelt a rat and the embassy plan fell through. The CIA failed to deliver the promised money to Nauru, and when

Nauru dunned the US government, the US government disowned its CIA negotiators. The Australian courts backed the US government.

Dowiyogo's other foreign exchange plan, also abortive, was to saw the mined-out coral pinnacles into polished slabs and export them as coffee tables.

In waste, the daddy of them all was Air Nauru, which lost $40 million to $80 million annually until it collapsed in 2005. Nauru was also keen to buy its own ocean-freighter fleet but luckily this did not eventuate.

Air Nauru serviced twenty-nine destinations but often flew without passengers. At its peak, Nauru's five Boeings could seat 10 per cent of the nation's population. In Australia, that feat would require 11,500 equivalent jetliners. Sometimes fare-paid Air Nauru passengers were bumped when politicians commandeered the jets for shopping in Hong Kong. This made Nauru a chancy destination for tourists.

The airline had colourful misadventures. One of its B-737s arrived in Nauru one day in 1980 with the pilot's face black, blue and bleeding. It had been waiting for take-off from Tarawa and a local resident invaded the plane and bashed the pilot. Why? Because during takeoffs, the 737s kept blowing the roof off the man's grass hut.

Soon after, an Air Nauru B-727 was outbound for Kagoshima, Japan, with – as usual – no passengers, three Australian cockpit crew, a Japanese senior hostess and three indigenous hostesses, nursing hangovers. A brawl erupted when the Japanese told the team to make coffee for the cockpit. The pilot, unable to separate the combatants, dumped fuel and returned to Nauru, where two Nauruan hosties got first-aid. (The Japanese hostie practised taekwondo.)

Air Nauru by 2005 had only one plane and that was repossessed in December. This delighted Australian protocol people. Previously, Nauruan presidents (there were about twenty of them between 1968 and last year) had demanded red carpet treatment for visiting heads of state when they dropped into Melbourne by Air Nauru for indulgences.

Nauru was able to resume transport when it acquired a B-737 via Taiwanese funding as a payoff for diplomatic re-recognition. This must have galled Beijing, which had coaxed Nauru away from Taiwan only four years earlier. US diplomatic traffic leaked by Wikileaks said Taiwan had been giving Nauruan politicians $5000 a month, and other parliamentarians $2500 a month, to keep the recognition going.

By 2004 Nauru couldn't pay its satellite phone bills, and lost contact with the world for a couple of months. Residents who, one local alleged, had used dollar notes for toilet paper, were now in shock.

The island however had turned the corner in September 2001, with Australia's Prime Minister John Howard and his "Pacific Solution" for boat people. The Nauru solution, which began with a $20 million down payment, was so effective that the flow of incoming boat people to Australia dried up. Among the windfalls to Nauru were about $100 million in foreign aid and ad hoc largesse. Australia, for example, gave Nauru an emergency grant of $1.2 million in 2003 to pay the public servants' Christmas wages.

Howard's compassionate successor Kevin Rudd scrapped the Nauru solution from 2007. But because this destroyed 100 jobs for local cooks, guards and clerks, the Labor government ramped up aid to compensate.

In August 2012, the boat-beleaguered Gillard government decided that Nauru was not a suppurating hell-hole after all, and sought Nauru's agreement to re-open the camps. As we have seen, Nauru could name its own price.

For respectability's sake, Australia is supposed to be leading Nauru into viability, via a Nauru–Australia Partnership for Development towards Millennium Development Goals. On the ground, progress is minimal.

Nauruans have a high fertility rate of about 3.4 births per woman. I have been unable to detect any funding for official family planning initiatives – only a third of women use any contraceptives, since "they wanted as many children as possible", and 85 per cent of female teenagers have not heard anything via the media about contraception. If health aid reduces the high death rate, the island's population will become even less sustainable on the coastal strip.

AusAid rates "gender equality" there a fail on health, education, services and private-sector business, and only a bare pass in the public service. Child mortality, though improved, is still seven times worse than in Australia.

At the outset of independence, Nauru litigated for compensation for the degradation of its mined land. In 1993 Australia settled for the formidable sum of $57 million upfront and $50 million in instalments. In fact, rehabilitation of the porous coral uplands is virtually impossible, so heaven knows where that money went. AusAid and the politicians did design a five-year rehab program in 2007 to be run by the Nauru Rehabilitation Program. AusAid now says, without a blush, "The corporation's focus has been on mining operations", and concedes that mining revenue is more valuable to the islanders than land rehabilitation.

The country today is ridiculously over-governed. It has eighteen members of Parliament (no women), six cabinet ministers, and thirteen ministries. There is one parliamentarian per 500 citizens. Power in Nauru runs via personal alliances, hence the high presidential turnover.

Nauru has joined a host of international bureaucracies such as WHO and UNESCO. Those generate avalanches of unread papers but Nauru's elite enjoy the junketing to world capitals. The forty-four-member Alliance of Small Island States (AOSIS) is currently chaired by Nauru's Ambassador Marlene Moses.

Nauru joined the fifty-four-nation Commonwealth in 1999 but found that this group, which includes similar basket-cases, is big on talk and small on handouts. When Nauru complained about its debt burden last October (2012), the secretary general Kamalesh Sharma offered some debt-management software.

In Nauru anti-corruption drives are often announced and never successful, partly because among any five Nauruans, two are relatives. No one has ever been convicted over the scattering of $1.8 billion to the four winds.

In 2010 a rare prosecution took place over an official's alleged misappropriation of more than $200,000, a large sum in the context of Nauru's low public service wages. Another recent case involved two local business men alleged to have exported $102,000 cash from the island without declaration. In 2010 the local police and the Australian Federal Police opened a case involving alleged foreign bribery of local politicians, which was dropped late in 2011.

Whither Nauru? At least it now has a thriving prison industry. Helen Hughes in her paper suggested that Nauruans end their mendicant stance and seek viability through basic agriculture, tourism, and sale of fishing, internet-domain and satellite rights. Secondary-mining of phosphate has become a further source of revenue.

Hughes concluded – and it still seems valid: "If Nauru does not adopt the economic, political and social reforms that will give it a decent and healthy standard of living, aid cannot help it. Donors that succumb to pleas for aid will be taking money out of their taxpayers' pockets and throwing it away."

She suggested Nauruans could apply for dual citizenship with Australia or New Zealand, in effect selling their island in exchange for an Australasian living standard. My own solution: offer them sovereignty over Rottnest.

Quadrant, Vol. 57, No. 1/2, Jan/Feb 2013

Amid the Glenn Beck Phenomenon

Glenn Beck is one of those conservatives that US liberals love to hate. When you see, as I recently did, how his words and ideals resonate with Americans in what leftists sneeringly dismiss as 'flyover country' it is very easy to understand why the left has declared him a public enemy.

It was July 5, the day after Independence Day. We pulled into the parking lot of a community hall at Dayton, Idaho (population 450), for an evening with religious-Right media phenomenon Glenn Beck. I opened the car door and we were buffeted by a pig-manure stench from working barns nearby.

We came from Logan, Utah, a larger town thirty-five miles south in the beautiful Cache Valley, bordered by purple mountains running north–south on each side, home to occasional mountain lions. My car companions were Mormons. So is Beck (and so are failed presidential aspirant Mitt Romney and 2 per cent of Americans). Two nights before, we'd also been part of Beck's audience, that time at the "Freedom Fire" pre-Independence Day entertainment at Utah State University's football stadium.

This article is largely about Glenn Beck, the apotheosis of religious-Rightism, but it's also about ways of thinking in middle America, unfiltered through the "progressive" media, where sneer is the default mode.

To a normally sceptical Australian, US religious-Right ways can be confronting. But the locals would probably view Aussies as unpatriotic, lackadaisical and sacrilegious.

Utah and Idaho are among the "fly-over states" of the USA, states beyond the pale for the east and west-coast liberal intelligentsia. Utah and Idaho are two of the most Republican states, with 73 per cent and 65 per cent support respectively in presidential voting. The philosophy in these parts is patriotism, piety, states' rights and bearing arms. Utah and Idaho are second and third-ranked (behind Kentucky) for gun ownership. One of my Mormon friends owns sixty guns (including muskets) — but he hunts and traps for a living.

At the Deer Cliff family restaurant, a waiter turned out to be a young son, a US Marine machine-gunner on leave. We chatted about deployments, machine-gun types and grenade launchers. I wasn't sure how much to tip him.

As for Beck, he talked about ninety minutes at Dayton, delivering the most accomplished oratory I've ever heard. He's been living off his eloquence for more than thirty years. My friends warned me he'd cry, and he did, at least six times.

When we entered the hall, two formidable black-clad police were off to one side. "Why are you here?" I asked them. "Mr Beck requested it," one of them replied, deadpan. It turned out that Beck was using a table-full of historic mementos worth more than $1 million as props for extempore history lessons, and they needed guarding.

Aged fifty, and six feet two inches, Beck is homely and bespectacled. He wore brown shirt, faded jeans and suede shoes. He held the audience of 700 spellbound, me included. No Australian speaker of any persuasion gets even near Beck's magic.

Beck is much loved in the mid-West, and last year he bought a family ranch at nearby Weston, Idaho (population 440). When he lards his speeches with prayers for crops and tales of his neighbour's horse eating Beck's grass, it rings authentic.

Most of his long speech was ad-libbed, but he may have cued parts of it from an iPad. No hired speechwriter could come up with such personal stuff. He began with a parable about his family life. He was building a small mountain home and insisted on junking the planned $1500 doors and matching cabinetry. Instead he scrounged a dozen mismatched $100 doors from saleyards, along with tired old dressers and vanity units. Beck was recreating the emotional feel of his grandfather Janssen's homestead, built from odds and ends: "Nothing matched, but in a way, everything did."

Janssen, he continued, was illiterate but a top machinist at the Boeing plant at Seattle – he used tricks to read the blueprints. Beck as a kid would do unpaid work for Janssen all summer vacation, feeding chickens, gathering eggs and cleaning out the coops. He slept in the hot attic with Janssen, who would tell Beck wonderful stories.

Beck then cut to the present, describing how on a hot night on July 2 he and his son (adopted) Raphe chatted about the day's events — rounding up cows, mending a fence, chasing badgers, Raphe trying his first ride on a horse. "I kissed my son good night as he snuggled close by my side, safe, content and sleepy. As I lay there smiling, I reflected on just how much I love and miss my grandfather." Here Beck cried. "It was at that moment with the help of the moonlight I could just make out my mismatched door." Here we cried.

Beck painted himself successfully as an everyman. He knows how to connect with a crowd. In reality, his main home in Dallas is on two acres and has seven bedrooms, and his childhood was not idyllic. But Beck at Dayton was inspiring his audience with the good stuff from his family life.

With his audience captivated, he moved on to messages of religion, morality and patriotism. He read from original letters penned by Abe Lincoln, flourished a Puritan's Tyndale English-language Bible, held up a bogus Swedish citizenship certificate issued to a Jew by Raoul Wallenberg in Budapest in 1944, and a violet star worn by less lucky Bible scholars in the camps. He also showed us the map used by Apollo 11's Neil Armstrong to pick a landing spot on the moon – it was covered in X's for unsafe and O's for safe. (His point was that Neil Armstrong's success was in the wake of selfless preparatory work by earlier Apollo teams.)

He had the microphone used by "Tokyo Rose" (Iva Toguri) to broadcast to US troops. It turned out that she was actually a patriot sending them coded warnings of Japanese bombing raids, and was secretly giving medicines to prisoners of war in Japan. But she was scapegoated by the US press and jailed for six years. When he first told this story on his broadcast channel last year, he actually used that seventy-year-old mike.

Beck was pushing back against the liberals' harping on America's dark past. Beck acknowledges the grim episodes — indeed, in 1866, only five miles from Dayton, US troops massacred several hundred Shoshones at Bear River, violence exceeded only by the massacre at Wounded Knee. But Beck emphasises the heroic and benevolent traits in America's story. Beck's history adviser is minister and Republican stalwart David Barton, whom Beck calls "The Library of Congress in shoes". Barton runs a case that America was founded as an explicitly Christian nation. He lacks credibility among academic historians.

I'll fast-forward to the ending of Beck's speech, skipping an hour on an emotional rollercoaster. He had an easel on stage still covered with a white cloth. He praised the global role and bravery of the American armed forces. (Why in daily Australian life are our own troops and veterans so invisible and unremarked?) He spoke of the uncertainty of success as the first boats hit the Normandy beaches in 1944. He said only one American flag survived the landing, the one on LST 493. Then he whipped away the cloth from the easel, and on it, in a gold frame, was that flag, with about a third of it missing, shot away. We all gasped. (I later found he'd paid $350,000 for it at auction.) Beck grew tearful. "I'm such a girl!" he confessed, and the audience laughed with him.

Beck's final words were the quotes from Lincoln's second inaugural, "with malice toward none, with charity for all" and Beck produced a bloodstained piece of sheet from Lincoln's deathbed.

Then aides with roving mikes took questions. The first was from a woman nearly 100 years old, who said her children, grandchildren and great-grandchildren were all Beck fans. "Thank you for what you have done and showed us, for leading us and motivating us to think for ourselves about important things we need educating about to understand. Thank you!" she said.

Someone asked him when he would create a public museum for his historical items. He said when he had $20 million to spare, but it was slow going because he rated other charities higher priority, including charities based on loving children who are not born. The audience applauded. Beck, by the way, earns $90 million a year from his media outlets, even more than Oprah Winfrey.

On the other side of the hall, another woman took a mike. She had lost a son serving in Afghanistan, she said (here another tremor went through the audience), and she was grateful to Beck for his patriotic messages helping to unify her country. She had two copies of the book *Lone Survivor* signed by Navy Seal author Marcus Luttrell and she said, "I want you to have one of them." Were those questioners pre-selected? I don't know. But the whole hall was in a mood of inspiration.

Beck gave the proceeds of the evening ($28,000 gross) entirely to local arts charities, and didn't charge either for his July 3 speaking stint at Logan. A year earlier, speaking at nearby Preston, Idaho (a metropolis of 5000) he raised $120,000 for local charities.

Beck has made foot-in-mouth comments in the past (much dwelt on by the media) but here's a positive anecdote. Some 60,000 Central American children have poured into the USA illegally in the past year as a result of Obama offering amnesties against deportation – much as Kevin Rudd's relaxing of border controls led to 50,000 asylum seekers flooding in here. Beck has condemned Obama's amnesty, but in mid-July he organised and led a million-dollar relief effort for the interned children at McAllen, Texas, involving truck-trailer loads of food and toys.

It was heartfelt Beck, alienating some supporters who thought he should let Obama's crisis fester. Mormons are by far the most anti-Obama religious group in the USA, giving Obama an 18 per cent approval rating, compared with 37 per cent approval by Protestants and 72 per cent by Muslims.

Another action example is that Beck, like many middle-aged Americans, loved Levi jeans. In 2011, Levi's creative directors came up with a television commercial featuring teenaged males in Levi's braving police riot lines, to the voice-over of poetry by Charles Bukowski: "Your life is your life, don't let it be clubbed into dank submission ... You are marvelous, the gods wait to delight in you." Beck took the view that Levi's was celebrating leftist rabble. He not only gave Levi an on-air pasting but launched his own US-made designer jeans, on patriotic themes and selling, online only, for $130. Levis quickly pulled its edgy ad. Beck's critics overlooked the fact that Beck's clothing profits go to his charity Mercury One.

The mainstream media is no friend of Beck. The Independence

Day fireworks organisers at Logan invited him at the last minute as a ten-minute patriotic speaker. Several Logan councillors objected that Beck was too "divisive" for such a role, which became the lead story for the valley's *Herald Journal*. The *Journal* painted Beck as a demagogue and twice in two days mentioned that Beck had got so angry on-air at his ranch that he once stepped outside to fire a gun in the air. The organisers responded by offering money back to any ticket-holder who objected to Beck. The day after, the *Journal* reported only three money-back requests. Then it ran a correction that even those three requests were unrelated to Beck.

As happens in small towns, we bumped into the Logan mayor Craig Peterson in the street, and he remarked that to have uninvited Beck to mollify three liberal councillors would have created a national furore.

At the event, Beck avoided speaking politically, apologising for every divisive statement he had ever made. The audience cheered his message about patriotism and unity.

The *Journal* led its report next day by saying that Beck received "an apparently warm welcome" – the first time I'd seen such an equivocal phrase. Running a ruler over the *Journal*'s report, I found there were twenty-three inches hostile, twenty-two inches "straight", and under two inches positive. The Letters page and on-line comments ran hot with Beck defenders.

This slanted reporting is nothing unusual. On July 29, 2013, the *Salt Lake Tribune* ran a guest feature by arts academic Alexandra Karl headlined, "Glenn Beck's nazi exhibit". She had probably never attended Beck's show, as she named the venue wrongly. Her conclusion was that because Beck owned and displayed Nazi memorabilia, he was part of the Hitler personality cult and "a sympathiser rather than a critic … It reveals more about Tea Party sensibilities and Beck's personal values than I dared thought possible." She highlighted one allegedly Beck-owned souvenir, "a satin handkerchief browned with Hitler's blood". This was in fact a napkin from the meeting room blown up by anti-Nazi plotter Count Stauffenberg in 1944, and Beck didn't own it, he'd borrowed it. He never claimed it was Hitler's blood.

More to the point, Beck was showcasing two themes of exhibits. One set involved seminal Americana from the country's struggle for independence and freedom, such as Abraham Lincoln's desk and a Bible brought to America on the *Mayflower*. The other set involved items related to tyrannies, as a "never again" moral lesson. The *Tribune* defended the indefensible by saying that Ms Karl was merely a guest columnist, as though her piece had appeared in the paper by magic.

The highlight of Beck's career is his "Restoring Honor" rally at Washington Mall on August 28, 2010. Beck's purpose was to honour US servicemen, who he considered were being disparaged by liberals. American conservatives – including my Mormon friends – swarmed to the event from all over the country. Beck and Sarah Palin (who prayed for ten minutes) spoke from the steps of the Lincoln Monument. They gave an award to (among others) Marine Sergeant James "Eddie" Wright, who lost both hands in a firefight in Iraq but now teaches hand-to-hand combat at the marines base at Quantico, Virginia. The rally raised $5.5 million for wounded veterans.

The crowd crammed the three kilometres of the Mall. The size of that crowd was the political take-home point, so how did the media handle that? I made my own estimate by comparing an aerial picture of an MCG grand final crowd (100,000) with the aerial of the mall crowd, and got a result something like four times, or 400,000. CBS News hired helicopter-borne crowd-count professionals and got a curious result of about 90,000. Associated Press ran an equally ludicrous figure of "tens of thousands". NBC ran an irrational number of "tens to hundreds of thousands", while the liberal *New York Times* was too embarrassed to mention any figure and settled for "enormous". Top estimate (Sky News) was 500,000. Beck joked that there was "over a thousand people".

A month later, US progressives staged a counter-rally called "One Nation". Despite unions busing in their members, the rally gathered a far smaller crowd which, unlike Beck's crowd, departed leaving the Mall covered in rubbish. Conservative blogger Michelle Malkin was the first person to notice that the rally organisers, which included the Communist Party of the United States, had later substituted, for their own rally, a picture online of the huge Mall crowd at the 1963 Martin Luther King "I have a dream" rally. The mainstream media didn't pick up on that great scoop.

Beck has come to national fame from a troubled background. At eight he began self-training as a talk-show host by playing back his improvised radio shows. He went on-air for real at thirteen when he easily won a competition for an AM radio gig, and at seventeen he successfully applied for a weekend FM job in Seattle, to the surprise of his new employers who found that they had hired a schoolkid. By twenty-one he was on a salary of $70,000.

But his home life was mess. His mother suffered alcoholism and depression and divorced when Beck was thirteen. Her new lover, according to Beck, was an abuser. Mother and lover went out on a small boat on Puget Sound and both drowned. Beck, who was fifteen at the time, has claimed it was a suicide pact.

Beck moved back in with his father. Beck says that his paternal grandfather sexually abused Beck's father, and Beck's father was later abused by a series of carers, mentors and preachers. This made the father dysfunctional and unloving, but not a sexual abuser. "My family was a shipwreck," he weepily told his radio audience.

Beck became an alcoholic and a drug addict, and says that he was high every day for fifteen years (allow for some hyperbole). His first marriage failed after producing two daughters. One suffered cerebral palsy. By the age of thirty he was washed up spiritually, a radio has-been, and suicidal. He was saved by Alcoholics Anonymous in 1994.

Beck met his second wife Tania in 1998 when she walked into the New Haven radio station to pick up a Sony Walkman prize. Here's Beck's description:

> I apologise, but guys will understand this. My wife is hot and she wouldn't have sex with me until we got married, and she wouldn't marry me unless we had a religion. I'm like, ah, you've got to be kidding me! I've got to go to church for this?

The result was that they tested various religious creeds and settled on the Mormon faith. Their quest also brought them to militant conservatism. His polemical style, especially after 9/11 and the Obama election, took him to top rating at CNN, then Fox News.

He scandalised liberals by, for example, calling Obama an anti-white racist, which gave his opponents ammunition for a boycott of Fox advertisers. Beck and Fox separated in 2011. (Obama had butted in to take the side of a black professor, Henry Gates, arrested by a white police sergeant. Both Obama and Beck backed down.)

Instead of hawking his talent to a new employer, Beck created his own branded channels, with the motto, "The truth lives here". These channels are run by his company Mercury Radio Arts, offering subscriber and streamed television, radio, publishing, stage and web content. Beck has also written twenty-two books, eleven of which have made the *Times* best-seller lists, half a dozen hitting the number-one spot. Typical titles include *The Real America: Messages from the Heart and Heartland* and *Cowards: What Politicians, Radicals, and the Media Refuse to Say*.

His stage shows are his one-man-band tours. They are also filmed and run in 300 to 400 theatres nationwide, much as New York Met operas find a global audience via film. His movie *Man in the Moon*, with an historico-political message, sold out 20,000 seats at the launch.

Barely sleeping at nights, he arrives at work on any morning with enough philosophical, entrepreneurial and political energy to keep his staff in turmoil for a week. He tosses off hours of radio and television chatting and sermonising per day.

Beck's a man to be loved or hated. There's not much in between. I stayed nine days in Utah, survived a wine-free family barbecue, and, unusually, attended church on Sunday. I stayed with people who overtly take pride in their religion, their community and their country. It was just luck that I twice got to hear their favourite son Glenn Beck speaking and to feel his impact.

Quadrant Monthly, September 2014

www.ingramcontent.com/pod-product-compliance
Lightning Source LLC
Chambersburg PA
CBHW032347280326
41935CB00008B/485